An Elephant at My Door

On Safari in Africa

Louise Ferraro Deretchin

STARSHINE PRESS
SPRING, TEXAS

Photography by Louise F. Deretchin unless otherwise specified.

ISBN: 978-0-578-84931-7

To my husband Joel and my children Jessica and Robin.
They are the greatest adventure of my life.

CONTENTS

I moved in with lions, was humbled by sand dunes, and shown what caring for the earth looks like. I witnessed sweetness in a leopard, satiation in a lion, and loving in a hyena. For the first time in a long time, I felt peacefully natural and very welcomed.

August 13-September 5, 2017

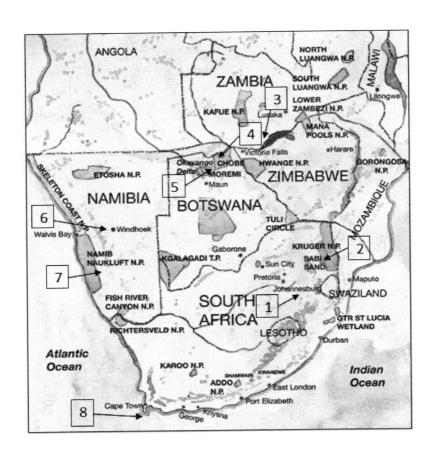

1 Johannesburg

2 Kirkman's Kamp

3 Waterberry Lodge

4 Linyanti Bush Camp

5 Pelo Camp/Okavango Delta

6 Windhoek

7 Kulala Desert Lodge

8 Cape of Good Hope

Chapter 1
THE APARTHEID PATH

The driver stares in disbelief at our luggage lying in the back of his truck and says, "Is that all?" My eyes meet his and I reply, "That's it," all the while thinking that I pack more for a weekend than I packed for this three-and-a-half-week trip.

Our two small bags look ludicrous lying in the bed of a Ford 250 pickup truck designed to carry a one-ton load. We'll be traveling on small aircraft from bush camp to bush camp in Africa and each of us is limited to a backpack and one soft-sided 12" x 24" x 11" duffle bag without wheels. The no-wheels rule allows the bags to be squished into tight spaces. To hold myself in check as I packed, I kept repeating, "One to wear, one to wash, one just in case," the precise instructions from friends who had been on safari and convinced us to go.

With everything loaded, we head to the airport to begin our adventure.

* * *

After thirty-two hours of traveling, I have little energy left, but what I see as we descend into Johannesburg sends a charge of excitement through me. I hold my breath as I look at pink-and-gold-tinged air that floats a thick blanket over golden grass. The band of color dissipates upward from the ground into a hazy blue sky. It is my first glimpse of South Africa and I want to hold onto it.

The plane completes its landing in Johannesburg, the starting point for a three-week safari my husband Joel and I have been planning for over a year. It's August, the end of winter in South Africa. Thirty-two hours ago it was summer in Houston where we stood outside our home watching the Uber driver load our luggage into the back of his pickup truck.

We exit the customs area and enter the confusion of the arrivals area. It takes a while for our tired eyes to spot the driver holding a hand-printed placard with our name on it and for our minds to compute that the sign is for us. I settle into the backseat of the car alongside Joel and ask the driver what causes the air to look pink and gold where it meets the ground.

His shoulders rise as he responds with a brightness to his voice, "That is Africa. It's always like that."

With only three hours of sleep on an airplane with seats that felt as if they were made from used cardboard, I'm too tired to pursue the question further. For now, my foggy brain is happy to enjoy the beauty of the muted colors.

We drive along highways flanked by typical urban signs and buildings and then through ordinary city streets with small businesses, pedestrians, and a mixture of non-descript housing. I feel as if I could be in any city in the world large enough to have an international airport. Toward the end of our forty-five-minute drive, the ordinary changes to upscale. Large, stucco homes in shades of beige nestle in luscious landscapes meticulously maintained. To a one, the homes are protected by walls and sculpted metal gates.

We arrive at *The Peech*, a boutique hotel on the outskirts of town that will be our home for the next two nights. Like the neighborhood it is tucked into, the two-story stucco structure is beautifully landscaped and gated. It looks like a private residence. We wait in the car outside the sizeable courtyard for an invisible hand to press a button that opens the metal-barred gate.

Inside, the hotel is decorated in dark leathers and wood accented with stone; the lights are dim. I'm not too tired to notice the casual luxury and to note that this may be the last bit of luxury we will have for the next three weeks.

It's too dark to make out anything other than silhouettes of trees and shrubs as a porter leads us through a garden area to our room in one of several two-story buildings lining the garden's edge. The room is beautifully decorated in warm colors with contemporary furniture. At this point, all that is important to me is the bed. I consider myself insane for having booked a tour for 9:00 the next morning. The tour will trace the struggle by the African National Congress (A.N.C.) to rid South Africa of the apartheid policy. I hope my mind will be up for it.

We forgo dinner in favor of an extra hour's sleep, shower, set an alarm, and go to sleep.

I wake up surprisingly refreshed. I inhale the cool crispness of the air and feel-good inside and out. Last night's silhouetted forms reveal themselves to be part of a well-manicured garden with robust shrubs and trees of varying heights. Flowers will appear soon, but not while we are here. My growling stomach reminds me I didn't have dinner last night.

A tall, blue-eyed, Nordic-looking man, with straight white hair sticking out both sides and the back of his baseball cap, approaches us as we enter the reception area.

"I'm Peter, your guide for today."

The opened shirt he's wearing looks like a Marimekko wall hanging with broad bands of black and white zigzags running from top to bottom. Beneath it, a black T-shirt decorated with a single-stem red rose that stretches from the neckline to the belt line peeks out. Beat-up casual shoes below his off-white, cotton slacks announce the casualness of the city and the tour.

"I'm early," he says. "Take your time. I just like to arrive early."

We take his words at face value and allow ourselves to enjoy breakfast. I order fresh fruit with my eggs. Joel orders pancakes. His eyes latch onto my melon pieces and berries.

"Would you like some?" I offer and of course he accepts.

Seated by a large window overlooking a picturesque garden, we continue our breakfast with soft conversation in the intimacy of the hotel's restaurant. Joel reminds me Peter is waiting for us. We grab our cameras and join him by his van, a spotless, late-model Mercedes. Joel and I settle into the middle row as Peter launches into a panoply of information. He tells us that South Africa is eighty percent Black African, nine percent Colored (a mixture of Black African with white European or Asian), eight percent white, and the remaining three percent Asian or other. I think of how simple the categorization is compared to what is used in the United States to identify the different shades of white, brown, and black.

Peter continues, "There are eleven official languages in South Africa; Zulu is the most commonly spoken one."

I wonder how people manage to communicate with each other given the number of official languages. I turn to Peter for the answer.

"Actually, there's a set of Zulu-like languages that are different from each other but understandable across one another," he answers. "In addition, everyone must study English plus one other language."

Peter has lived in South Africa all his life. He is conversant in multiple African languages as well as Afrikaans, his native language. He seems to speak American, too, because, to us, he has no British or other discernable accent.

He goes on. "Johannesburg was built around gold mining. At one time it was the world's largest producer; now it ranks about eighth. However, it has eighty percent of the world's resources of platinum."

I toss around platinum and the numbers in my head amazed at the wealth and almost miss what Peter says next.

"Coal and diamonds are among minerals mined in South Africa."

The mineral wealth of the country is staggering. But I'm not seeing platinum and diamonds reflected in the areas we drive through as we approach the downtown. The closer we get, the more I sense diminishing vitality. There's a quietness, a lack of bustle. It conjures up images in me of Detroit where I lived in the 1970s; it was not in full decline yet, but slowly leaking life. I turn my attention back to what Peter is saying.

"Under apartheid, the Central Business District was classified 'whites-only' which meant Blacks could work and shop in the city but not live in it. During the 1980s and 90s, with crime increasing and the uncertainty of the impending demise of apartheid, businesses and residents began to flee the CBD. As the buildings emptied, the CBD fell victim to drug lords and squatters."

He parks in a garage and we walk through the downtown to the fifty-story Carlton Center Office Tower. There, we crowd into a glass elevator with other tourists and ride to the top for a panoramic view of downtown

Johannesburg. Peter points out buildings that are empty, entire blocks abandoned, and sectors earmarked for redevelopment. Looking out from the tower, we can imagine the vibrant city that was, and see evidence of the painful transition it is going through.

"Efforts have begun to reclaim buildings by ousting drug lords and squatters; some structures are too far gone to reclaim. Twenty percent remain empty. Many are still occupied by drug lords."

I can see that the patches of redevelopment constitute large undertakings but are miniscule compared to the size and breadth of the downtown area. Joel, having worked on urban redevelopment projects in Albany, New York and Detroit, Michigan, has a ton of technical questions to ask Peter about who is sponsoring the redevelopment, the strength of commitment from the business community, financing, and the plan for execution; all elements are critical to success.

Like Peter, Joel has perfected keeping a neutral expression on his face as he listens to answers to his questions. In private, he says to me, "They're not doing enough. It's a waste of time. It needs to be of sufficient scale to turn the downtown around."

Perhaps having a thriving new business center built in the suburbs is a disincentive to wholeheartedly investing in the rebuilding the old downtown center. I'm glad that something is being done but have no illusion about how long it may take or the likelihood of progress outpacing the festering problems.

On our way out, we pass photographs of street scenes, people, and miners on ledges digging for gold. Joel tugs at my elbow and, with a nod of his head, draws my attention to a picture of Mahatma Gandhi displayed in a glass case. I stop to read what is written below the photo and am amazed to find out that in the early 1900s, before leading non-violent protests in India to free it from British rule, Gandhi was an active opponent of apartheid in South Africa.

Later, I learn that the scope of Gandhi's anti-apartheid efforts was narrower than what I was led to believe. Gandhi, as it turns out, formed the Natal Indian Congress to campaign against having the upper-class Indians lumped together with Blacks. An early action, and one that he won, was to petition the Durban Post and Telegraph Office to create a third entrance to keep Blacks separated from Indians.

Gandhi explained his grievances in a letter he wrote in 1896 in which he states, "In the Durban Post and Telegraph Offices, there were separate entrances [one] for *Asiatics and Natives* and [one for] *Europeans*. We felt the indignity too much and many respectable Indians were insulted and called all sorts of names by the clerks at the counter." [from the Collective Works of Mahatma Gandhi, Vol. 1, p. 367].

He felt indignity. I felt disappointment learning he was not the embodiment of social justice; he wasn't perfect.

As a result of Gandhi's efforts, the previous two entrances were restructured into three: *Europeans*, *Asiatics,* and *Natives*.

We exit the tower and walk back to the garage. On this sunny day, it looks like a normal city with cars and pedestrians moving steadily along uncrowded streets and sidewalks. The destruction behind the building façades easily evades a visitor's eye.

Our guide points to the Carlton Hotel. "It took seven years to build. It was the jewel of the Carlton Center. In 1997, fifteen years after it opened, it closed. Fear and crime led to shutting it down."

The building looks solid and in good condition. I ask, "Will it reopen?"

"Not likely," Peter answers. "It has long been stripped of trim and furniture. Part of the roof is open to the elements and the interior is going to waste."

He adds that the new city center in Sandton, a northern suburb of Johannesburg, is doing well. He uses "we" when he speaks of the hope he shares with others that the growing pains will ease as the government is made to abide by the constitution, and corruption is challenged in the federal courts.

It is the pedestrians that give me the most hope for Johannesburg—they show the city is alive at some level. Perhaps, in not too many years, a vibrant city will re-emerge.

We leave the downtown and, as conversation continues, step back in time into the history of the struggle to end apartheid. Peter begins by telling us that apartheid had its roots planted when the Dutch set up an area for re-supplying cargo ships passing the Cape of Good Hope en route to the riches of India. The local tribes provided the cheap labor necessary to make re-supplying of ships economically and practically feasible.

Peter adds, "The practice continued and is still the de facto practice even though apartheid is legally ended."

Peter's forthrightness always surprises me—there is no sugar coating, but also no condemning of what is going on in South Africa's struggle. It just is what is.

He continues, "It will take longer for the social and economic changes to occur—social change, because of the need for trust to be re-established after the violence that erupted when passive resistance failed; and economic change, because of poor education of a large part of the Black population and their having lived for generations as the underclass."

Seated back in the van, I ponder where I would begin to build a new government with a population that has neither been allowed to participate in government nor prepared to run a country as large as South Africa. Leaders, good and bad, always emerge no matter the circumstances, but where would the skilled managers who make the government work come from? I think about how incompetence and self-interest can slip in; how easy it would be to sideline the monstrous task of re-forming a government in favor of seeking prestige, power, and financial gain—the problem South Africa faces at this time.

We head to the northern part of Johannesburg and Liliesleaf Farm. I turn to Joel and ask, "Have you heard of Liliesleaf Farm?"

"No. This is all new for me."

"Same here."

We continue along city streets and then enter a treed area bright with sunshine. A sign says Liliesleaf Farm is ahead.

Deceptive in its peaceful setting among grassy fields and trees, Liliesleaf Farm is where a critical turning point in the struggle to end apartheid emerged. Frustrated by the lack of progress using non-violence and with the government's heavy-handedness in suppressing the call to end apartheid, leaders of the liberation movement met in secret at Liliesleaf Farm to plot an alternate course.

We park the van and follow signs along the pathway to the farmhouse that recount the events leading to the A.N.C.'s decision to change from non-violence to targeted violence in the struggle for equality.

A video plays in an auditorium in one of several small buildings on the property. It begins with Nelson Mandela addressing a cheering crowd in 1948. His upbeat message rings out with a call for equality for *all*. The video continues by tracing non-violent acts being met with indifference by the government and, all too often, violence against the Black population.

In 1955, after seven years of non-violent activism, the Congress Alliance consisting of the A.N.C. and its allies, compiled the Freedom Charter based on demands collected from a cross section of South Africans of all backgrounds, genders, ages, and color. The basic tenets of the Charter were equality, opportunity, and dignity for all. Peaceful protests, negotiations, and passive resistance continued, but the government's rejection of the Charter fanned the flames that led to violence as an option for protest. The government prosecuted 156 men and women activists in a treason trial that lasted five years. The trial was a powder keg and the government was playing with matches.

As the video progresses, tensions rise and so does my heart rate. There is not a sound in the auditorium. I don't think anyone is breathing. Joel is stone-still. The next clip begins.

On March 21, 1960 at Sharpeville, a South African Township, several thousand protesters descended upon the police station to protest laws requiring Black Africans over the age of sixteen to carry a passport in their own country. What started as a peaceful, festive-like event, with thousands offering themselves to be arrested for not carrying passports, turned ugly as the crowd swelled to about 20,000. Rocks may have been hurled. Police responded with fire. Sixty-nine protestors were killed and over 200 wounded, mostly from bullet wounds to their backs as they fled the chaos that broke out.

The image of people being shot in their backs was more than South Africans of any ethnicity could bear. Freedom Fighters realized peaceful protests, as a strategy, was not working; something different had to be done. With the help of the Communist Party and Moscow, the A.N.C. leadership acquired Liliesleaf Farm and began meeting there in 1961.

When the video ends, the audience is slow to rise as were we. I knew about the struggle to rid the country of apartheid; it played out from my childhood to my growing into adulthood. I knew about the violence from reports on television, in newspapers, and, later in life, from friends who fled South Africa. But I didn't know about the peaceful optimism with which it began and the brutality with which the movement was met long before it developed a military wing of its own.

We leave the auditorium and walk wordlessly to the one-story farmhouse. I stop to read a sign on the side of the structure printed in large, white letters.

> It was an old house that needed work and no-one lived there. I moved in under the pretext that I was the houseboy or caretaker who would look after the place until my master took possession. I had taken the alias David Motsamayi, the name of one of my former clients. At the farm, I wore the simple blue overalls that were the uniform of the black male servant.
> Nelson Mandela,
> *Long Walk to Freedom*, 1994

The A.N.C. hired a white European couple with two young children to move to the farm and be the façade for the leaders as they secretly plotted more aggressive, violent means, including bombings, to end apartheid. Among the leadership were Sisulu, Mbeki, Mhlaba, Goldreich, Bernstein, and Wolpe, their names reflecting the diversity of support for ending apartheid.

By 1963, aware of the danger of meeting at the same location over a long period of time, the leadership planned to make their July 11, 1963 meeting the last at Liliesleaf Farm. The purpose of the meeting was to finalize plans for guerilla warfare against the government. Care would be taken to not harm civilians.

As the meeting was underway, a laundry truck pulled up. The van's rear doors flew open and armed police flooded out. The leaders had no time to escape or destroy plans and diagrams they held in their hands. Arrests followed; those who escaped went into exile. Nelson Mandela was not among the eleven present—he had been arrested previously and was on trial. However, he had directed the workings of the A.N.C. at Liliesleaf Farm even while imprisoned and awaiting trial.

Maintaining a neutral expression and voice, Peter, our guide, fills us in on speculations that continue to exist on how the farm was compromised. He says, "One theory is that a neighbor may have become suspicious when he saw whites and Blacks together shaking hands, something very unusual for the time. Another is that the A.N.C. was exposed from within, perhaps by someone opposed to use of violence. Yet another is that the United States, and to a lesser degree Great Britain, had been following the A.N.C.'s activity. When Moscow and the Communist Party in South Africa became involved through the purchase of Liliesleaf Farm, red flags went up and the CIA turned its eyes toward the farm. It gathered information and turned it over to the South African government, enabling the arrests."

I stare at a display board with a web of lines linking countries to events that led to the arrests, preferring not to believe the United States would have worked against the Freedom Fighters. But in 1963, the Cold War was in full swing. Just one year before the arrests, Nikita Khrushchev, premier of the then Union of Soviet Socialist Republics, planted nuclear weapons in Cuba, ninety miles off the shores of the United States. His actions precipitated the Cuban Missile Crisis that brought the world to the brink of nuclear war. At that time, any international actions Russia took were viewed as threats to our own country. While I understand the United States' action in its context, it still strikes me as being in opposition to the equality we have been striving for since the birth of our nation, a striving that resurged in my lifetime with the battle for school desegregation begun in the 1950s.

Farmhouse at Liliesleaf Farm.

Peter, with his straightforward delivery, tells us, "With the July arrests, the government celebrated what it believed to be the end of the anti-apartheid rebellion. Of course, that wasn't the case. It had, however, succeeded in crippling the liberation movement for more than two decades to come. On June 16, 1976, that changed."

I never expected an in-depth history lesson. I thought this would be a light day filling empty space in the itinerary. Instead, here I am caught up in the story of the struggle, seeing the places firsthand, seeing pictures and videos of the people involved, and hearing their words. For me, the struggle changed from being clinical to being very real and very human. Having lived through this period in history, I am disturbed by my ignorance. I knew about the violence, but not the prolonged patience exhibited preceding the violence. To hear and see, documented by voices and filmed events, that peaceful, reasoned actions to achieve a just cause had no effect until violence stepped in, weighs heavily on me. I can't help but think about the race riots that occurred in my country at the same time and continue to flare up today and wonder if we will ever reach the point where we can skip the violence and move from reason to solution.

Peter, barely leaving time for my own thoughts to brew, continues.

"On the morning of June 16, 1976, between 10,000 and 20,000 Black public school students in Soweto gathered for a peaceful march to protest the decree requiring that their main academic courses be taught in Afrikaans, the language of South Africans of European descent, instead of in English, the language traditionally used. Bantu, their native language, would be used for religious instruction, music, and culture. Students felt they had struggled to learn English and did not want to exchange it for a language that was not as universal and, consequently, not as useful to them. Students from different schools merged as they moved forward planning to take their protest beyond Soweto.

"Before the children could make it out of Soweto, the military moved in. Soweto has only three access points; it was easy to seal off the area. The police set a dog loose on the children. The children responded by killing the dog. A policeman lost control, fired a shot, and more shots followed. Everything got out of control. One-hundred-seventy-six people were killed, thousands of others injured."

The killing of children stabbed at the hearts of the people, Black and white. Videos and photographs leaked to the press showed students neatly dressed in school uniforms, singing as they marched. And then shots, followed by screams, could be heard as people panicked, scattering in every direction. A photo of a dying thirteen-year-old boy being carried away in the mass of bloodied confusion hit the newsstands nationally and internationally. The people had had enough. Patience exploded into violence and the anti-apartheid movement was revived.

It took almost another two decades for apartheid to meet its demise, but with its June 16th actions in Soweto, the apartheid government, in its intransigence, had sealed its own fate. In 1994 South Africa's first democratic election was held and it voted to become a constitutional democracy with a Constitution Court to uphold the newly accepted Constitution of South Africa. Nelson Mandela was elected president. Apartheid was no longer the law.

With my head full of facts and my heart shredded by stories of struggle and sacrifice, I take a mental break as Peter launches into the period after the election and the government's structure. I hear enough to know that he is disappointed in the disarray and corruption that set in after Mandela's time as president ended, but hopeful that the Constitution Court is becoming effective in fighting the corruption that is dragging down the country.

I focus on the people and the land that we pass as we drive along smooth, paved roads. The colors of muted pink and gold I had seen in the evening air as we touched down in Johannesburg last evening are echoed in the land. It must be the dust from the earth suspended in the air that sparkles in the late afternoon sun. We drive on. We are on our way to Soweto.

Chapter 2
SOWETO

It must be at least noon when we approach Soweto, one of the townships ringing Johannesburg. Like the others, it was established as an area for Blacks to live when apartheid policy forbid them to live in cities. For years following the Soweto uprising, the sound of the township's name resounded with violence and fear. Now its name is spoken with curiosity and, perhaps, a hazy knowledge of its history.

I think about *Born a Crime*, a memoir by the comedian and television star Trevor Noah, about growing up in Soweto among shanties and dirt streets in the 1980s and 90s. By then, white flight from the cities was rampant, rents were down, and Blacks began moving into the emptying buildings. Trevor's Swiss father and his Xhosa tribe mother rented separate apartments in one of those buildings. When they decided to have a child together, they knew that under apartheid policy sexual relations between Blacks and whites was a crime punishable by imprisonment. In essence, they became criminals, and Trevor was their crime.

As we approach Soweto, Peter draws our attention to informal settlements, expanses of land covered with homes forming irregularly patterned quilts of corrugated metal, cardboard, and wood. "Soweto borders Johannesburg's mining district," he explains. "Illegal immigrants from Tanzania, Zimbabwe, and other troubled African nations come here in search of a better life."

I survey the informal settlements visible on either side of the road. The constant flow of immigrants fills in remaining spaces and presses the settlement's perimeters outward. The inhabitants live as squatters in shacks without water or basic sanitation. Their corrugated tin roofs atop lopsided houses are weighted down with tires and rocks to prevent them from slipping or blowing off in storms. Zigzagging dirt paths, shaped by the haphazard positioning of homes, make navigation through the settlements for outsiders and public services almost impossible. Privacy is minimal and separation from potential outbreaks of disease impossible.

The only brightness I see comes from the colors of clothing strung on lines to dry.

"The settlers come in hope of safety and a better life, but the rate of influx is too great for South Africa's economy to absorb," Peter continues.

I slump back in my seat as I think about the squatters' choice to live in abject squalor rather than live with the terrors they face from intertribal warfare, unstable governments, and hopelessness in their own countries. Yet, among the shanties, a woman stands in her doorway. Her hand is on her hip; a smile is on her face. Another woman takes long, graceful strides through grass as the sun shines on her. It could be a scene from anywhere if you extract the metal and cardboard.

Glancing back at us through the rearview mirror, Peter, his voice tingling with amazement, says, "An enterprising person *even sells* packaged sets of walls and a roof to the immigrants for little money—little to us that is—so that they can erect a house in a couple of hours."

I look out the window and snap pictures as we speed by hoping to capture the breadth of the settlements along with the immensity of the problem.

Joel spots a cluster of one-story, concrete homes and asks "Those look like government housing. Are they?"

"Yes. The government has been leveling informal settlements it has vacated and builds solid houses for the settlers on that land or other land. Sometimes the government turns vacated land over to the township for community use. It's a challenge to get ahead of the problem."

He pauses and then adds, "Difficult as it is, we remain optimistic, as we should, that the settlement situation will be worked out."

A woman with a baby crosses the street by an informal settlement.

Homes in an informal settlement.

I am more than ready for sunshine to splash into my thoughts. I get my wish as we turn a corner, enter Soweto proper, and pass a sign that reads VILAKAZI STREET, Soweto's most famous street. The homes of two Nobel Prize winners, Nelson Mandela, the leader of the anti-apartheid movement, and Desmond Tutu, an activist and Archbishop, are just down the block from the sign. Mandela died in 2013, Tutu still lives here.

One glance down Vilakazi Street and I know I'm going to love it! Shops and restaurants line both sides of paved streets. Racks of garments in bright patterns that mix reds, greens, and blues with golds appear at intervals along the sidewalks. There are no pastels here, only colors as sharp as the sun. I can't wait for Peter to park the car.

He parks in an asphalt lot. Leaving us standing by the car, he walks toward a loosely gathered group of men, each attentive to, but none approaching, us. Peter passes a few South African rands to one of the men to watch our car and returns. He tells us he doesn't mind paying; they need the money.

I hear music and hope we head in its direction. School children dressed in brown V-neck sweaters with grey slacks and skirts linger on a corner. Across the street from them, Zulu dancers in solid brown traditional costumes sing and dance to music they beat out with their hands and sticks. Beads, seeds, and patches of bristle adorn their hair and drape from the necks of women and bare-chested men. I'm torn between taking pictures and moving with their enticingly joyful rhythms. The camera wins out, at least for a while. I snap away, but I can't stand still. The dancers sing and dance long enough for pictures and for my body to echo their rhythms.

Zulu dancers in Soweto.

An unobtrusive basket lies nearby; the option to leave money is up to us. Joel drops few bills in. He and Peter are ready to move on long before I am. It's well past noon and lunch looms large in their minds. Like a pair of laser beams, they head straight toward a restaurant down the block. I, however, am drawn to every splash of color I see. I grab a protesting Joel and drag him toward the open door of a store.

"We can't shop now. Peter is heading to a restaurant," he says in a low voice.

That's a pretty lame excuse as far as I'm concerned. Besides which, it's too late to get me away. Foot-tall African dolls with soft, bright-colored wraps, beaded clothes, hair and eyes, and wire-wrapped legs have a magnetic hold on me.

"Ask Peter to wait a minute," I say, one foot already inside the store.

Joel obliges, Peter paces outside. I finger silky fabrics, swoon over the African dolls.

Joel drags me out promising we'll come back after lunch. "We'll have more time to shop then," he says.

I'm not sure Peter has allowed any time for Joel to keep his promise, but I have already pushed at the limits of Peter's patience. He appears to be one who lays out a schedule and sticks to it. I move on.

Just down the block is Sakhumzi, an open-air restaurant, one of Peter's favorite places to eat. At the buffet, we fill our plates with vegetables, fruits, breads, and meats—some are familiar, others are not, all are colorful. I don't ask questions, just take a seat at a slatted table along a railing that separates us from the sidewalk and eat the delicious food.

Sidewalk musicians a few feet away entertain with antics, songs, and dances to the accompaniment of a guitarist. Their rubber-boot clad feet stomp out rhythms. Their faces are a study in intrigue and jocularity. I take several photos knowing I will want to paint their portraits. I have painted portraits of African women; it's time to move on to African men.

Gumboot Dancers in Soweto.

"Those are Gumboot Dancers," Peter explains as my eyes drop to the calf-high galoshes they are wearing.

"The dance tells of working in the dusty gold mines. In the dance they symbolically beat their legs and bodies with their hands and stamp their boots the way miners do to rid themselves of the dust after a day of digging."

Peter adds, "The mines are narrow, deep, becoming deeper and more dangerous to work in."

I picture workers in dark hollows, digging for gold nuggets. A miner trapped farther down, gasping in dust-filled air, no one able to reach him. I erase the video playing my mind, turn back to the rhythms and the songs, and admire the beautiful lines of the performers' faces.

We leave the restaurant and head toward the car. I make sure I'm in the lead so that I can march the three of us into the store we passed earlier. Phantom images of its colorful merchandise and dolls had shimmered over my plate throughout lunch; I'm determined not to miss an opportunity to see them again.

Inside the store, long dresses hang on circular racks and from the ceiling on racks that stretch from wall-to-wall. The safari neutral colors I'm wearing look dead rather than neutral set against the bright, geometric and floral-patterned fabrics that surround me. I buy a long, white, sleeveless dress covered in shapes printed in black, mustard, and chocolate. Joel hands me a necklace made with chunky mustard-colored beads to go with it. I want the dolls—one cloaked in dark blue and gold, one in emerald green—but I can't justify spending more money on myself. I buy them for my daughters instead.

Dress shop on Vilakazi Street where I bought my dress and the dolls.

African doll made by local women to support their families.

We leave Soweto and move on to Constitution Hill and the Constitutional Court building. Here is where the hope lies for South Africa's new government. A plaque hanging inside the lobby reads:

> *The first Constitutional Court of South
> Africa, established under the Constitution
> of the Republic of South Africa, 1993, was
> opened by President N.R. Mandela on
> 14.02.1995. The Constitution is the
> supreme law of the land. Let justice be
> administered in the Court without fear,
> favor or prejudice.*

This is the highest court in the land. Here cases of corruption within the government at the highest levels are beginning to be heard. Prior to the hearings, rampant corruption went unchallenged. According to Peter, the court hearings are a major step forward in setting South Africa back on its feet.

The daylight dims signaling it's time to return to the hotel and pack for our flight to Sabi Sands tomorrow— the beginning of our safari. We say goodbye to Peter, freshen up in our room, and head to the softly lit dining room for dinner. Joel orders springbok, a member of the antelope family. Neither of us has ever heard of it. I play it safe and order salmon. The meals arrive. Joel tastes his meat and tells me it is delicious.

He asks with a note of hesitancy in his voice, "Would you like to taste it?"

I can see, reflected in his face, the internal battle between having been generous and wishing he hadn't asked. He knows what usually happens. If I prefer his dish, he offers to exchange meals with me and I accept.

I taste the springbok. It is exquisite. I have never had red meat that is so delicate. I find it so amazing that I can't bring myself to deny Joel the pleasure of dining on it. I don't ask him to switch; I watch the pleasure in his eyes as he savors each bite. Thoughtfully, he doesn't utter another word about its greatness. He just asks, "Is the salmon good?"

"Delicious!"

We sip wine and enjoy. Surely, after this meal, we will have sweet dreams.

Chapter 3
SABI SANDS

One to wear, one to wash, one just in case runs through my mind as I place in my duffle bag each of the three near-identical outfits I'll be rotating through for the next three weeks. Each folded neatly into its own Ziplock bag makes packing and repacking a cinch. Best of all, the only decision I will have to make each day is which shade of green to wear.

I tuck the African dolls, wrapped in bubble wrap, into the last corner of space I have in my bag; Joel has pressed my new dress into his. At the bush camps, our clothes will be laundered each day except for intimates—the religion of the staff prohibits them from handling what they call *small things*. I'll be washing my own, so will Joel. With backpacks slung on our shoulders, we say goodbye to luxury, and get ready for grunge. I can't wait to dig into this adventure.

We climb onboard a South African Airlink plane parked on the tarmac at Johannesburg airport. About twenty passengers are seated two-by-two. Fifty minutes later we arrive at Skukuza Airport in Kruger National Park soon to be immersed in safari life. Signs for arrivals take us past a sculpture of an elephant standing in the center of its private alcove. Joel hurries me along, not letting me stop to take a picture. Outside, guides from each camp are lined up like boy scouts on review wearing khaki shorts and shirts, standing straight with feet apart, one hand behind their back and one holding a sign with a name on it. We spot our guide, a sturdy-looking guy. He introduces himself as Bret, our game ranger for the next three days, and then leads us to the luggage. In what seems like one continuous, swift motion, he flings both duffle bags onto his shoulders and relieves us of our backpacks.

"Is that all?" he asks.

"Yes."

"Good job!"

I wonder why he's praising us. And then I look around and see others have traveled with every size suitcase short of a trunk. I guess we won't be seeing them on the small aircraft.

We climb into a safari vehicle—an open-top, modified Land Cruiser with three rows of stadium seating behind the driver. We're the only passengers. As we bump along narrow roads, driving over sand mounds that are the equivalent of ski moguls, Bret explains that Kirkman's Kamp, the place we will be staying, is in the Sabi Sands Game Reserve, a private game reserve that is adjacent to Kruger National Park.

He tells us, "The reserve is 65,000 hectares," and translates for us Americans, "That's about 161,000 acres."

I'm holding the bar in front of me, leaning forward, straining to hear what he is saying over the sound of the engine and the wind in my ears. His South African accent compounds my difficulty. The wind, however, is a blessing; it's keeping me cool in the 100^0 temperature. Bret apologizes for the heat and says it will cool down.

Joel and I by a safari vehicle at Kirkman's Kamp.

The heat is not my focus of interest. It's superseded by the scenery of this different land. The yellows and browns of tangled grass dominate the view filling in the spaces between leafless shrubs and occasional trees, each with unblocked access to the sky. I delight in the sculptural form of the long, bare branches backlit by the bright sky. I scan the dry grass searching for whatever may be there. I love the emptiness of the landscape. There's so much and so little to see. I feel at home here. I smile thinking that I am a dry-grasslands and desert person. I love this scrubland as I do the seemingly barren parts of New Mexico where I spend my summers. For me, neither is barren, just simplified, devoid of competing images. Their subtle colors and exposed forms invite endless challenges to discover nuances and to bathe in the pleasure of doing so.

I tune back into Bret, "There used to be a fence on the east side of Kruger separating it from Sabi Sands," he continues. "It was put there in 1961 to protect animals from an outbreak of foot and mouth disease. Then they had to build a fence on the west side of Kruger so the animals would not move westward out of the park. In 1993, when the threat of disease was over, the fence was taken down so that the animals could roam freely again."

He stops the history lesson to point to zebra, which he pronounces like Debra with a Z. He points out impala, more zebra, and even springbok, small and as delicate-looking as befits the dinner Joel was served in Johannesburg. Bret calls out the names of other animals that his trained eyes see; I see most of them fleetingly and try to remember their names. A half hour later, Kirkman's Kamp appears among the shrubs and trees in the middle of an island of sand and grass. Outside the one-story main building, female staff dressed in white blouses and khaki skirts line up to greet us with song; their hand clapping provides rhythmic accompaniment. I'm smiling from ear-to-ear. A man, also dressed in khaki and white, stands nearby with rolled-up, damp washcloths carried on a tray; the refreshing coolness of the cloth against my face and skin is appreciated. A chilled fruit drink completes the welcome.

We step inside the main building and step back in time into a 1920s colonial hunting lodge filled with European antiques intermixed with hunting paraphernalia and trophies. It feels, at once, both exclusive and comfortable. From an open book on a table we learn that the original owner had been an avid hunter and later became an assiduous protector of game.

Kirkman's Kamp, Sabi Sands.

A cold lemonade, served in an informal room with overstuffed leather chairs, casual tables, and a formal bar, hits the spot before we leave the lodge to settle into our room. As we cross a large, open, sandy area, a staff person cautions us to never walk unaccompanied between buildings in the early morning hours or at night. The absence of fences allows animals to walk freely throughout the camp. He also reminds us that the animals *are* wild. As a final caution, he tells us never to go down to the Sand River which flows behind our room—it is a much-used waterhole, especially now as water sources begin to dry up. All this is said matter-of-factly—not a hint of concern in any word. We are ready to relax into the animals' world.

Our room is one in a row of eighteen guest units that form one single-story building. Each has its own entrance from the outside and accommodates two adults. A quick calculation reveals that there can be no more than thirty-six guests at Kirkman's Kamp at a time.

A king-size bed occupies the center of a spacious, sunlit room decorated in light colors. Black and white photos of game and white game hunters flanked by Black African tribesmen hang on the walls. They appear to have been taken in the early 1900s. I admire the clarity of the gallery-sized photos where blades of grass are equally as sharp as specks in the big cats' eyes. I hope my new Nikon camera can do as good a job.

A separate bathroom with a large soaking tub and separate shower adjoins the sleeping area. Glass doors open from the bedroom onto a private veranda overlooking shrubs and the Sand River, the river we have been warned not to go to. A selection of spirits set on a table in a corner of the room invites imbibing. A laundry bag lays on a bench. The bag will be collected each morning and the laundered clothes returned to us by end of day.

Absorbed in the casual luxury of the lodge and our room, I don't think things can get any better. But then we are served lunch on the wooden deck at the back of the main building. Broad umbrellas shade tables covered with linen. A huge tree with white blossoms drapes the middle of the deck. Colorful birds hide among its leaves. We are assigned a butler to take care of all our dining needs; he will be ours for our three-day stay. I keep thinking that somewhere along our planned safari, the hotel-like room will become a tent and the spacious shower a bucket of water. In the meantime, I will indulge myself in total luxury.

Bret stops by as we finish lunch to let us know to be ready at 3:00 p.m. for a game drive. I'm already ready! He gifts each of us with a reusable water bottle—disposable ones are not allowed—and then lays down a few rules, the main two being, "Don't stand up in or get out of the vehicle," he explains. "Any action will cause an animal to react—it will either run away from you or run toward you."

An enactment of what Bret tells us plays out in my head as he continues, "We come around a corner and a leopard is there. The natural thing to do is to jump up and take a picture. A guy did that. The leopard saw motion and charged. The guy was lucky. The leopard ran past him. Remember, don't stand up. A leopard could be in the bushes near you and you won't even see it."

I feel the warning shoot through me. I would be the one to bolt up, trigger finger on the camera shutter release.

He continues, "Unlike Kruger National Park where you can drive any color or shape car, at the private reserves only brown or green safari vehicles are allowed. The animals have learned to trust the vehicles. That's why we can get close and why the animals stay around while we watch them."

He adds that, unlike Kruger, in Sabi Sands, we are not restricted to driving on the roads; we can track animals across the bush, into the water, or wherever they go.

At three o'clock, we're back at the patio filling our water bottles and snacking on biscuits and tea. The reusable water bottles are given to guests upon arrival to reduce the amount of plastic that pollutes the environment and endangers the animals. Disposable bottles or cups are nowhere to be seen.

Bret points to a line of six vehicles and tells us ours is the first one. Another couple staying at Kirkman's Kamp is already seated in the first row. With cameras slung from our shoulders and broad-brimmed safari hats to protect us from the sun, we introduce ourselves and settle into the second row. A brief conversation reveals that the couple, Jillian and Craig, are on their honeymoon. They live in Durban, South Africa, down the coast from Sabi Sands, and frequently take weekend safaris. My ears perk up when I hear "Durban". I remember that's where Gandhi took a stand on the post offices' apartheid policy.

I can't resist checking out what Jillian is wearing. I think about how Joel and I so carefully inquired about what to wear: no black, white, or blue (blue blankets are used to attract and trap tsetse flies). Plaids, patterns, and bold colors are out. Long sleeves and a hat for protection from mosquitoes and sun are a must, sturdy shoes recommended. Apparently, the couple with us never got the appropriate-game-dress memo. Jillian has on a black tank top. No hat and no sturdy shoes for her—sandals are fine.

I glance at other vehicles that are loading up and see that baseball caps are the head cover of choice, hiking pants optional. I look like a newbie in the safari world. Oh well.

"What would you like to see today?" Bret asks.

"Leopards!" comes from Jillian and Craig.

"Anything with four feet," from me.

Joel doesn't get to say anything before the decision is made to find leopards.

Richard, a game tracker, joins us. He comes from a family well-respected for its tracking abilities, Bret tells us by way of introduction. Richard smiles. Like Bret, he is in khakis, but he is lean not stocky; like us, he's wearing long hiking pants. He slides into the front seat next to Bret. A rifle lies across the dashboard in front of them. It's in a zipped-up case. I wonder what good the encased rifle would do in an emergency. Do Bret and Richard practice unzipping cases?

Bret engages the engine and we're off. The sand moguls are as jarring as they were earlier today, but now they are thrilling as well. With the game vehicle pointed straight at the Sand River, we head for the area where a leopard was last sited. At this time of year, winter, the river is more a collection of streams than a river. Without hesitation and without slowing down, Bret shoots across. As I reach for the grab bar in front of me, I see that the wind has wrapped Jillian's long blond hair around it leaving no convenient place to grab. I balance and bump and grope for a stronghold anywhere. This is like driving at thirty miles an hour over urban potholes. I turn to Joel and see that there's a smile on his face and a twinkle in his eyes that reflect the excitement I am feeling.

We splash through the river water and stop on the opposite bank. Richard spots tracks in the damp sand, a leopard's pad and four toes clearly visible. He hops out and follows the tracks until they disappear into the water. Quietly and slowly he continues to search the ground for clues. We sit in the vehicle, silent, our eyes scanning for signs. We wait there quite a while. I am willing to give up on leopards and try something else. Richard returns and confers with Bret. I can't make out what he says but can hear his tone is soft, speech melodic.

A second safari vehicle pulls up. Another game tracker comes to speak to Richard. Both take off on foot. Bret hops back into the vehicle; "They think the leopard has gone back into the bush. They're going to circle around left on foot. We'll drive to the right and meet up with them."

Zoom. We're off. This time I grab the bar before the wind covers it with hair. Hair gets tangled in my fingers anyway. I apologize.

We slow down as we make a turn, all eyes searching. Mine are glued to the ground looking for tracks and don't see what is right in front of us until the vehicle stops short. Three white rhinos graze about twenty feet ahead. The largest of which, a male, stands in the middle of the road. It's my first photo op! I snap away, mostly taking pictures of the big guy. The female and the baby are partially hidden in the grass.

As I snap shot-after-shot of the male, I begin to think there is something strange about his face, a face that is not beautiful to begin with. He is missing his big horn! The female, on the other hand, has an impressively long one. Its upward curve makes it resemble a scythe. The baby, small only relative to the mother, is beginning to sprout horns. I switch my focus to them. I comment that I know that white rhinos don't derive their name from their color, which can be dark, and ask how you can distinguish them from black rhino.

"White rhinos have flat jaws," Bret responds.

Now, I feel like a rhino expert!

White rhino with a missing horn.

Richard calls in. He reports that he linked up with another group and that they have found a rhino horn. We report back that we found the rhino that belongs to it.

The horn, Bret tells us, will be brought back to the lodge, stored, catalogued, protected, and turned over to authorities. Prized in other cultures for its believed aphrodisiac powers, the horn's value is immense. This rhino probably lost its horn defending territory. It would not be alive, and the horn would not be left behind, if a poacher was involved. He then tells us that white rhinos are rare in other places but plentiful in Sabi Sands. No count is kept of the population for fear of attracting poachers. Rhinos are being poached by the hundreds each year in South Africa alone.

Namibia, I find out, was the first country to introduce dehorning as a preventative action. The program, accompanied by increased security, has met with success. Significantly fewer dehorned rhinos are counted among the killed. However, dehorned rhinos become vulnerable again as their horns grow back. Even while hornless, they are sometimes killed for the remaining stub that is left behind to ensure regrowth.

Bret tells us Sabi Sands also is well-known for its leopards. Elusive and shy, they are hard to find. But, here, they are plentiful and comfortable.

Now I understand why Jillian and Craig were so quick to say "leopards" when asked what they wanted to see. I also begin to understand how little I know about the places we are visiting. I wrapped myself so thoroughly in the logistics of getting from place to place, what to bring, and how to bring it that I didn't delve into what we would be seeing and doing. Maybe that's not so bad—each thing I discover here makes me feel like I just opened an awesome Christmas present.

We move on. An occasional animal darts across the road, mostly impala referred to by locals as the McDonalds of the bush—they are both abundant and fast! Radio calls are exchanged by game rangers and trackers in different vehicles about where they have searched and where they are headed. Bret calls out things as he sees them, but from the second row of seats, with wind blasting through my ears, and the bumpy road rattling my eardrums, I miss most of what he is saying. I make a mental note to make sure I ride in the front row next time.

We are two hours into the game drive when we get the message we've been waiting for, "We found her." And then, "Her cubs are not with her."

That doesn't matter. I'll be happy to see just her.

Bret steers the vehicle off the road and into the grasses. Dry twigs and small shrubs snap beneath the wheels as we rush to the siting. We are on the hunt. Minutes later, Bret points to an area. All that's visible in the grey light of early evening is a movement of the grass. It's not until the leopard begins to come closer that we can see her. With every glimpse of her as she ambles though the dry grass, the rapid staccato snap of the shutters on Joel's and my cameras can be heard. The other couple's cameras aren't firing with the same urgency; they have been on safari many times and probably have tons of pictures already.

The leopard disappears into the bush. I take a quick look at the photos I have taken and see that I have lots of pictures of blades of grass with occasional spots visible behind them.

Bret starts the engine and heads out to where he thinks the leopard is heading; he has not given up on seeing the cubs. We drive along sandy roads and in and out of the bush stopping and backing up to examine tracks. Craig is particularly adept at spotting movements. He and Bret have an ongoing dialogue I cannot hear from the second-row seat. I just let my eyes follow the trajectory of one or the other's arm, hoping to see what they are observing.

"There she is," Craig says softly.

I crane my neck, but don't see her at first. And then she emerges into a clearing. Our vehicle parallels her movement as she saunters along. She doesn't seem bothered by us. She settles into a grassy area where she poses for us, first standing and then sitting giving us profile shots. There is no doubt that she is royalty, we are paparazzi.

Her body flattens as she lies down; there's not a bit of tension in the movement. Her tail lifts and falls, accentuating her length and grace. Her face is almost sweet. We are less than thirty feet from her with nothing between us. She is at home, we are visiting.

Female leopard in Sabi Sands.

We leave the leopard and get back on the road. A few elephants cross our path. Seeing them casually walk into view feels like an everyday experience after the rush we had from tracking.

As the sun begins to set, Bret stops the vehicle and sets up for a sundowner, a tradition on safaris. He and Richard lay a table with an array alcoholic beverages, coffee and tea selections, and snacks to enjoy while we watch the sky change from grey to deep pink and the sun turn red.

Back at the camp, dinner awaits on the veranda. We dine on duck in a wine reduction under sparkling stars in a dark sky. Too tired to think, we shower and go to bed soon after we finish eating. There'll be no sleeping in tomorrow morning; we need to be up by six for the next game drive.

I fall asleep thinking that nothing could top today even though our game ranger said tomorrow may.

Chapter 4
CUBS AND PUPS

A bang on the door startles us. It's 6 a.m. It's Bret making sure we're awake. We bolt out of bed and begin what will remain our morning drill while on safari. With a splash of water on our faces, we reach for a ziplocked bag, dress in its contents, grab a jacket and head for the patio by 6:20 where a display of coffee, juices, biscuits, and fruit decorates a long, linen-covered table. By 6:45, we're ready for the game drive. Today's objective: lions and cape buffalo.

Four massive male lions, believed to be from the same litter, troll Sabi Sands and Kruger National Park killing male lions or other cats they consider potential competition. So far, they have slain thirty-six lions and taken over nineteen prides destroying any cubs they encounter so that only their line will survive. Each one, because of its size and pugnacity, is fearsome; traveling in a pack, they are formidable.

I wrap my hands around my hot coffee mug to keep warm as I listen to Bret and picture monstrous lions. Although engaged in what he is saying, I keep one eye on the safari vehicles, waiting for Bret to point out where ours is in the line of six. I'm determined to be in the front row; I don't want to miss a word Bret says today. He gives the signal; I tug at Joel's arm and try to look nonchalant hurrying to the vehicle.

Hot water bottles tucked under blankets await us on our seats. We place them on our laps welcoming the warmth on this chilly morning. The honeymooners, Jillian and Craig, don't seem to mind being in the second row. They're easy. Richard, our game tracker, stands alongside the safari vehicle. He waits for us to get comfortable and then slips in beside Bret.

As we head out, I ask if anything can be done to stop the slayings by the marauding lions. "Human intervention is not allowed. The killings will continue," Bret says. "With the odds stacked against winning a battle with the four brothers, the head pride male may choose to run away. But that's almost a death sentence in itself. It would be hard for him to survive on his own."

"If there's no intervention, how would their reign end?"

"As they take over more and more prides, their territory may expand to the point where it is impractical for the four to remain together. They may divide up the territories."

I wonder how lions decide who gets what.

Bret continues, "If they divide up, each will become more vulnerable and can be picked off one at a time. Or, the band may stay together. The bonds males form when they are young last a lifetime. They'll continue killing other lions until they get too old to defend themselves against younger, more powerful males. Any way it ends, it will be ugly."

Later, I learn what *ugly* means as I watch a video of an aging member of a coalition of killer lions being destroyed by a younger band seeking revenge for the killing of one of its own. The band comes upon the killer lion separated from its coalition. Working as a team of distractors and attackers, the revenge-seekers bite through the spine of the old lion. Unable to raise his paralyzed hind quarters, he continues to battle, his front paws swiping, his mouth open and challenging. The young lions, capable of killing the old one outright, choose instead to cannibalize him starting at his rump while a member occupies the still-menacing lion at its front. His attempts at defense become increasingly feeble as he slowly sinks to the ground. The image of him looking back over his shoulder, seeing his hind quarters being devoured is stuck in my mind. For me, that is about as ugly as ugly can get.

As we drive along, Bret, with his eyes scanning the sand for tracks, continues to tell us about bands of lions, the most notorious of which were the Mapogos, "rogues" in Zulu. Around 2002, the five alpha males, all brothers, formed a coalition with a powerful male that joined their pride. The coalition moved into Sabi Sands in 2004 where they reigned as indisputable kings for seven years. Their hunger for domination led them to kill over 100 lions in a single year, taking over more territory and prides than any other coalition ever had done. Their exceptional size and beauty attracted biologists, trackers, rangers, and visitors to the preserves. Their ruthlessness, and the length of their reign made them legendary, so much so that they became the subject of a documentary, *Brothers in Blood*.

I ask if the current coalition has been named.

"Not yet."

A call comes in. The plans to look for lions and cape buffalo quickly change. The leopard cubs have been spotted. The cubs, a few months old, are thirsty and are heading toward water. We take off with the determination of a tow truck heading toward a car accident. I'm still hanging onto images of massive lions but figure a brief diversion to cubs might not be bad. Besides, none of the game rangers have reported seeing the lions.

We bump down the riverbank as softly as a safari vehicle can. There before us are two cubs wrestling with each other—practice play for hunting skills they will need. They separate. One sits still, the other chases something too small for us to see. They run, jump, play tag within the confines of the narrow sandy cove. They are like children at a playground; but, unlike children, they pause to listen and sense their environment. Joel and I click away.

Bret says, "This is pure gold!" He is as excited as we are, maybe more so, to witness the cubs romping. From his reaction, we come to realize how rare a sight this is to see.

We follow the cubs from the riverbank into the tangled grass and thorny bushes. The safari vehicle cuts its own path, running down thorn bushes the height of small trees. A two-inch long stiletto plucks off Craig's baseball cap; Richard jumps out and retrieves it. We crouch down to avoid having more than a hat plucked. Jillian and Craig, in the row behind us, are seated higher and need to crouch lower. The cubs disappear, but Bret seems to have a sixth sense about where to find them. We spot them slinking along shrubs and then climbing onto low branches. We don't see the mother, but Bret assures us she is nearby. The cubs slow their play and after a while, flop down on tree limbs lying near the ground, their bodies wilt into a state of relaxation that only a baby without cares can know. They watch us watch them. The urge to reach for one to cradle against my shoulder is strong. The image of the mother leopard lunging at me is stronger.

Leopard cub at Sabi Sands.

By now, another safari vehicle pulls up near ours. We decide to leave. Bret checks in with other rangers. No lion sightings. The four brothers must have crossed back into Kruger. We drive to an open area where Bret and Richard set up a folding table on an outcropping facing the river. They place sugar cookies on the table alongside hot coffee, tea, cocoa, and, of course, a selection of spirits—scotch, vodka, and gin. Joel and I watch a small herd of elephants, partially hidden by trees, graze across the river. Bret, Jillian, and Craig carry on conversation. Richard casually stands nearby.

It's 9:30 a.m. when we head back to Kirkman's Kamp, an hour away. Caught up in the adventure of tracking lions and then cubs, I am surprised that three hours have passed since leaving the lodge. Along the way back, we pass zebra, giraffe, and small and large antelope—springbok, kudu, nyala, and impala. To me, they are like endless candy in an unbounded candy store.

A nyala grazing just off our veranda welcomes us back to our room. Joel plops on the bed; I sneak in some souvenir shopping at the camp's store and then sit on a porch at the main building, writing in my journal.

A nyala by our veranda.

At one o'clock, I wake Joel telling him there are great-looking salads being served for lunch. He is still full from last night's dinner but keeps me company anyway. Three o'clock and the afternoon game drive comes quickly. We head out to see a hyena den where mothers and their pups currently are hanging out. With a thoughtful resonance to his voice, Bret says, "I love hyenas; they're fascinating." He pauses and then adds, "They're my favorite animal."

I'm not so sure that I will share his enthusiasm. I think of hyenas as ugly, sneaky creatures that prey on the kill of others.

Bret continues, "The female hyenas are larger than the males. They are born with, and continue to have, male and female genitalia. You can look at a pup with an obviously extended penis. It looks like a male, but you really can't tell." He adds, "The adult males don't have anything to do with the females except for mating."

This is getting interesting, but I'm still not sold on hyenas having favorite animal status.

We pull up right to the edge of the den, a shallow sandy area protected by a rock overhang. Two mothers, resting with their eyes closed, are unfazed by us, but remain alert to the four pups' movement. Dog-like in looks, but not dogs, hyenas actually are in the mongoose family. Bret tells us that a hyena can smell a carcass two miles away. That increases the likelihood of finding a meal while reducing the number of times she needs to leave her pups unprotected at the den.

Silently, we watch the romping pups with smiles on our faces, but inevitably a chuckle or two escapes. Puffy little balls when they snuggle, totally mischievous when they unfold, the pups behave like puppies in a pet store window. Two of the four are beginning to get their spots; the other two are still all black. One, seemingly determined to let no one rest, races around the den and then dislodges a pup snuggled next to its mother by wedging its own body between them. A moment of nestling later, the wayward pup extracts itself from the mother and engages another pup in a wrestling match. The match ends abruptly as both pups come to check out our vehicle.

Hyena with her pups.

Bret tells us that one time a pup retreated from the safari vehicle showing signs of fear. The mother threw it against the tire and, as the pup retreated, threw it back again and again until it showed no fear.

I tried doing something like that at a swimming class for my then one-year-old daughter. It didn't work. She screamed louder and louder until the instructor asked us to leave.

Bret's fascination with hyenas is beginning to rub off on me and then he clinches it with, "Unlike baby leopards that need to eat meat to survive, hyena pups get all the nourishment they need from their mother's nutrient-rich milk."

I *see*. The hyena female is engineered for independence and survival. She needs a male briefly and minimally, can feed off other animal's kill but is an effective hunter as well, and is a self-contained source of food for her brood. Superwoman!

We leave the hyenas as the late afternoon sun washes the den in golden light. It appears the rogue lions have not re-entered Sabi Sands; we won't be going in search of them today. Word has circulated that a dominant male leopard has made a kill and hauled it high into a tree. Richard knows where to find it. Off we go.

Along the way, we pass a mother and baby hippo submerged in a pond except for two small mountains of mid-section and two sets of eyes. As we watch the mounds hoping to see some movement, Bret tells us that Kruger had a problem with overpopulation of hippos. The problem reached a dangerous point and caused a dilemma given the policy of not interfering with nature. As it happened, nature took care of itself.

Hippos have extremely sensitive skin and must remain under water in daylight hours to protect themselves from the sun. At night, they leave the water to graze. During the 2015 rainy season, October through March, Kruger experienced the worst drought ever recorded. As the drought continued into the 2016 season, rivers and water holes dried up and vegetation grew increasingly sparse. Hippos were forced to travel farther away from protective waters to find grazing areas while the sun was still blazing. Starvation added to the agony of scorched skin. Thousands of hippos died and the hippo population returned to a viable level.

My stomach clenches and my skin prickles when I think of what an agonizing death that must have been. I can see the blistered, peeling skin worsening as the hippo walks distances in the sun seeking, but not finding, soothing water deep enough to cover its enormous body. Images of bloated corpses that had to choose between staying near water or having food, neither choice a good one, cross my mind. I'm glad to be distracted from my own thoughts by being jostled by the safari vehicle and searching the bush for live animals.

We come upon a white rhino and her baby grazing about thirty feet off the road. The mother presses her young one close to her body as we approach. We watch for a while and then drive to what looks like a combination of picnic shack and lookout by a waterhole. As the sky turns to grey, we sip sundowners and wait to see if the dominant leopard will come to the waterhole. He obliges. While we watch him drink, we learn from Bret that female leopards have territories with boundaries. A male's territory may overlap more than one female's. To become the dominant male, a leopard must establish and defend a territory, not allowing any other male to roam within it.

"Ousting a dominant male is very difficult," Bret says. "If it should happen, the ousted male would become nomadic. He'd be forced to roam, unable to remain in one place for long or else he would be killed by the dominant male in that territory."

As the leopard ages, he loses strength and speed, his teeth wear out making it harder to hunt successfully and to defend his territory. At some point, the throne is relinquished to a younger, stronger male and the older one becomes nomadic.

Having quenched his thirst, the leopard walks along the side our stationary vehicle with no urgency evident in his stride. After he passes, the engine comes to life with a low rumble and we follow him to the tree where he has hidden his kill. In the dim evening light, we barely trace the leopard's form as he sprints up the tree. Hyenas circle at the bottom waiting for the carcass to fall. One wrong move and the leopard will have bought dinner for them and he will go hungry.

The grey sky turns to black. Richard shines a spotlight on the tree. An impala carcass dangles from a branch more than twenty feet up. From his perch on a limb next to his kill, the leopard studies the carcass, considering how to approach eating dinner. Having dragged the carcass into a difficult-to-reach spot, he has made it difficult for himself to eat. He begins to tear tentatively into his dinner. A nearly torn-through leg starts to fall. A lightning-fast paw snatches it up. The leopard then grips the impala in his jaws and drags it to a more secure limb farther up. The hyenas will not feed off his efforts tonight.

We leave the leopard to his dinner and return to Kirkman's Kamp for ours. Tables and chairs are set up in a boma—a circular communal area enclosed by fencing made from saplings and left open to the sky. A barbeque dinner of ribs, antelope, sausage, potatoes, stir fry, mushrooms and onions, and dessert is served buffet style. We sit at tables for ten instead of our usual private ones. I give up trying to avoid gaining weight. The incredibly delicious, baked-on-the-premises bread breaks down the last crumb of willpower I have. The African staff chants traditional songs. Some break into dancing singly, others join in groups of two or three, sometimes mimicking the movement of animals, other times following patterns of foot movements. They are having so much fun with their voices and displaying such dance prowess that I want to join them. But I don't, fearing my movements would look stiffly formal compared to the natural flow of their bodies matched to the rhythms beat on a single drum.

Tired though I am after our wonderful dinner, I need to shower before going to sleep. I'm afraid the smell of barbeque that permeates my clothing and hair will bring the fearsome lions to us instead of us going to them. Tomorrow, we will search for the rogue brothers again.

Chapter 5
KILLERS AND KINGS

The wind that began kicking up last night continues into this morning. It is the first time we have needed to wear both our vests and jackets. The hot water bottles and blankets on the safari vehicle will be appreciated twice as much today.

There's no lingering over coffee and biscuit. The word is out that the killer lions have crossed back into Sabi Sands. By 6:30 all the vehicles scatter with a single mission—find the lions. Teams of trackers and rangers from Kirkman's Kamp will keep in close communication with each other and with teams from other resorts in the preserve.

The door has been removed from Bret's side of the safari vehicle so he can search the ground for tracks more readily. To aid tracking, Richard rides high on a seat perched on the left front fender. Bret drives to where the lions were spotted. Joel and I sit in the first row of passenger seats, Jillian and Craig in the back. None of us is speaking. From the slow sweep of Joel's head and unblinking eyes, I can tell that, like me, he is intent on spotting any movement that might betray the presence of the lions. A layer of anticipation tamps down the building excitement.

Richard, our game tracker, on the left fender. Bret, our game ranger, at the wheel.

The area is vast; none of the other safari vehicles are in sight. Bret slows, stops, and then backs up. He points to lion tracks distinguished by the large size of the pad and four toes. He concludes that the lions passed this way sometime this morning and are heading in the direction we are traveling. Seated behind Bret, I also see tracks; but the ones I see look like they are pointing in the opposite direction from the ones Bret and Richard are following. Knowing I sometimes see things backwards, I say nothing. Besides, I've amassed very little tracking experience growing up in Brooklyn, New York.

Richard jumps off his seat and walks ahead, disappearing around a bend. Bret examines nearby tracks more closely and sees that there are tracks on top of the lions' tracks indicating the tracks may be old. He searches the road for more clues. What he finds is ambiguity and possibility. He gets back in the vehicle. We catch up to Richard at a *Y* in the road. He thinks the lions have backtracked. We drive back to where we first saw tracks and follow the tracks I had seen before.

Richard gets ready to go on foot into a large area of dry grass, the brownish-gold color of lions. Bret tells him we'll circle around counterclockwise and join up with him. With a firmness in his voice I have not heard before and his eyes fixed on Richard's, he adds, "Stay in touch." The command covers, but doesn't hide, Bret's concern.

My eyes follow Richard, a solitary figure entering a place where lions can easily hide. Joel is silent with eyes fixed on Richard as well. I check out the zipped-up rifle case on the dashboard and notice the zipper teeth are separated part-way down. I wonder how long it would take in an emergency to extract the rifle from a case with a broken zipper. But I don't ask, not wanting to give life to something horrific just by having thoughts of it.

I watch Richard, armed only with a two-way radio, walking tall in the bent grass and wonder how he can do that with such confidence when we are repeatedly reminded that just standing up in the vehicle could trigger an attack. My thoughts flip between thinking he's confident and he's crazy. I settle on he must know what he's doing.

We bounce along, dodging branches that whip through the open vehicle. No word from Richard. We keep going. No Richard, no lions. More distance, more thorn bushes mowed down by the front of our vehicle.

The radio crackles. It's Richard. He's found the lions.

Bret throws his hands in the air in excitement, yells for us to hold on, and takes off like a banshee. I swear, if one of us were plucked from the vehicle by a thorn bush, he wouldn't notice we were gone. We vault over bumps, logs, rocks anything that gets in our way, and scoop up Richard waiting for us in the tall grass. With his flat palm and four fingers extended together he points the way to where the lions are hidden. Two of the four lions disappear into the brush as we approach. We are within fifteen feet of the remaining two when Bret cuts the engine. Not a sound comes from any of us.

One of the lions, partially hidden by the bush, tears into a slab of ribs left from a well-dined-on cape buffalo carcass. Focused as he is on his dinner, he is still watchful. Without interrupting his meal, he lifts his head and we can see the intensity of his yellow eyes. The second lion lies on his side in a patch of grass soaking up the sun. A look of contentment spreads across his broad, sleepy face. His belly is distended from the feast he has enjoyed. He appears to be asleep, but with any movement, his eyes slit open just enough to assess the situation or ward off any intruder's impulse to come closer.

In a stage whisper filled with excitement, Bret exclaims, "Look at those manes! They're massive." Without moving his eyes from the feasting lion, Bret continues with a low, steady voice, "A lion's mane is light colored until he is about six years old and then it turns brown. That signals the maturation of the lion. The larger the mane, the more fearful it appears to other lions and the more attractive it is to females."

The manes of these lions are thick and turning dark—no problem attracting the ladies. They have already taken over nineteen prides. I wonder if their thirst for dominance is insatiable.

A member of the band of lions with remains of a cape buffalo.

Another member snoozing.

Bret points to a circular area of churned-up sand alongside our vehicle. "That's the struggle and kill site." He adds, "It's not easy to take down a buffalo; they're big and mean. If these lions are anywhere near as skilled as the Mapogos, they can take down full grown male giraffes, rhinos, and hippos."

We're no more than ten feet from the resting lion. I estimate it would take a stride-and-a-half and a fraction of a second for him to be in our laps. A blade of grass sticking up by the side of the vehicle creates a slender blur in the center of every portrait I take of him. I'm afraid to speak or reach past Joel to bend the grass down. Finally, I get the courage to whisper, almost to myself, that the blade is in my way. Bret hears me, nudges Richard with his elbow and tells him to get the grass out of the way. Richard snaps his head toward the lion and then whips it back to Bret with disbelief shooting from his eyes.

"Not the grass by the lion! The one behind you," Bret tells him. Relief washes over Richard. A burst of involuntary laughter lets loose from all of us. The lion opens his eyes and then closes them again. Richard snaps off the blade of grass and I get a better shot.

Bret tells us about a tourist, "He wanted me to give him the rifle and let him stand by a resting lion. I refused. He said, 'I don't want to kill him; I just want a picture with him.' Crazy tourists."

I exempt myself from being included in the *crazy tourist* category.

Bret continues, "Lions have nothing to fear from any other animal or us in this preserve. Their only enemies are other lions. With the coalition these brothers have formed, they don't even have to worry about that for now."

The lion eating ribs has had enough of being disturbed; he drags the carcass farther into the bush. As he walks away, we can see his massive size. I multiply him by four and understand why, given the opportunity, other males run away.

Another safari vehicle pulls up. We decide to move on. Bret's phone rings. The mother leopard has been spotted, this time *with* her cubs.

Chapter 6
THE HUNTING LESSON

The leopard cubs are hungry. The smaller of the two cries out. Bret shakes his head; he's concerned over its distress. "The cubs have gone without food for too long," he says. "The mother's been away hunting. She's come back to lead her cubs to the kill."

As we follow the family, we watch the little ones meander in front of their mother, sometimes walking, sometimes running, looking back over their shoulders frequently as if to ask, "Are we going the right way?" They have never been this far from where their mother left them while she hunted—a place with trees to climb, grass to hide in, rocks to romp across, and a river with cool water to drink. Now, they are in new territory marked by sand, dry low-lying grass, desiccated shrubs, and mostly leafless trees. They're highly visible in the open space; their only escape from predatory animals are the trees.

In a flash, the larger of the two cubs sprints toward a tree fifty yards away. The tree's thick, long, undulated branches covered with dark leaves is an ideal place to hide a carcass in this otherwise barren area. The second cub follows suit. They know that the first to arrive at the kill gets to eat until it's fully satisfied. If the kill is substantial enough, there will be leftovers for the second cub; if not, the cub will go hungry.

The larger one reaches the tree first and with great speed and agility climbs among the branches hoping this is where its mother has nestled a carcass beyond the reach of other predators. The smaller one sits at the base of the tree and whimpers from hunger. The mother comes, sits next to its cub, and comforts it by gently brushing its head with her tongue.

Joel asks, "If one cub proves to be dominant and repeatedly finds the food first, what happens to the other one? Will it starve to death?"

Bret answers, "If that happens, the mother will hide two kills and lead each cub to a different site."

Mother leopard soothing her hungry cub.

No carcass is found. The larger cub scampers down and the three move on. After a while, the weary cubs sit down in the grass to take a rest. The mother nudges them to get up; they resist. She prods further. They give in. Using subtle movements of her tail to communicate with her little ones, the mother encourages them to find the kill on their own.

Another leaf-filled tree, another disappointment. By now, I am scanning the horizon along with the cubs looking for the next possible hiding place. I spot one, so does the bigger cub. It dashes up the trunk to a branch where a rodent stands suspended between action and no action. The cub lowers his rear quarters and raises his right front paw. A staring match ensues. With the lightness and fluidity of air, the cub further extends its paw and holds it in mid-air a few inches short of the rodent. In the stillness surrounding the prey and the predator, I feel as if I am seeing silence.

From behind me I hear Craig say, "C'mon, baby. You can do it!"

The cub hesitates, withdraws his paw, and then retreats.

"Ahh! You almost had it," he says.

We continue following the cubs. As with yesterday's game drive, distance goes unnoticed and time is measured by what we're seeing and doing instead of by the pulsations of a clock. It's only when we leave or return to the lodge that we are aware of the time at all.

We move on, abandoning the cubs in their search for the kill. We learn later in the day that the mother continued marching the cubs farther, but no ranger or tracker stayed with them long enough to see them reach their goal. Perhaps there was no carcass stashed away. Perhaps the mother had to move her cubs to a new location fearing they might be discovered if left in the same area too long. Or, perhaps she had been waiting for all of us to leave.

With a chuckle, Bret says as he drives along, "We were supposed to have a surprise for you forty minutes ago."

Twenty minutes later, we arrive at the surprise destination, a flat area surrounded by trees where cloth-covered tables are set with plates, napkins, and silverware. Plastics and paper are not used in this eco-protective country. Service people stand at the ready behind a string of buffet tables with fruits and salads lining one end and large pans of bacon, sausage, and eggs covering the other. It's after eleven. I wonder out loud to Joel if we should save ourselves for lunch; but the look we give each other says, "Let's eat."

"We'll skip lunch," Joel volunteers.

When we return to Kirkman's Kamp, Joel naps while I write in my journal seated on a deck at the main lodge. A nyala comes and grazes no more than three feet from the hassock on which my feet rest.

Around two o'clock, the heat begins to wear me down. I decide to return to the room but, just out of curiosity, I take a detour to check out the lunch menu.

Moroccan vegetable soup
Tabbouleh and a variety of other salads
Wild rice risotto
Homemade ice cream

I go to the room to wake Joel knowing he would not want to miss risotto. Groggy though he is, he hears risotto and ice cream and quickly becomes a willing conspirator in abandoning the no-lunch resolve.

By 3:30 p.m., we have refilled our water bottles and are back riding through the brambles. Richard, perched on the seat on the front left fender, takes out a small machete to slice our way through the branches that threaten to stab us with dagger-like thorns.

Bret wants to show us an area he loves. "It's so beautiful," he says.

The place he brings us to, one filled with an abundance of dark, leafy trees and lush shrubbery, is a surprise in this dry climate, but not novel in its beauty for us. Joel and I live among greenery. For me, the openness in the barren areas and the absence of leaves revealing the sculptural limbs of trees are more exciting. Nevertheless, I can enjoy the lusciousness of this area that springs from a water source not visible from the road we are on.

We come upon four rhinos grazing in shrubs just off the side of the road. They bolt farther into the bush and form a huddle, presenting their backsides to the road. They're perfectly still, trying to camouflage themselves as boulders. It might have worked if we hadn't seen them scramble.

Bret explains that rhinos have very poor eyesight and, with the wind blowing, they can't hear well either; hence, they are quick to hide. We don't stop to watch their motionless, boulder-like bodies. Word has come that elephants are by the water. We head to the Sand River and down its short but steep bank.

A nursing herd clusters across the river. Nestled against its mother, a very young calf nurses. He finishes and then reclines, pushing himself against the side of a large, but still young, calf. The bigger one tries to prod the little one into getting up, but it just tumbles from side-to-side rubbing against the other's body, refusing to leave it alone. A third calf, the biggest of the three, joins the middle-sized one in tousling about the smallest calf. The play gets a little rough. The smallest one cries out and the mother comes to its rescue. With the sweep of her trunk, she pushes the larger ones off the little one while emitting a squeal of admonishment. I laugh at the universality of the mother's utterings. I can almost hear ring out from her warnings, "Leave him alone. He's smaller than you are!"

Mischief maker little elephant calf along the river.

Bret signals it's time to leave. We head along the bank and then into a part of the riverbed striped with wet sand and water. With Richard seated beside him, Bret aims the vehicle down the riverbed's center, swerving and splashing in the soppy sands, testing the limits of our vehicle's ability to plow through tire tracks etched by earlier vehicles; our wheels further deepen the ruts. Windblown and jostled, we enjoy every minute.

Several minutes into the ride, Bret and Richard hop out of the vehicle to examine the depth of a pool of water in front of us. Barefooted, pants rolled up, ankle deep in sinking sand, they look at each other, chuckle, and nod. The gleam in their eyes is apparent even from where we are seated.

They climb back in and, with a focus on what lies ahead, they put the engine into gear.

I don't know for sure if they both agreed that we could get through this patch of water, but if they did, they were both wrong. The wheels plunge forward just far enough into the muck to have us committed when all four start to spin, digging us deeper into trouble. We passengers jump out to lighten the load, but it doesn't help. Bret and Richard survey the situation. Richard gets a jack and begins raising one wheel at a time as we use the lone shovel and our feet to shove sand under each wheel. When all four are sanded, Bret throws the vehicle into reverse. We move about two inches, begin spinning, and repeat the jacking process.

Others with bigger feet than I have seem to be doing a better job of pushing sand under the raised wheels, so I step back to enjoy the scenery. Standing barefoot in the warm, wet sand, I leave my own footprint next to a lion's paw print. I gaze at the sky still lit by the afternoon sun and trace the clouds to their reflection in patches of water. As I do, I see something slinking toward us. Its slow trot makes it clear it is not in a hurry. Its profile, with high front haunches and low-slung hind quarters, makes it clear it's a hyena. Its presence looks so natural in this riverbed, that I have no concern as I watch it meander along. It's only when the hyena is at fifty yards and closing in that my internal warning system turns on.

I get Bret's attention and point to what's approaching. He says, "Don't worry about it. It's not interested in us."

I hope he's a better judge of hyenas than of the vehicle's traction in wet sand.

Stuck in the Sand River.

Hyena checking us out.

As I keep one eye on the hyena and one on the jackings-up, a story Bret told yesterday looms large in my mind. According to Bret, one of the workers at the lodge had been out drinking. He returned to his room and fell asleep on the couch without locking his door. A hyena walked in and killed him.

"A hyena won't bother you," Bret said. "But the guy was lying down, asleep. For the hyena, he was fair game."

The story translated into two lessons for me:

> Lesson 1: Keep your door locked.
> Lesson 2: Don't look dead if a hyena is around.

I have no intention of lying down in the sandy riverbank. Apparently, the hyena has no plans to wait for me to do so either. Satisfied there is nothing of interest, it ambles off. I turn my eyes and camera toward the pale pinks and blues of the early evening sky creating paintings reflected in the ribbons of silvery water.

For more than an hour, our efforts to extract ourselves yield little results. Bret, despite multiple urgings from Craig, refuses to call for a Range Rover to tow us. Joel and Craig show signs that they have had their fill of making the useless rounds of jacking-up wheels. Richard, usually patient, quiet, and willing to leave decision-making to Bret, has mutiny stirring within his normally serene eyes; he's the one who has been pumping the jack handle while others push sand. I don't mind the time passing here on the riverbank; I'm busy taking photos as the light begins to change. Finally, when evening threatens to close in, Bret makes the call for help but insists on continuing the effort. As a rescue vehicle appears in the distance on the opposite bank, Bret becomes more determined and the jacking becomes more intense. Backing up in second gear with Joel and Craig pushing at the front, and Richard pulling on a tow rope at the rear, Bret maneuvers the vehicle onto more solid ground.

We are good to go just as the Range Rover arrives. The driver looks disappointed; but Bret looks like he just won a championship wrestling match. With slyness written all over his face, he explains that there's a pink-baseball cap tradition at the camp. If a game ranger gets a vehicle stuck, and, much to his embarrassment, needs to be towed, he is crowned with a pink baseball cap which he must wear around camp until he can pass it on to the next driver who requires rescuing. I suspect the current pink-cap wearer will be sorely disappointed when he hears how close he came to, but missed, passing the cap.

We are behind schedule getting back to see the lions. Somehow, Bret knows they are going to cross the river and is hoping we are still in time to catch the four of them lying around together before they do. By now, it is almost dark and getting darker by the second.

"Hold on," Bret calls. Our hands snap automatically into position on the bar in front of us. I bet we are travelling at fifty miles an hour around corners, over rocks, and up and down inclines slowing only when we leave the road and enter the bramble. Richard, from his seat on the front fender, snatches the spotlight from its stand. His posture radiates intense concentration as he sweeps both sides of the road ahead, watching for anything poised to cross our path. Few words are exchanged between Bret and him as Bret barrels ahead. The competence and trust these two men have in each other is amazing to observe. We are so lucky to have them as our ranger and tracker.

We arrive at the place where the lions are expected to cross; they're not there. We wait awhile in the darkness. Impatient, and afraid we'll miss them, Bret decides to try another location. As we bounce down a bank one tire at a time at another site, we see other vehicles are already there. Bret maneuvers into a spot from which we can see the lions in the dim lights cast by other vehicles. We see only two brothers, not four; one is asleep and the other is preening.

We wait silently for something to happen. Meanwhile, Richard shines the spotlight on the ground near each lion so we can see more clearly their every movement. Mostly, we watch them breathe. Every move, and even their breathing, is a moment of fascination for me. Their huge manes remind me of the MGM lion that roars at the beginning of movies. As a child, I was scared stiff of that lion. I would squeeze my eyes shut, stuff my fingers in my ears, and push my body into my mother's seeking her protection. And now, here I am in the dark, with nothing between me and two magnificent killer lions and I feel not an ounce of fear.

Lion along the riverbank at night.

"They have to roar," Bret whispers. "They are separated from their brothers. They'll call to each other to meet before crossing. You have never heard anything like it."

"C'mon. Get up!" he pleads. But they lions don't move or make a sound.

When the second lion lies down, I give up hope. They look like they are settled in for the night. I turn to Bret and ask, "Is it unusual for them to be sleeping now? I thought lions are nocturnal."

"No. They sleep for about twenty hours a day."

Now I know what animal my husband is related to!

Bret desperately wants us to hear the lions roar. He keeps repeating, "They are going to roar. They have to roar. They are separated from their brothers. They have to roar!"

He struggles to find words to describe the magnificence of the sound. We wait until well-past the time we're expected back at the lodge for dinner. Bret is more disappointed than we are that we need to leave without hearing a roar. Joel and I are curious about, but really don't know, what we are missing; we can only suspect its grandness.

Chapter 7
BETWEEN PLACES

My objective today is to have nothing eventful happen so that I have nothing to write about. Finding time to make entries in my journal, download photos, and get some sleep has been difficult. I can manage two out of the three—the first two—but poorly at that. Perhaps Zambia and Victoria Falls will provide me with just a few simple things to say and much needed sleep.

We leave Sabi Sands in South Africa and head for the airport; we're on our way to Livingstone, Zambia. My hope for an uneventful day begins to fray shortly after we settle into the car for an hour-and-a-half drive to the airport. The driver is also a tour guide for Kruger National Park and can't resist delivering a monologue. I can't resist listening.

"Look! There are impalas. They are the McDonalds of the bush. They are fast and they are everywhere!" He laughs. It brings a smile to my lips and gets a chuckle from Joel; we've heard this before and don't mind hearing it again. The driver adds that the dark markings on the back of the impala's rump even form a letter *M* arched like the ones on McDonalds' signs.

We drive along a smooth, wide road, the air is crystal clear, and the sunshine brightens everything in sight. I lazily look out the window and see that a fence, at least ten-feet tall, runs along the left side of the road.

"It's an electrified fence that goes around Kruger and Sabi Sands," our driver says. "It's there to prevent the animals from getting into the villages."

I look to the right and see that in the open, flat areas, there are homes and small businesses scattered in a village, one of several we pass.

"If a lion, leopard or other animal dangerous to the people finds its way into the village, it is tranquilized and brought back to Kruger. A buffalo, springbok, giraffe or other edible animal is captured, butchered and given to the village for food."

It crosses my mind that amongst the low-lying, concrete houses a giraffe's presence would be outstanding. Calls to Kruger to capture the escapee must buzz through the phone lines in anticipation of the feast that lies ahead. While I might pass on eating giraffe, I'd be first in line for springbok. The lingering memory of its deliciously delicate flavor is enough to start me drooling. Kruger, as it turns out, has a butcher shop on its premises. In addition to donating butchered wayward animals, the park slaughters animals at different times of the year and sells the meat to the villagers.

I flash back to the sun scorched hippos and think that Kruger might have been able to use them for food, reducing the competition for vegetation and water during the drought and, perhaps, saving some of them from a torturous death. As if reading my mind, our driver tells us that as the impact from the drought intensified, by September of 2016 officials at Kruger decided to butcher animals and distribute the meat to villagers.

"People were starving, and the animals were going to die anyway," he tells us. "Hippos at small ponds were targeted most. They mark their territory with an explosion of feces. As they defecate, they spin their short tails to spread their mark farther. In small ponds, that's enough to pollute the water and make it unusable for other animals."

The visual of a hippo-sized explosion is too much to take in. I miss the next few sentences and pick up with the driver telling us that cape buffalo were butchered, too.

"They consume a lot of vegetation. Killing a cape buffalo means more food for many other animals."

"What were the hippo and buffalo populations at that time?" Joel asks.

"Seventy-five hundred hippos and 47,000 cape buffalo. That was the highest number there had ever been."

"How many did Kruger slaughter?"

"The plan was to slaughter about 350 hippos and buffalos; but I don't know how many were killed."

As Joel and the driver continue talking, I'm tossing around in my mind Kruger's decision to slaughter the animals, an act in direct opposition to its policy of non-intervention with animals' lives. Even now, as a band of marauding lions continues to add to the thirty-six lions it already killed and to its takeover of prides, the park has no intension of violating its non-intervention policy. The drought's disastrous effect must have pushed the policy past its limits. At some point, non-intervention must have become an actor in the tragedy.

It's not until later that I read about the mixed results of interventions at the time Kruger was declared a National Park in 1926. By 1900, elephants had been cleared from the area primarily by poachers. With the declaration of the National Park as a protected area, the elephants flourished, reaching a current population estimated at 20,000. A second intervention instituted at the time dealt with the human side. Communities of hunter-gatherers were relocated to outside the park. Authorities hadn't realized at the time that they were removing one of the most important drivers of the Kruger ecosystem. The hunter-gathers had been an essential part of the equation in controlling animal populations.

I take in the information and wonder if current communities of hunter-gathers could be reintroduced into the park today and given the dual role of managing animal populations and protecting them against poachers. I think about the communities that were displaced and the challenges they must have faced in a new area not knowing the patterns of the animals' movements and behaviors, locations and use of waterholes, and sources of edible plants. I think about how families had to give up favorite places to explore, recreate in, and share with new generations. How did they survive the disruption? Did they? Could a current community of hunter-gatherers survive being relocated into the park?

As I entertain the possibility, I consider how delicate the balance of nature is and how limited our foresight is in predicting consequences beyond our immediate circumstances and knowledge. I also think about how, even today, we uproot whole communities, mostly impoverished ones, disrupting ways of life and support systems, to build high-rise buildings, shopping centers, and event venues to meet, and often just to stimulate, demand. Planners may provide similar or better structures; but how can they re-create the intricacies of a support system?

Farther into the drive, we pass several commercial farms of tall, dark trees densely planted. Lined up like soldiers alongside the road, they render the view beyond them impenetrable. Their straight trunks are used for utility poles. As we get closer to the airport, the land turns from flat to hilly. Acres of citrus trees, tobacco, peanuts, mangoes, and avocados lie just beyond either side of the road. The grand display of bright greens lightens my spirit.

We arrive at an African bush-themed airport complete with a thatched roof and an interior decorated with woods from a variety of African trees. A skycap engages Joel in conversation telling him about his family, children, education, and plans. I catch enough snippets to know Joel has gotten wrapped up in the man's life and is about to hand over an overly generous tip. It's happened before. The words *Kind Heart* must be embroidered somewhere on Joel's chest. It's one of those things about Joel I get to step back from and enjoy.

We board our airplane, a comfortable thirty-seven seat jet, and head to Zambia three-and-a-half hours away. Upon arrival, we join the tail end of a long line of travelers waiting to purchase KAZA Visas, the single visa that permits entry into Zimbabwe as well as Zambia. It will allow us to see Victoria Falls from both sides. The line is slow moving, but having grown up in Brooklyn, New York, we are used to long lines. We're just grateful we are inside a building and not standing in the sun.

Up ahead, there seems to be some confusion slowing the processing. Forty-five minutes later, a tour group of thirty people is all that stands between us and our visas. Joel asks their tour guide what's happening. The airport has run out of stamps for the KAZA Visa. Not knowing if we even need to go to Zimbabwe, and being short on cash, we decide to forgo shelling out an extra $100 to purchase separate visas for each country. We'll settle on the one for Zambia only.

By the time we get to the luggage area, it is virtually empty; just two blue duffle bags remain with a smattering of conventional luggage. Joel grabs his bag; I hesitate at mine.

"That's not mine," I say as my eyes scan the bag. It's blue, the same size, but looks wrong. The name on the tag confirms it is wrong.

An image of a thirty-person tour group grabbing bags flashes through my mind. They have left the secured baggage claim area. Without explanation, I call to Joel, "Stay here in case I can't get back in."

I shoot past a guard, and exit into a large, rectangular room with glass doors at the far end. Beyond them, a crowd of people is loading onto a bus to who-knows-where. I run past a man with our name on a placard, acknowledging him with a wave, and head to the sliding doors. I see my duffle bag near the top of the pile of bags waiting to be loaded. As I approach the automatic doors, they don't open. I step back and approach again. No luck. I run to a second set of automatic doors; they don't open. I race back to the first. By now my heart is pounding. Whizzing through my mind is that we are staying no longer than three days in any one place; it would take until the end of the vacation for the luggage to catch up with us. I can survive on three outfits for three weeks, but not just one, the one I have on.

I'm making pleading sounds and banging on the doors as hands reach out to grab the bag next to mine. In the reflection, I glimpse the man with our name on a placard running up behind me. I turn to see him flapping his arms like a giant bird gone mad. His flapping works; the doors open. I pause just long enough to marvel at how clever he was and then rush through the doorway and slap my hand on my duffel bag.

"This is mine," I exclaim as thirty people turn in synchrony to look at the crazy lady laying claim to a piece of their luggage.

"Deretchin," I point with an emphatic finger to the name on the tag. "See, Deretchin. That's my name!"

I sound like I'm pleading for my life! The group leader checks the name on the luggage and apologizes. He walks back with me to the terminal to collect his ward's luggage, and I to collect Joel who must be wondering what has happened to his wife.

With bags in tow, we head to Waterberry Lodge in Livingstone, our home for the next three days. When we arrive, I am struck by how different it is from Sabi Sands where the absence of greenery lays bare the contours of the land and outstretched limbs of trees. Here, the grounds are a manicured garden of green lawn, flowering trees, and trimmed shrubs. Paved pathways instead of sand connect the main lodge to the generously spaced, mushroom-shaped guest cottages, each with a thatched roof over a white, stem-like stucco body. Our unit sits on a shallow bank no more than fifteen feet from the fast-flowing Zambezi River. The distance from bank to bank looks swimmable by an athlete except for the hippos that populate the water.

The river is the longest east-flowing river in Africa. Its 1,599-mile journey begins in the northwest corner of Zambia. From there, it works its way through eastern Angola, flows along the border between Namibia and Botswana, and then travels along the border separating Zambia and Zimbabwe where it topples over the Victoria Falls. From there, the river continues to Mozambique where it empties into the Indian Ocean.

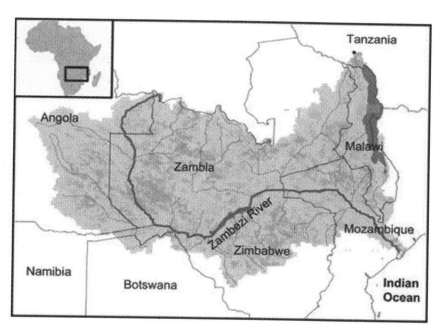

Zambezi River's path through Africa.

Joel and I take a few minutes to linger on the deck taking in the mesmerizing beauty of the waters. The view of the river from our room is unobstructed; it's just us and the river.

A king-size bed dominates the main room of our cottage. Netting, suspended from a rod encircling the bed, gracefully drapes over the entirety of the bed. The netting gives a royal feeling to the room. It's not long before we realize that the netting is a forewarning of the bugs to come and the reason for which all our clothing is in Ziploc bags. Black bugs the size of ladybugs creep along the white walls and on the white sink and commode in the bathroom. There's no point shooing them away; there are too many. This is their home and they are not about to yield territory.

Inside our cottage at Waterberry Lodge.

We leave our bags zippered and head to the main lodge, an open structure at the high end of a sloping lawn that rises from the river. After a refreshing glass of iced tea, we settle down with the lodge director and talk about activities they have available. Joel asks about kayaking, one of the selections on her list. I watch how quickly the current is moving and think that if we kayak downstream, I hope someone motors us back up.

"Kayaking is not for the faint of heart," says the host.

That's me. Faint-of-heart.

The sandy land we see across the less than quarter-mile wide river is Zimbabwe. In between us and it are hippos. It's hippos that are the threat to kayakers, not the current; they are three to eight-ton bundles of aggression. Not too many conversations later I learn that a couple was kayaking down the Zambezi when the husband turned around to look at something. When he turned back, his wife was gone. If Joel sneaks in reservations for a kayaking trip, he's going alone.

The host tells us the hippos like the well-watered, sweet grass of the lawn the lodge overlooks; they come on the property to graze at night. She ends with a caution; don't drink the tap water—it comes from the river.

We sign up for an evening cruise and retreat to our room to settle in. Under siege from a return attack of turista, I take Imodium to quell the cramps and we cancel the pre-dinner cruise. It's not until a half-hour later, when I down yet another pill, that I realize I'm drinking from the tap and not from the pitcher of potable water provided. Instead of dying, which I thought I surely would, I find myself feeling better in time for dinner. I conclude that whatever was in the river water did battle with whatever I had inside me and won—a conclusion borne out over the next few days by my not being plagued by attacks any longer.

Dinner is served by candlelight on the deck overlooking the river, its ripples sparkling with moonlight. The food is very good, but not exquisite like it was at Kirkman's Kamp. There are other guests, but no hippos; we dine alone as do other couples at tables for two or four. We return to our room after dinner, Joel to sleep, me to catch up on downloading photos and making entries in my journal.

By 11:00 p.m. Joel has been asleep for a couple of hours; I'm trying to keep my eyes open to finish labeling photos. The only thing keeping me awake is Joel's snoring. When it gets annoyingly loud, I go to the bed to shake him only to find he's not snoring. The sound is coming from outside. I laugh quietly to myself; the noise is from hippos grazing around our cottage! I listen to their different grunt patterns with interest instead of annoyance:

> Grunt-grunt-grunt-screech
> Grunt-grunt-grunt grunt-grunt-growl
> Snort

It was the snort that had me believing it was Joel snoring. Joel's peaceful demeanor sends a message to my brain to turn off the computer and go to sleep. I push aside the insect netting gracefully draped over our bed and melt onto the mattress. I close my eyes thinking about how much I miss the starkness of Sabi Sands and that nothing can compare with the experiences we had tracking and watching animals.

Chapter 8
SCENE AND UNSEEN

Up, breakfasted, and out by nine, we are ready for a trip to Victoria Falls. Our guide, Mr. Kandenga, meets us at a small, shaded parking lot tucked into a garden.

"Call me Mr. K," he announces as we approach. Sunshine bounces off his shaved-to-bald head and highlights the dark reddish-brown tones capping his rounded cheeks.

"First we'll go to Victoria Falls," he says. And then, lowering his voice speaking in a conspiratorial way, "For lunch, I will take you to my favorite place."

I express concern over not having visas that would allow us to see the falls from the Zimbabwe side.

"Don't worry about that. *I am* your visa," he says.

I look at him as if he is a Superhero.

Relieved, Joel and I settle into the back seat of Mr. K's meticulously cared for white sedan. As soon as he starts the engine, he begins a monologue. He speaks so softly that his words are barely audible to me. Still dragging from not having had time to catch up on sleep, I don't want to expend my last bit of energy trying to listen to what he's saying. I let Joel carry on the conversation. I pop out of my semi-comatose state when I hear Mr. K say, "There's a village." He points to the right side of the road and casually adds, "We'll stop there on our way back." I mentally switch Mr. K's statement to "We'll *definitely* stop there on our way back."

I have never been to an African village and hope I get a chance to visit one where I can be a fly on the wall watching the villagers go about their everyday lives. I'm not particularly interested in going to one where villagers prepare a show and have crafts to sell; although, that could be fun, too.

A few minutes later, we park the car on the Zambia side of the Victoria Falls Bridge and begin our walk across. The flat, 650-foot expanse carries rail, pedestrian and vehicular traffic, and links Zimbabwe to Zambia. The arched underside rises 420 feet above the Zambezi River.

We gaze over the right railing and catch our first view of the falls. Through a bend in the narrow gorge, we can see long threads of sparkling white water slithering down a nearly vertical wall.

Mr. K points to the water beneath the falls tracing its flow through a channel and into a swirling pool. "That's the Boiling Pot," he says. "Rafters put in the water near there. They go through the Boiling Pot and cross under the bridge to the other side."

I picture myself yanked from the shore before I get both feet in the raft, spun in the pool, and then spit out onto rocks and snatched by raging waters. My imaginings are as close as I care come to rafting through the Boiling Pot.

We pick up the pace and walk to the opposite end of the bridge. Near the Zimbabwe entry point, Mr. K leaves us and disappears for several minutes. When he returns, we look expectantly at him thinking that he has arranged for us to cross into Zimbabwe. Instead, he suggests we walk back across the bridge and take in the views on our own. My eyes dart to Joel's. He shrugs. We move on.

The views of the turbulent water tumbling through the narrow, cavernous gorge are spectacular. Mesmerized by the sound, we don't notice that Mr. K is standing just a foot or two behind us until he speaks. He points to a section of swirling water where we stand looking out over the bridge and tells us, "That is where most rafters overturn and have to be rescued."

It's August, the beginning of low water season when rafting is most intense. Class five rapids flow beneath us. There are no ripples, just non-stop, white-capped waves that plunge over rocks and surges of water that shoot out as if from a fire hose. The thrust of the river's flow is fascinatingly beautiful, but its potential destructiveness doesn't escape me.

We turn our attention to a bungee jump platform secured to the edge of the bridge. A couple that could be honeymooners looks intent as they get harnessed together. When we get closer, I can hear a nervous giddiness coming from the woman as she receives instructions. Her companion is dead quiet. As the countdown to the leap begins, a cameraman takes up position ready to immortalize the adventure for the bungee jumpers. I look down to the river and wonder if they will muster the courage to leap; it's a forty-story drop from the bridge to the river.

They leap. Their screams leave a steady trail of sound fading behind them.

The jump into the gorge.

Couple swinging over the Zambezi River (see arrow).

As they swing back and forth between canyon walls in a wide arc over the roiling waters, I survey the bottom for a rescue point and wonder how they will be extracted. I learn later that jumpers are winched back onto a catwalk at the lower level of the bridge.

While the river is impressive at this low-water-level time of the year, the views of the falls from the bridge are not. We leave the bridge and drive to the Victoria Falls National Park entrance gate. Joel and I look at a map of the park area as Mr. K takes care of entry fees. We see that a path to the right leads to the Knife Edge Bridge and extensive views of the falls. Mr. K points us to the left, a wooded area. We argue; he prevails. He hands each of us a slingshot and a few small rocks and proceeds to show us how to use them.

"There are baboons. They will snatch things from you. If they come near you, you scare them away with this," he says raising his slingshot and firing. "They are dangerous."

We walk along a treed path pausing at one or two places that provide scenic views of the falls, but they are too far in the distance for us to see or hear water cascading. Only the greyish upper part of the falls is visible.

Mr. K, who keeps a keen eye out for baboons and his slingshot at the ready, brings us to a tree on which a six-inch fungus grows. He tells us that villagers, when collecting honey, burn fungus to produce smoke. The smoke dazes the bees, making honey collection a lot less painful. He tells about a robbery in the area, and then another robbery, and yet another and then cautions us to be on guard. By now, my mind has left my body behind. I can see from Joel's shifting from foot-to-foot that he is as eager as I am to explore another section of the park, the one to the right of the entry that listed the Knife Edge Bridge. But there is no nudging Mr. K along or stopping the robbery stories and warnings. Clearly, he wants to point out things that go beyond seeing the Victoria Falls; but how can we be curious about things beyond the falls when we haven't seen the falls yet?

We're relieved when we turn around and head toward the park entry. As we get close, a group of teenage girls, tourists like we are, clusters on the path chatting and giggling. They fail to notice baboons lurking in the woods nearby. Their laughter turns to screams as the marauders surround them. Having spotted the baboons as they launched their offensive, Mr. K is already on his way with a weapon and pebble artillery in hand to rescue the terrorized teens. A couple of well-placed shots and the baboons retreat. One girl remains frozen in place looking at the slingshot in her hand. "I forgot I had it," she says laughing through her tears.

At last we are back at the starting point and can follow the path to the right. To our dismay, Mr. K marches us past the turnoff for the Knife Edge Bridge. We follow him onto a path that goes behind the falls, past a view of the Victoria Falls Bridge, and then to the top of the falls. Islands of rock in the broad, plateau-like surface form pools of water fed gently by the Zambezi River. The placid scene gives no clue to the vertical drop and plunging waters that lie beyond the plateau's straight edge. At this time of year, it is safe to wade into the water without fear of being swept over the edge by the force of the current as hippos, crocodiles, and tourists have been. I'm tempted to roll up my pants and step in the ankle-deep water; but elect to enjoy watching others splashing and taking pictures.

Playing in the water at the top of the falls.

Once again, we head to the turn off for Knife Edge Bridge, a walkway along the gorge's edge that faces the falls. As Mr. K leaves us to explore on our own, he says, "Meet me back here in forty-five minutes."

FORTY-FIVE MINUTES! We spent an hour and a half hearing about fungus, baboons, and robberies, and a few minutes on top of the falls. How can we cover what we want to see in less than half that time?

"He'll wait for us," says Joel.

"But he has plans for our lunch," I say. Food is very important to me.

We compromise and give ourselves an hour.

The views as we approach the bridge are worthy of more attention than we give them with our sixty-minute clock ticking down. They provide snapshots of sections of the falls seen through tree limbs and leaves. As we begin our walk across the bridge, I pause, Joel moves on. Experience tells me I should go with him because he always finds interesting things to see or do. But I'm drawn to what I am seeing; I need to remain still.

Unlike the curved, Horseshoe Falls we saw last May from the Canadian side of Niagara Falls with voluminous water plunging over its sides, Victoria Falls, at this time of year is a 5,604-foot wide, vertical wall of lacey veils of water sliding down exposed basalt rock. Here, in May, the water would have been gushing from its 354-foot height, dropping twice the height of Niagara Falls. By the end of September, it may be completely dry.

Guides, with which I shared my plans to visit Victoria Falls, told me that I may be better off visiting now, in August, because I can see the rock formations that comprise its massive walls. At peak flow times, February through May, the mist created by the thunderous falls can rise over 1,300 feet, obliterating the view and creating an inverted rain that drenches visitors traversing the Knife Edge Bridge from their shoes up. It must be incredible to experience the power of the water at full force in this narrow gorge. But here I am, delighting in the patterns of brilliant white streams lacing through, and bouncing off, steps of water-sculpted black rock.

I linger on the bridge, taking photo after photo. I can see no more than a third of the falls from the Zambia side, and can capture even less of its one-mile breadth with my camera lens.

A section of Victoria Falls, the largest mass of falling water in the world.

As I reach the end of the bridge, a view of falls on the Zimbabwe side inserts itself where the walls of the gorge appear to converge in the distance. Dense mist rises from a flood of plunging water creating a massive blast of whiteness that obscures the rock's intricate patterns. The view provides me with a glimpse at what I am missing and reinforces the value of what I have been able to see.

Center Back: Mist rising from the falls on the Zimbabwe side.
Right: Falls on the Zambia side.

I catch up with Joel. Neither of us is done looking, but it's past an hour and it's time to find out what Mr. K has planned for lunch.

Victoria Falls Bridge (back left). Top of the falls (back right).

We drive into Livingstone and pull into a small parking lot in front of Olga's Italian Corner. Why an Italian restaurant? Why not an African—something I would much prefer? Mr. Kandenga and I seem to be on different pages. Joel notes that Olga's prides itself in making homemade pizza crust, bread, and pasta. He seems happy with that.

We settle in at the far end of the thatch-roofed, open-air restaurant. There are several tables but only one other is occupied. After surveying the menu, we decide to go with pizza. I order a Margherita pizza with mozzarella, tomatoes, and basil. Joel orders the crocodile meat pizza. He usually bails me out by giving me his dish when I choose something exotic to eat and don't like it. I don't know if I will be able to return the favor.

As I'm enjoying my first slice of pizza, I shoot a glance at Joel; he is already on his second. I work up the courage to ask for a taste. We exchange slices. I gingerly bite into the crocodile meat and find it is chewy but otherwise without a particularly distinguishing flavor. At some level, I'm grateful for that.

Joel asks about a poster at the entry to the restaurant concerning a school. Our waitress tells us that all the profit from Olga's goes to training youth in a trade—culinary arts, tailoring, and plumbing among others. The restaurant is one of the "operation locations," businesses where students can be employed. Our waitress and the chef have come through the program. I'm intrigued by it and impressed with the restaurant, the food, and the service. I'm also beginning to understand Mr. K.; he's showing us things he sees as important. For him, satisfying our tourist needs is necessary but secondary.

We step out into the sunshine and see Mr. K waiting for us by his car. As I slide into the back seat, I ask him about the village we passed and if we could stop there.

"There is not enough time to go there. We would not make it back for the evening cruise," he tells me.

"I'd rather visit the village," I say.

"We're going to a village tomorrow," Joel reminds me.

"I want to see both villages! Besides, we can do the cruise tomorrow night."

Wisely, Joel objects no further. Mr. K is not as easy to direct. "First," he tells us, "we will stop at a street market."

That's okay with me. Given how little opportunity we have for shopping on this trip, and how little room we have in our duffle bags for souvenirs, the market may be the perfect place to pick up small gifts.

My pent-up shopping drive explodes as soon as I step onto the sidewalk. I'm struck by the profusion of color as I peer down the center of the block-long corridor of shops. Clothing, baskets, bowls, and carvings hung from high to low on the street and stall sides create a tunnel of excitement. Unorthodox combinations of lime green with yellows, oranges, reds, blues, blacks, and whites generate a visual energy that catches my breath. Symbols of elephants and hyenas incorporated into broad horizontal stripes on pants and tops recall images of the safari at Sabi Sands. Polka dots add levity. As an artist, I marvel at how the cacophony of colors and form somehow work together.

Sidewalk market in Livingstone, Zambia.

The vendors pitch their goods with a smile accompanied by humor. When we don't make a purchase, they still have a smile ready should we return. Something catches Joel's eye and he stops just inside one of the shops. He fingers three-inch, round plates with scenes painted on their curved, plaster surface. I show him one I like.

"Two are enough," he says holding his two—the ones with animals painted on them. Mine has scenery on it. I relent and put it back.

The vendor watches my eyes and then says to Joel in a soft voice, "Your wife likes this one."

The vendor's smile seals the deal. I slip an extra one into the sale and we leave with four tiny plates, each wrapped tightly in newspaper.

We pass shops with baskets, shoes, and clothing as we work our way to the last stall where a carver displays slender, ebony carvings, each a foot high, lined up like soldiers. I browse casually, but Joel examines the carvings individually. I join him admiring the workmanship.

"Here is the village chief and his wife," says the carver with pride filling his words.

I look closely but can't tell them apart.

"Look. Here is his beard!" a triangle at the bottom of the chief's chin. "This one," he says pointing at the other, "is the chief's wife." His voice betrays a tinge of surprise or hurt, or maybe both, that I couldn't tell the difference.

"Oh! Yes. I see," I say quickly.

We were thinking of buying just one, but we can't leave the chief without a wife. As the vendor wraps the two carvings, he tells us that the wood comes from the core of the ebony tree. The core's extremely fine texture renders the tree's growth rings indistinguishable and its grain barely, if even, visible. The carvings that come from the jet-black wood are sleek and glossy, sensuous in their look and feel.

Our two carvings come from skinny branches but are beautifully black with parts of the tree's brown exterior bark clinging to their edges. More substantial pieces would be prized by sculptors and priced accordingly.

Mr. K signals us to leave; it's time to head to the village. I don't know what to expect but no doubt Mr. K has his reasons for choosing this village for us to see.

Chapter 9
KALODI VILLAGE

Gravel crunches under our tires as Mr. K eases the car onto the shoulder of an asphalt road that cuts through Kalodi Village. A pregnant woman waits to cross from the other side of the road. Her dark, short-cropped hair caps her dark brown skin; her smile matches the brightness of the crisp sunlight. Her smile is for a neighbor across the road.

I marvel at the grace with which she wears her lapa, an African wrap skirt made from a rectangular cloth tucked around her waist. Bold swirls of blues and black decorate the straight fabric that falls to her ankles; a grey and pink T-shirt tops off her outfit. On her back, a toddler rides bundled into a gold and blue kanga, a cloth cleverly wrapped to provide a seat for the child and openings for his arms and legs to move freely.

We follow Mr. K into a mini cul-de-sac of mud huts. Worn outer layers expose the huts' substructure built from vertical saplings lashed to horizontal ones. Posts, made from the trunks of young trees placed at the corners and intermittently along the walls, lend support to the structures. Reddish mud, the color of the earth we are standing on, fills the rectangular spaces between the bound saplings. The white, fine-grained, protective outer layer is made from termite mounds formed with excretions that pass through a termite's digestive system. Thatched roofs or ones made from corrugated metal weighted down by large stones top the houses. The weighted-down roofs bring back memories of the Himalayas where Joel and I first saw such roofs in small villages as we trekked along mountain paths.

I'm as still as the air that surrounds me as I scan the scene trying to take in everything in the mini cul-de-sac. I've never been to an African village. Mr. K points to a stack of reeds that lie drying on the sun-soaked ground and explains that the reeds will be used for weaving mats. Metal and plastic pails, empty gasoline cans, cast iron pots, and ceramic dishes are neatly stacked alongside the houses. The bare ground looks swept clean. No one is in sight; there is no movement. The stillness makes me want to whisper.

A rooster appears, strutting across the open area, checking out a pot set on a low-burning, open fire. It flashes through my mind that he is searching for a missing girlfriend. A woman steps out of a hut that is well-maintained with a thick, even coating of white termite-mound material. She wears a pale green lapa with a giraffe printed down the front. A double strand of white beads decorates her pea-green, scoop-neck top. She looks uncertain about why we are here. We are unexpected company in a village that is not set up for the entertainment of tourists.

A sneaker-and-shorts-clad toddler comes tumbling past the woman. She catches up with him, takes his hand, gives us a warm smile, and walks her child back into her hut. I don't know if she wants her privacy or if she is leaving us to explore undisturbed. Either way, she is gracious in accepting our presence.

Kalodi Village near Livingstone, Zambia.

Barely visible in the shadow of a doorway of another hut, a girl leans against the opening, watching us with a shy smile. She looks as if she would melt into the darkness if we approached. The structure she is standing in looks like a collapsing camping tent for two, thrown together with dried, tall grass and covered in part with bright-yellow plastic tarps and grain sacks. A plastic bag with a picture of Red Square and "MOSCOW" printed across its top is pushed aside from the doorway. She wears what looks like a spaghetti-strap undershirt; her plain black skirt hangs straight on her slender body. She retreats deeper into the shadow when she sees that our curiosity echoes hers.

I wonder about the shabbiness of the structure and ask Mr. K if the girl lives there.

"No," he answers. "No one would live in something like that. It is a bathroom or a place to wash up. They are built from discarded plastics. Most homes have one or share one with others."

Young girl peeking out a bathroom doorway.

As we move farther into the village, I hear music and begin to follow the sound. Across a flat, grassy area, several women dance to contemporary African music; a dozen or more children play nearby. I reach for my camera and hesitate; I don't want to intrude on the fun they are having, nor do I know if they would be annoyed by being photographed. As I'm considering *should-I-or-shouldn't-I*, the women spot me and wave me over. Joel creeps up behind me and says, "Let's go." I can't restrain myself any longer; I quickly snap a picture, and off we go.

The music we hear comes from a radio powered by a solar panel. The huts are closer together in this part of Kalodi Village than where we entered. The red mud and the substructure are exposed more than covered, hung cloths or corrugated metal rather than wood boards are used for doors, and the common area, which is everything outside a hut's door, is alive with people. This part of the village has the feeling of being the-other-side-of-town, not too unlike where I grew up in Brooklyn with buildings close together, crowded apartments, and people of every age gathering outside. It was the place to catch a breeze, laugh, play, and tell stories.

The women are dressed in colorfully printed lapas and plain T-shirts; one is in jeans. Children have on any manner of matched and mismatched colorful clothes, shoes, no shoes, and flip flops; boys are in shorts or pants, girls in skirts and dresses. We join the fun and then become the fun.

Joel, always the gentleman, asks if it's okay to take pictures; I have guilt written across my face betraying the photo I sneaked. The women say, "Sure. Sure," and the photo frenzy begins. He snaps a picture of children and then rotates the camera so they can see themselves on the LED screen. A chorus of "me, me, me" erupts as more children descend upon Joel asking for photos to be taken. The number of children grows from one dozen to two. I smile watching Joel as his joy matches the children's. Soon the women beckon him to photograph them. Joel obliges; I inherit the children.

Women listening to music by huts with exposed substructure.

Joel photographing children at Kalodi Village.

In their eagerness to be included, the little ones crowd into the camera waving with arms extended straight out to the lens. They look every bit as sprightly, happy, and well-fed as the children I see on playgrounds back home. I snap a couple of pictures with their hands blocking their faces and then ask them to keep their hands down. They look a little confused over the request but do it anyway. With each click, the children push forward grabbing for the camera to see their images. I give up protecting the LED screen and just peel little fingers off the telephoto lens. A boy, about age four, staggers under the weight of his little sister as he lifts her up to the camera so she can be included in a picture. An adolescent assumes a typical teenage boy's stance for his photo. I laugh to myself thinking about the universality of the body language of teens.

Children eager to be photographed.

Adolescent striking a pose.

I notice a lanky teenage boy holding a baby in his arms and standing apart from the others. Unlike the sprightly children surrounding me, he has a dull look in his eyes. When the other teens move away, he comes closer and asks me to take a picture of him with the baby cuddled against his chest. I take one and then he asks for money. I'm taken aback; I haven't been asked for money anywhere I've been on this trip. I glance over and see Joel handing out dollar bills as he and the women laugh and have a jolly good time. Later, when I ask Joel why he gave out money, he tells me Mr. K suggested it.

I turn back to the boy and tell him I don't have any money with me; it's true. I let him know I will ask my husband for some later.

Joel waves me over; the ladies want to be photographed with him. I extract myself from the children, promising to return. With each picture I take, it seems there is one more woman who wants to be included and another picture to be taken. No matter how many women join in, and how they rearrange themselves, one remains attached to Joel's right side. She's young and she looks as if she is laying claim to him. I watch with a wife's eyes, not able to suppress the sting of protectiveness and jealousy I feel. The sting fades quickly as I get caught up in the laughter and excitement that continues long after the dollar bills run out. The women, like the adolescent boys, strike poses—glamour shots along with affectionate ones showing their babies. As an artist who paints people, I am delighted with this opportunity. Some of these faces will find their way onto my canvases.

Joel with the women and Mr. K.

Women posing for a glamour shot.

Children shared and loved among the women.

Later, when we return to Waterberry Lodge, the lodge director tells us that the villagers are so poor they cannot afford to buy mirrors. That is why they are so excited about seeing themselves in photos. I ask, if I print up pictures when I get back home, would she be able to get them to the villagers. She says that it would be wonderful and that she would have Pasco, a waiter from Kalodi, bring them. As promised, I send copies in duplicate hoping everyone will get at least one photo of themselves.

When Mr. K signals that it's time to head back to Waterberry Lodge, I make sure Joel gives money to the boy with the baby. Joel's out of one-dollar bills, so he gives the boy a five-dollar bill and tells him to share it with his friends. As promised, I return to the little ones for more photo taking. The boy with the baby continues to linger nearby. There's a quiet sense of urgency in his eyes. As we are about to part, the boy makes it clear he wants us to see something. He brings us to a six-foot-round mud and wire enclosure and beams as he lifts the wooden lid. Inside are six hamsters with brown, white, and grey markings. I photograph the hamsters. He glows. I smile.

A final shot of the children.

Waving goodbye.

As we drive away, I turn to Joel and say, "Did you notice there were no men?"

The reply comes from Mr. K. "It's Sunday," he says. "Men are playing football over there." He points to a field beyond the bushes.

I close my eyes. I want to hold onto images of what I just experienced: the sunlight, the simplicity of the villagers' lives, their joy in the music and their children, and the spontaneity of their welcome. Would I like to trade places with them? On some level, yes. Could I? Probably not. Would they like to trade places with me and the way I live? Possibly, but I'd have to warn them it gets complicated.

Thank you, Mr. K, for bringing us here.

Chapter 10
TUKONGOTE

We motor upstream on the Zambezi River in an aluminum skiff that has little more to it than a hull, an outboard motor, and seats. Joel and I sit up front in bucket seats facing into the wind, our guide, James, steers from behind. The early morning sun and light down vests keep us pleasantly warm on this chilly day. As we steer head-on into the nearly foot-high waves, the boat lifts and drops in a steady rhythm. Invigorated by the air and movement of the water, I smile at Joel. He's letting his white-speckled beard grow; I call him Hemingway. I like the beard; maybe he should keep it.

Having seen Victoria Falls, I have a greater appreciation for the river and its destination. I think about the activity options we were offered when first we arrived at Waterberry Lodge; they included kayaking on the Zambezi. On a morning like this, paddling upstream would be impossible; paddling downstream, struggling to avoid being caught in a current rushing toward the falls, would be a pleasure-killer. I can just imagine Joel calling to me, "Paddle, goddamit!" as my muscles burn and my strokes remain useless.

James points to a line of hippos between us and the shore.

"You have to keep your distance from them. They are aggressive and unpredictable." He adds, "They're very dangerous."

No need for the warning; I have no desire to pet them.

I eye the menacing-looking heads protruding from the water and see what looks like the dominant male. He's at the center and slightly forward of the pod. His head outsizes any other. A ton-and-a-half of power floats beneath him. As dangerous on land as in the water, he can reach speeds of nineteen miles an hour on his stubby legs—I can run about three miles an hour. Walking from the main lodge to our cottage at dark, grazing time for hippos, will have more of an edge to it now.

We skim by other pods well-spaced along the way; each territory is about three football fields long. The territory is staked out by a single bull for the sole purpose of establishing mating rights.

"How many females do you think are in that pod?" I ask James as we pass eyes staring at us.

"Maybe ten. There could be more. I've seen some with as many as thirty."

"Are there any other males in a group?"

James tells us that a young bachelor can remain in the pod as long as he is submissive. If he isn't, either the bachelor leaves to stake out his own territory or he fights the bull in a jaw-to-jaw battle. The loser, if he's lucky enough to escape, clambers ashore to hide in tall grasses until his wounds mend or he dies.

The water calms as we round a bend. A slender crocodile suns on a sandy spot near the shore's edge. His still-watchful eye is shut to a slit, an undulating line of teeth protrudes from his closed jaw. Farther along, women wade ankle-deep in water washing laundry; children play close by at the edge of the riverbank, but not in the water. We have arrived at our destination, Tukongote Village.

At a clearing just past the laundering, James maneuvers the boat partway onto the shore where we are greeted with a wave by a four- or five-year-old boy in pajama bottoms, a T-shirt, and a yellow baseball cap. He fetches a friend wearing a Superman shirt to join him in the welcoming. The women look casually at us; some take time from their chores to smile.

Informal greeter at Tukongote Village.

Close to the riverbank, a sun-wrinkled, elderly man sets a fishing net in the water as he sits in a mokoro, a hand-carved canoe chiseled out from the trunk of a mongongo tree. The pale-yellow wood from the large tree is prized for mekoro (*plural of mokoro*) because the wood floats and won't sink. As we watch the fisherman adjust his fishing net, he watches us and what transpires on the shore. He, we find out, is the village chief.

Village chief fishing in a mokoro.

We follow a wide, dirt path into the village. It's quiet even as boys bounce past seeming to dance to music playing inside their heads. Girls carry laundry-size plastic bins tucked under their arms while steadying another on their heads. Outside a hut, two children cluster around a cast iron pan set on a metal burner. They await a serving of food being cooked by a boy. We pass an outdoor kitchen with treated mud sides; its thatched roof floats above a one-foot-high opening left for ventilation. We take a peek inside and see a metal grill set atop eight-inch rocks at each of its corners. Charred wood coated with ashes remains piled neatly beneath it.

Nearby, a garden with bright green, leafy vegetables catches our eyes. A fence of twigs and saplings protects it from animals eager to graze. At the garden, pre-teen boys descend upon Joel to strike poses for the camera and view themselves on the LED screen.

We pass a woman smoothing a coat of termite-mound material onto the exterior of her hut. I don't know if it's her face, her posture, or just the care emanating from the swirling movements of her hand that makes her so beautiful to me. Whatever it is, she is beautiful. Another possible painting!

Woman applying protective coat of termite-based material.

The village is near the top of the economic structure as far as rural Zambia is concerned. The uniform condition of its huts testifies to that. Kalodi Village is close, but not as high. A contributing factor to its lower ranking is that, unlike Tukongote, Kalodi lacks access to the river, a ready supply of fish and water for crops. In a country with eight to nine months a year without rain, the absence of a readily available water source is significant.

James rejoins us. He still has his sunglasses perched on the visor of his baseball cap shading the upper part of red-brown face. His smile dimples his well-rounded cheeks. He points to what looks like the beginning of a new structure—saplings, equally spaced and lined up in a row, with cord strung between them marking where cross-branches will be placed.

"This is probably going to be a new bathroom," he says. He then points to a nearby structure and says, "This is the one they are using now. It must be getting full. The new one will replace it. They will close and seal the old one."

I recall reading about the Bill and Melinda Gates Foundation challenge to engineers to build a toilet that doesn't require a sewer system and processing plant. The current system used at Tukongote is to dig a deep pit away from the water and throw ashes down to help with decomposition. It's not ideal, but it is much more hygienic than defecating in the open. Perhaps the Gates Foundation will find a more effective, practical solution. Prototypes are underway, including one that converts solid waste to compost, but the high cost of production remains a major impediment.

Farther into the village, we come across cattle herded behind a branch-and-barbed-wire fence along a tree-shaded stretch of the riverbank. Some cattle are hefty; others have backs that sag. I ask if the cattle are raised for food.

"They are not eaten," James explains. "The number of cattle you own shows how wealthy you are. The cattle are currency. A groom's family can pay for a bride with cattle. They can buy things and pay with cattle."

Just beyond the pen, we come to a gathering area where music is playing. We follow a boy and girl, about four-years-old, holding hands, as they head toward the communal area. The children stop under a raised table made from branches. Still holding hands, they bounce up and down in rhythm with the music. Cleaned pots and pans piled on top of the table in plastic bins dry in the sun; a man and a woman stand alongside the table talking. Unlike the colorful patterns I have seen on other lapas, the one the woman is wearing looks like a political ad. It has "2016" printed near the top; at the bottom, there is a picture of two men paddling a boat and the words "Patriotic Front." Twenty-sixteen is the year Edgar Lungu, the head of the Patriotic Front party, was re-elected president. Zambia's government enjoys relative stability attributable, in part, to its having avoided much of the post-colonial upheaval other African nations experienced; its stability, however, doesn't shield it from claims of voter fraud at election time.

I stop by a teenage girl grinding grain. With both hands, she raises a wood pestle that is taller than she is by two feet, and pounds it into the grain in a wooden mortar that is carved wide at the top and tapers inward toward its flat base. I tried grinding grain, *once*. It was in Southeast Asia. I found out quickly that it is the strength and rhythm of the person doing the grinding that makes it appear so easy. After three or four strokes that crushed not one grain, I handed the pounder back to the woman who looked half my size and twice my age. She laughed.

I smile watching the girl and then ask, "What are you grinding? Is it corn?"

She smiles back and says, "Yes."

"What is it for?"

"Nshima," a finely ground, white cornmeal boiled in water, a staple in the villagers' diet.

At another high table a few feet away, a woman cleans fish. Her smile is welcoming as she holds up what looks like a catfish no longer than her hand. I ask if I can take a picture of her. She laughs shyly and says, "Not of me; of the fish."

She continues to laugh as I focus in on the fish. When we step away, Joel says, "Did you take just the fish?"

"Yes," I reply, "but my hand moved just as I snapped the picture and the woman accidentally wound up in it."

Joel shakes his head.

A gathering place for music and chores.

The underlying serenity I sense in the village makes me promise to simplify my life. How healthy everyone looks continues to impress me. I'm beginning to believe it is attributable to the outdoor living and the quality of their food. The villagers' diets appear to be based largely on what they grow, raise, or fish. Eggs, fish, and an occasional chicken or goat are their sources of protein. There's no McDonalds nearby. Villagers, in general, can't afford prepackaged meals with dubious nutritional value and lists of ingredients that read like the contents of a test tube. Unlike our country, which is plagued with obesity, there is no sign of obesity here. The people are neither runway-thin nor well-rounded; they each seem to be right-sized for their stature.

As if reading my thoughts, James says, "Many of the men have to find jobs outside the village to support their families. This leaves a greater burden on the women to care for the crops and animals. There is just so much the women can do. The less they produce, the more they have to buy. That is expensive. It means that the men have to work away from the village more and can help less."

I understand the conundrum and sense a tightening spiral. I also see so much that is worth holding on to. In Tukongote and Kalodi as well, the children I saw are spirited, charming, joyful, and healthy-looking, traits that appear to carry into adolescence and adulthood. I hope the villagers can hold on to these traits as change moves in.

I am crushed when I learn that the life expectancy for men is fifty-nine years and, for women, sixty-four. I am told by the lodge director that it is a great improvement over what it was twenty years ago when the life expectancy was forty-two. The HIV epidemic that raged in the 1990s and early 2000s contributed heavily to skewing the statistic. Over 200,000 had died from AIDS, most in their twenties and thirties.

Adolescent girls at Tukongote.

We leave the main part of the village and follow a wide, dirt path with a smattering of bare trees on either side. The path leads to the Tukongote Community Preschool. A sign, "Welcome to our school. We love to play. We love to learn," painted across the bright yellow wall of the entrance, greets its students and visitors. Beneath the greeting, photos and stories portray the history of the school's development.

Entrance to Tukongote preschool.

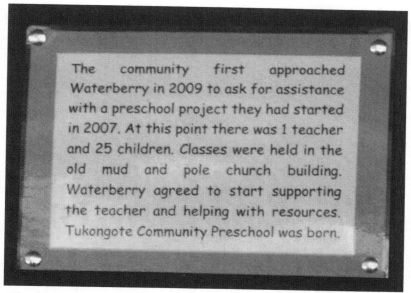

The beginnings of Tukongote school told on a bulletin board.

Teacher and children with original school in the background.

Inside the preschool that opened in 2017.

School is not in session, but I can imagine the voices that would fill the room. The school has seventy-five students and six teachers, up from twenty-five and one teacher when the villagers first started it in 2009. Bright yellow, red, and blue furniture, mats, and walls decorate the classroom. Children's work, written in English, is on display. Plans for expansion, adding grades, teachers, and children, are underway.

The Waterberry Lodge, where we are staying, plays a major role in supporting the village children's education. The preschool was built, and a primary school added, through the villagers' determination and the lodge's efforts. Funding sources for teachers' salaries are secured by the lodge through sharing profits made from sales in their gift shop, fund-raising activities, and donations, many from guests, such as we, who visit the school.

In villages where there is no school, the nearest school may be as far as nine miles away. Where the walking distance is prohibitive, government-run boarding schools are provided as an option for children beginning at age seven. The boarding schools in rural Zambia are poorly funded by a government struggling economically. At school, as many as three dozen children may be supervised by one person. Children, who find it too emotionally difficult to be wrenched from home where they are surrounded by people who share in caring for them, frequently run away from boarding schools, ending their education. Without a twelfth-grade education, they will lack the basic requirement for getting a formal job later in life. The children of Tukongote are lucky their community is determined to have their children educated and have found a partner in Waterberry Lodge that is dedicated to supporting their efforts.

I learn that Tukongote means "to go together." It is the word used to describe openbill storks when they fly together in a group. The stork is the logo for Tukongote. How befitting the village.

Our visit began with a little guy greeting us at the river's edge and ends with a farewell by another little guy. He's about five-years-old but looks like an old soul as he saunters toward us with a confident smile and hands tucked into the pockets of his knee-length, denim jeans. His smile sets the mood for the rest of the day.

A smile for our send-off.

We return to the lodge and have barely enough time to absorb our morning's experiences before heading back onto the river. This time, Joel and I are taken to a small island for a private picnic for the two of us. When we dock, we see a waiter poised behind a buffet table covered with an array of salads, fruits, fries, and chicken. Two small tables with placemats, wine glasses, napkins and silverware are set nearby. The waiter and our guide, James, head off to another part of the island leaving us with chilled, white wine to complete the mood. As they leave carrying their lunch buckets, I call to them, "What are you having for lunch?"

"Polenta!" they call back, using the Italian name for their lunch, a name that tourists are more likely to be familiar with than "nshima," the local name.

I love polenta. For Zambians, it is ordinary, just as it was for my mother who grew up in a small village in northern Italy. I still chuckle at this peasant food's rise to gourmet status in American restaurants.

"We'll be back in three hours for you."

Three hours! Joel and I look at each other with a *what-will-we-do-for-three-hours* expression in our widened eyes. It turns out not to be a problem. We watch highways of currents in the river slip past each other in counter directions, sip wine, take in the sunshine, and enjoy a leisurely lunch. No books, no internet, just each other.

A glass of wine with sky and water.

We take to the river one last time for an evening cruise. As we glide along with other visitors to the lodge, we pass baboons playing on the riverbank, a foot-long baby crocodile resting on a tree root along the bank, birds displaying brilliant colors, and a final treat, a purple and blue-tinged sunset shimmering over the water. Perfect!

Chapter 11
BACK TO THE BUSH

Our driver, Jonah, waits in the crisp sunlight on yet another glorious morning. We drive on familiar roads and streets in Livingstone, passing lush greenery and then houses, shops, and restaurants. We wind our way through the quiet city and out again onto paved roadway lined with grasses and scattered low-growing trees. An hour into the drive, the land changes from lush to nearly desolate, the sun from crisp to harsh. We are on our way to the Kazungule Crossing from Zambia to Botswana and our next safari. The juncture of four countries—Zambia, Zimbabwe, Namibia, and Botswana—lies at the midpoint of the Zambezi River at the crossing.

On our approach from the Zambia side, we move to the left side of the road, bypassing trucks creeping along the right side. We continue passing slow-moving vehicles. Soon their slow movement becomes no movement at all. We continue driving along what seems to be an endless line of parked haulers.

I ask why they are parked along the road. Jonah explains, "They are waiting to cross the border. Sometimes they wait as long as a month."

I gasp.

We wind our way toward the front of the line, passing enclosed semitrailers, flatbeds, and trucks with strapped-down grey, yellow, or faded red tarps covering their cargo. Men, in groups of twos and threes, hang out in a vast sandy area near the crossing point, some stand alongside their trucks. Most are slender in build rather than broad and muscular as I think of truck drivers being.

A shanty-like building, surrounded by emptiness advertises showers, another, a room for rent. A few food stands dot the sandy area. It's strangely quiet here. Things and people appear to move slower than time.

Our car slides alongside a flatbed truck weighted down with thick disks, two to three feet in diameter, stacked two deep and secured with a web of heavy chains. The shape and rough grey surface of the cargo leave me guessing what it could be.

"That's copper," Jonah informs us. "It is probably going to China." China is one of Zambia's major trading partners.

I've never seen raw copper ore. Its dull grey, stone-like surface gives no hint of the beautiful shiny reddish-brown or green-patinaed metal it becomes. I wonder if Zambia is managing the exit of its natural resources wisely or, if because of its need for money, it's giving away its wealth too quickly and for too little.

Jonah tells us that most of the trucks are loaded with copper and mining supplies making their way from the copper belt of Northern Zambia and the Democratic Republic of the Congo to the southern seaports of Africa.

As he talks, I look out the window and see men and women climbing in and out of the cargo areas. They move with no sense of urgency. Having sweated through many hot summers in Houston, Texas, I have learned that moving slowly, sometimes, is the only way to survive.

"They are inspectors. Each truck must have its load inspected before it is allowed to cross the river," Jonah tells us.

The time-consuming inspections only half explain the daily bottlenecks at the crossing that make Los Angeles' roads look like speedways. Once cleared to cross, the trucks are ferried one at a time across the quarter-mile wide passage. Zambia has three ferries, but only one in operation today. Botswana has only one ferry. Patience is a necessary virtue here.

A crane and construction materials across the river signal that something may be underway to give relief to the congestion. Further inquiry reveals that Botswana and Zambia are building a road and rail bridge at the crossing between the two countries.

We park the car and begin the business of leaving one country and entering another. Our driver walks us to a small wooden building where he leaves us to queue up with other people. Left unclear of what we are supposed to do, we queue up as directed. Other travelers, most African, some European, seem to have more savvy, or confidence, than we do. We follow their lead.

A clerk hands us a short form written in English that we fill out and return to him to be stamped. Just as we complete our transaction, Jonah reappears and drives us to a small dock where a man waits next to an eight-passenger rowboat with an outboard motor attached. Jonah speaks with the man in a local language, most likely Lozi. We listen without understanding until the man flips through a few pages of paper and shakes his head. We understand enough to know something is wrong.

"He says you are not on the manifest."

"That can't be. We have paid in advance." Joel says. He checks the manifest a few times with the man and our driver. Our names are not there.

Meanwhile, I'm trying to remember where I buried our itinerary, receipts, and contact numbers should problems arise.

A few quick words pass between Jonah and the manifest holder.

Jonah turns to us and says, "He will call his office."

Scenarios race through my mind, everything from pleas to verbal warfare, neither of which can be conducted absent a shared language.

The phone call ends and the man with the manifest motions for us to climb into the boat. The adrenaline buildup leaves me stunned; there will be no battle. I recover quickly and pop into the boat (maybe Joel pushes me, I'm not sure). I count us lucky to have had someone with us to smooth things over. Spending days with the truckers and the small shacks trying to get things sorted out is far from appealing.

The motor revs up and we move through the waters of the Zambezi River, narrow and calm at this point along its journey. We are the only passengers on the five-minute ride. Shipments of copper and cobalt from Zambia, gold, ferroalloys, chromium, and diamonds from Zimbabwe, diamonds, copper, and nickel from Botswana, and, from Namibia, copper, uranium, gold, and zinc pass over the same spot we traverse barely aware of the juncture's critical nature. When the bridge is complete, it will give the landlocked region easy access to the north-south transport corridor from the Democratic Republic of Congo to the coastal city of Durban, South Africa.

My mind drifts, wondering what impact the bridge will have on the countries and their people. Will the accelerated transfer of goods require more or fewer trucks? Require more or fewer drivers? Increase mining production? Deplete resources more quickly? Give families more time together?

I don't have much time to entertain thoughts before arriving at the Botswana shore. A shuttle bus, parked a few feet away, waits to take us to an airplane serving bush camps. Twenty minutes later, the shuttle leaves us off at a wide, dirt pasture that serves as a runway for arriving and departing flights. There are no delineated lanes, just an expanse of dirt edged with scattered, low-growing trees. A ten-passenger plane sits alone mid- field.

Our bags are taken from us and stored in a cargo area. We climb stepladder-like steps pulled down from the passenger door. A row of single seats lines each side of the plane; we claim the two front seats across the aisle from each other. The plane fills with other travelers. The Botswanan pilot, young, calm, and confident, climbs into the cockpit. I wish I could describe myself in the same way. The only other time I was in a small plane, I said numerous prayers, mostly for the flight to be over.

The pilot announces we will be making six stops. I know little about flights other than that takeoffs and landings are the most dangerous parts. I'm hoping Linyanti Bush Camp, where we are headed, will be the first on the list. He rattles off the names of the stops; Linyanti is the sixth. That means six takeoffs and six landings. An alarm bell vibrates inside my head.

At the third landing, Joel says to the pilot, "I notice you circle the landing area a couple of times before landing. Is that to test the air currents?"

"No, it is to scare animals away."

On our next approach, I make note of elephant dung lining the edge of the landing field. By now, I'm quite confident in the plane and the pilot—in fact I'm enjoying the views as we fly low over of dry bush and grassy plains with rivulets of water. I get a bird's eye view of the

Okavango Delta, a geographical wonder for which Botswana is famous. The delta will be the site of our next camp; but now, we are heading to a bush camp nestled inside the western boundary of Chobe National Park, a forested animal reserve in Botswana.

By the last leg of the trip, we are the only passengers left onboard. As we touch down, Joel nudges me to look at the only other plane at the landing site—a plane that is even smaller than ours. It's painted camouflage pea-green and tan. On its side in bold, black letters are the words "BOTSWANA DEFENCE FORCE."

"That's the Botswana Airforce," Joel says with a glint in his eyes.

We chuckle at the thought but soon realize that Botswana is known for its huge herds of elephants and that the plane is most likely for tracking down poachers.

A safari vehicle waits at the edge of the landing field; We climb in and join a family of four who arrived earlier. As we bounce along, there are the usual questions: Where are you from? Where have you been? Where are you going? How long will you be on safari? The common thread through it all is that all of us are excited about sharing what we have seen and eagerly await our next experiences. We don't have to wait long. A breeding herd walks through the forest no more than fifteen feet from us, paralleling the road we are on. I ooh and ahh with every calf that walks by, barely paying attention to the giant mothers. They, in turn, hardly take time for a curious glance at us as they quietly lumber forward.

Breeding herd walking by our safari vehicle, Chobe National Park, Botswana.

Sam points out a pan-shaped circle of dust. "That's a waterhole."

I'm reminded that we are at the beginning of dry season. Our friends who had shown us pictures of their safari that were the impetus for our journey into Africa, had gone in May when the waterholes were filled with water and a variety of species frequently could be seen sharing the resource.

The other passengers arrive at their camp to a greeting of singing and rhythmic hand clapping that can be heard as soon as the vehicle approaches the camp's lodge.

We arrive at Linyanti Bush Camp at 2 p.m. to a hand clapping and song greeting of our own as we step onto the clearing and into the hot sun. This is the first tented camp at which we will stay.

Cullen, the host, shows us to our tent surrounded by jungle except for a narrow footpath that leads to its door. The tent is an enclosed rectangular structure with a pitched canvas ceiling and tan canvas walls hung between wood posts. We have been told by our travel agent, that no permanent infrastructure is allowed in bush camps. The tents and lodges are designed to be collapsed, transported, and reassembled easily so camps can be relocated when their presence begins to encroach upon the animals' movements and lives.

"Try not to use lights," is our first instruction. "Always turn them off when you leave." That noted, the instructions continue.

"We are on solar power. If you want to take a shower, take it in the afternoon, otherwise you may not have enough hot water."

I glance at the small water tank outside our window and make note to take a shower before Joel does.

Although this is the adventure I have been eagerly awaiting, I'm not sure I'm ready for it after being spoiled completely with our own butler, gourmet meals, and luxurious accommodations at Kirkman's Kamp in Sabi Sands. At this point, I'm hoping Linyanti is the bottom of the line accommodation we'll experience and that the next will be better. I'm sure Joel can read my face because he slips beside me and says, "The next camp is the one with the bucket shower."

As we enter, Cullen tells us the canvas shades are drawn against the heat of the sun. They can be rolled up by hand and fastened with Velcro straps, one at each end. He advises us to keep the shades drawn until later in the day. Behind the shades, screens cover large, window-like openings. It's warm in the room, but not uncomfortable; I'll remember to use the shades.

The room is plain but spacious, well-kept, and looks quite comfortable with a king-size bed, nightstands, a sofa, and chests for our clothes. A wood door opens into our private bathroom. A large, round copper sink faces the door, a screened commode area is to the sink's right, and a shower to its left. A glass door opens from the shower onto a deck that runs the length of the back of the tent. Just outside the door, a claw-foot tub, with a European style hand-held showerhead attached to its faucet, sits in the sun.

"Would it be all right to take a bath in it?" I ask the man showing us the room.

"Yes," he answers with a smile.

I see that a narrow path and brush lie just on the other side of the deck and ask, "Do animals walk past here?"

"Oh, yes!" he says, and his smile gets bigger. "Come. The chef has prepared a snack for you."

Joel in our tent at Linyanti Bush Camp in Chobe National Park.

With that, we head to the lodge walking through a dry, cleanly swept, dirt area shaped like a cul-de-sac. We pass two other tents separated by dry grasses and scraggly trees along the way; more tents are off to the left of the lodge. At the lodge, a tented building left open front-to-back, a mini feast awaits. Platters of beef steak, potato salad, mushroom salad, cheese, crackers, kiwifruit, and an unknown fruit the size of a small orange that is cut in half exposing seeds in a gooey-stringy substance, line the center of a long wood table. The sweet tooth in me quickly sees dessert is missing.

I've grown accustomed to having dessert with both lunch and dinner during this trip. On my way to Linyanti, I pledged to give up the lunchtime desserts. But, like New Year's resolutions, the pledge was doomed to be short-lived. I turn to the fruit with gooey seeds for consolation. It turns out to be delicious and as close to dessert as I will come for now.

I just have a few minutes after lunch in which to change from a plaid shirt that has dark, muted shades of blue and brown to a khaki safari shirt. I wasn't planning on changing and didn't think it would matter what I'd wear after having seen a woman on safari in a black, spaghetti-strap top. Thinking I could relax my adherence to safari dress code—no prints, no tsetse attracting blues—I casually asked Cullen, the host, if it was okay to wear what I had on. I saw his nostrils flare as he dragged his eyes slowly over my shirt. I got the message.

When we reach the safari vehicle, we find another couple already occupies the first row. Joel and I take the seats behind them. Stanley, our ranger/driver, introduces himself and we are off in search of lions spotted earlier in the day. Stanley, a chatty fellow, can easily be heard from the second row. There is no need to see his face to know there is a big smile on it; the timbre of his voice betrays all. He is quick to tell us that he is a licensed truck driver. He looks the part, being a big, burly guy. From the way he drives, I swear he's envisioning racing to get to the head of the line at the Kazungule Crossing. Jostled left and right around turns and up and down across rises and falls in soft sand, I find myself wishing I had a saddle with stirrups instead of a bench seat with which my butt is trying desperately to maintain contact.

We locate one of the lions lying in the grass. He looks old and battle-scarred, lacking the threatening power that exuded from the killer lions we saw earlier on our trip. He tries to outlast our gazes, but eventually resigns himself to surrendering his peaceful spot and begins to stroll. Stanley maneuvers the safari vehicle to remain in front and alongside the lion. Doing so, means we are shooting pictures into the sun. But Stanley has an eye for angles and makes sure we have plenty of good ones for capturing the lion.

Lion sighting at Linyanti.

Given how unspectacular our day has been, doubts begin to build in my mind as to how eventful this leg of our trip will be. I don't mention my concerns to Joel and decide to tuck away the doubts and settle into whatever Botswana has to offer.

We give up looking for more lions and head to the river to stop for a sundowner. Just as with Sabi Sands' sundowners, we are served wine, spirits, and snacks. At sunset, a white-hot sun, ringed with yellow, blasts a brilliant hole through the red sky streaked with orange and purple. Silhouetted trees meet the sky at the horizon. The river glows red. Islands of grass in the water become black stripes. I stand cuddled close to Joel; we don't need to speak. For me, the magnificence of the sunset goes a long way toward seeing Botswana with fresh eyes.

It is dark when we arrive back at camp. After we freshen up, Stanley knocks on our door and beckons us to come. Holding a flashlight, he guides us to the boma. The wide opening in its sapling fence allows animals to flow freely in and out. The respect for the animals' ways is a reminder that we are the guests of the magnificent creatures we are seeing.

Stanley tells us, "The boma is where a husband and wife or neighbors come if they are angry with each other. Here they can work out their problems."

"Would someone be here to help them?" I ask.

"Only if they want someone."

Tonight, the boma has another purpose. When we enter, we see a fire blazing in the center surrounded by chairs set in a semicircle. Guests from multiple nearby camps have taken seats. We are surprised by the number of people—the camps, small in size, are well hidden from each other creating the feeling that the experience we are having is uniquely ours.

We join the other guests with drinks and chatter. A whisper of chanting voices becomes louder as the staff, still dressed in beige camp uniforms, enters the boma. They face the guests singing African songs. Soon dancers join them and take turns mimicking animals. Cullen, our host, spreads his arms, drawing his elbows back behind him and thrusting his chest forward like a giant bird with expansive wings. Another dancer creeps low to the ground twirling like a leopard engaged with its prey. Stanley, our ranger, moves his feet in rhythm with the songs and then plunges one foot forward as if crushing a snake. Two bars later, he repeats the plunge.

The performers work their way into a line that begins at one end of the semicircle of guests. Continuing to move to the rhythm of a song, each staff member escorts a guest to a seat at a table.

The music and dancing end, but the high spirits continue as we share stories and comments about ourselves. The chef announces he has prepared a traditional African dinner. His pride is apparent as he points to each item on the buffet table explaining how each is made:

Polenta made from white cornmeal

Oxtail stew

Mashed beef (yes, it is mashed)

Chicken curry

White bean mash

Apple crumb tart with whip cream

As a person who lives to eat, I barely contain my excitement at having a traditional dinner. I taste every dish, some twice, and savor the experience.

Smiles abound as we leave the boma and are escorted back to our tents. Joel and I settle into bed happily exhausted at 9:30 wondering what else the next day could possibly bring.

Chapter 12
HORNS AND HOOVES

Fresh morning air, laced with the smell of brewing coffee, greets us at the back of the lodge. A circle of chairs surrounds a glowing fire. Thin pieces of firewood, spread like sun rays, lie flat on the ground with their tips pointed into the flame's center. As the fire dims, a ranger pushes the sticks a bit farther in, keeping the fire glowing while consuming only as much wood as needed.

Staff, dressed in warm jackets, stand by clutching steaming mugs, waiting for us to get started with breakfast so that they can eat as well. They don't have to wait long; the cool air stimulates my ever-eager appetite. The morning light is still grey when Joel joins us and we fill our bowls with hot cereal and our plates with warm biscuits.

Breakfast at Linyanti Camp.

We are the only guests going on safari this morning; the first row of seats behind the driver is guaranteed to be ours. Stanley, our game ranger, waits by the safari vehicle wearing his large, dark sunglasses instead of having them perched on his forehead as he likes to do. To fend off the morning chill, the staff has placed warm folded blankets on our seats. The ride is a lot less rough from the first row than it was from second until Stanley calls back to us, "We need to check on the lions."

He shifts into a different gear and goes all out demonstrating his prowess at the wheel. We are thrown left and right as he speeds around turns, change directions, and flies over obstacles. I am convinced he would be a great demolition derby driver. I worry about Joel's neck and his bulging discs; he may be an inch shorter by day's end. Meanwhile, I take the blanket I have been given to sit on and fold it into the small of my back to provide some relief from a mounting soreness.

Stanley, our game ranger/driver.

The bumps and jolts go on and on, but our search comes up empty. Finally, Stanley says, "We will look for lions later. Now we will look for cape buffalo."

I'm happy to switch from looking for lions to looking for cape buffalo. Soon after we enter an open, area, Stanley points to the horizon across an expanse of flat, dry land.

"See the brown dust? That's cape buffalo."

A small band of reddish-brown air rises above the ground in the distance, but I see nothing that resembles buffalo.

"Of the big five most sought-after animals on safari or to hunt, cape buffalo are the most dangerous. If you injure a buffalo, another one will ambush you and kill you."

Mentally, I run through a list of the big five—lion, leopard, rhino, elephant, buffalo. I would have placed any other most-dangerous-to-hunt animal ahead of the buffalo. With their huge, heavy bodies that can weigh as much as a ton, and relatively short legs, I would not expect them to move well; but according to Stanley, they can reach speeds of over thirty-five miles an hour. At close to a ton, that would be a lot of power heading your way.

Stanley wants to get a better look. He aims the safari vehicle directly at a nearby mound the size of a truck and, without hesitation, charges up to the top. He says something I don't quite catch as he pops out of the vehicle.

I turn to Joel and say, "Did he say we just drove up a termite mound?"

Joel shrugs his shoulders and says, "That's what he said."

The mound beneath me now has my full attention. I recall a foot-long, mud tunnel going up the side of my house that sent me scrambling for a termite exterminator. The mound we're parked on is nearly a third the size of my house; we would have needed a tow truck to get rid of it.

Squinting, Stanley pans the horizon, "I'm not sure they are buffalo. They may cross into Namibia before we can get to them."

He shifts his binoculars to the right and spots zebras and wildebeests. Not knowing for sure if cape buffalo are on the horizon, or if we can get to them, we opt for zebras and wildebeests. Before leaving the mound, Stanley points to a tree at its top and says, "Did you notice the tree?"

I was so busy looking out across the plains that I hadn't looked up.

"That is a sausage tree," he says with a broad smile. The devilish glint in his eyes makes me think he is joking.

I don't believe him until I look closely and see the tree has an abundance of light-colored, sausage-shaped fruits, each dangling from a branch by its own string; I still only half-believe him, or at best think that is what the locals have nicknamed it. It's not until I look up "sausage tree" on the internet that I find the tree really is known as a "sausage tree." Mammals, including baboons, elephants, giraffes, and hippos, love to eat its fruit. Although the unripe fruit is extremely poisonous to humans, when ripe, it can be baked and eaten. Roasted, it is used to flavor beer.

We drive across the open expanse of dried grasses to the herds of wildebeest and zebras. As I watch the animals, I notice that they cluster with their own species as they move in unison from place-to-place. Even though the species are distinctly different, they have found they can live peacefully side-by-side.

Wildebeests, "wild beasts" in Afrikaans, are also known as gnus among native Africans. The former nomenclature cloaks the animals in an aura of fearsomeness. But to me, their elongated, jowly faces and slumped posture make them look more sad than terrifying. Perhaps gnu, a name that conjures up a neutral image, if any image at all, would be better.

Wildebeest.

As we watch the herds, Stanley keeps an eye on the red-brown cloud on the horizon. He decides to take a chance on tracking down the cape buffalo. We grab onto anything we can as we shoot across the plains and into a swampy area that tries to suck the vehicle's wheels out from under us.

"You need the heart of a soldier to get through this," Stanley says proudly. He then adds, "I have the heart of a soldier!"

That said, he thrusts the vehicle into the marsh, changing direction, testing paths, backing up. Joel and I hold tight as we lurch through tall, dark green plants and equally dark soil that testify to the richness of the delta for which Botswana is well known.

"We won't get stuck," Stanley says.

Joel and I remain silent. We don't want to distract our soldier-hearted driver; we want him to be successful or else we'll be knee-deep in marsh with whatever creatures inhabit it.

Stanley tries going forward. The wheels spin out and the tall grasses push back. He throws the vehicle into reverse. The engine roars, but we go nowhere. Joel and I look at each other. The last time this happened, we spent the better part of an afternoon digging out from water-saturated sand in the Sabi River riverbed.

Stanley announces that he is giving up on getting to the cape buffalo. Fortunately, we had not penetrated too deeply into the marsh. He succeeds in doing a one-eighty with the vehicle. With our backs to the horizon, he plows through the marsh. The front wheels barely touch dry land when Stanley spots something else to aim for.

"Look. There are vultures circling. Let's go see where they land."

It takes just a few minutes to find that a mostly-eaten buffalo is the vultures' object of interest. All that remains is its head and an emptied, dry carcass. It isn't great to see, but at least it's something.

We pull up to a group of vultures standing nearby in a patch of flattened grass. Most are dull grey, but a few boast bright, purplish-blue feathers and stand taller and larger than the others. I comment on the contrasts in size and color.

"There are different kinds of vultures in Botswana. They feed together." Stanley explains, "They don't fight for the food because they don't compete. The ones with big beaks eat the big pieces. The ones with small beaks like little hooks, pick at the hard-to-get-to pieces."

Two species of vultures in Botswana feeding together.

Stanley continues to scan the horizon as we sit quietly in the game vehicle, watching the vultures shift from spot to spot. Like us, they are waiting for the next something to happen. Suddenly, "Buffalo!" rings out from Stanley's voice. Without uttering another word, he swings into action. Joel and I have become adept at reaching for the grab bar in front of us at the slightest sign of enthusiasm from Stanley.

The cape buffalo are on the move. As we aim for the reddish-brown dust cloud rising in the distance, we can make out dark humps breaking through its bottom edge. As we draw closer, pointy horns that curve in toward each other appear among the dark humps now more distinguishable as massive bodies. A flock of white egret-like birds circle the herd as it advances in our direction. The herd is in the flat, grassy area now. We close the gap between us and them quickly. Stanley positions the safari vehicle parallel to the herd of at least a hundred buffalo, but he doesn't stop or even slow down.

With all the jostling from side-to-side, we can't steady our cameras enough to snap pictures. We call out to Stanley, "Hold it!" and then "Wait!" but our voices are drowned out by the engine. Finally, "Stop!" reaches his ears.

We photograph the passing herd enmeshed in its cloud of sandy dirt stirred up by the pounding of their hooves as they move swiftly alongside us. They stretch out in a long line no more than four-deep. Calves, about two-thirds grown, mix with adults, moving at the adults' speed and even jutting ahead at times. Before we are anywhere near finished photographing, Stanley begins to speed away. He wants to get ahead of the herd and away from the dust.

"Wait! Wait!" spills from my mouth. "We want the dust!"

"Ohhh!" he says with a smile and then waits for us to give the okay to reposition.

We shoot more photos and signal Stanley to move on. The buffalo slow their pace and bunch up, grazing as they move forward. I can see why Stanley wanted us positioned ahead of the herd; it's a lot easier to get a still shot with oncoming animals than from alongside ones that are moving away.

The eyes of some bulls remain fixed on us, even as the rest of the herd grazes. I have seen sentries like that with herds of elk pausing at a meadow in front of my summer home in the Southern Rockies. As most of the elk herd lay down to rest, a few remain standing on high alert along the periphery of the resting elk.

Herd of cape buffalo.

When I use my telephoto lens to get a closeup of a mature bull, the horns come clearly into focus. They look as if they are plastered on top of the buffalo's head and parted in the center. They droop down and then flip up like a 1950s women's hairdo. But there is nothing dainty about these animals. They are massive and mean.

Mature male cape buffalo.

We stay put for several minutes, just watching until the herd disappears. I try to fix images of it in my mind but know that they will be replaced by other adventures. Photos will rekindle the memories; they'll be good, but not as complete as being here in the moment.

We leave the plains and head to the river a short drive away. A line of hippos, all facing the same direction, look at us from midstream in the clear, narrow waters of the Linyanti River. They appear to be floating motionlessly in the water but, in the shallow waters, they are standing. Their eyes, ears, and noses remain above the surface so they can employ all three senses to stay alert. Alert they are. I can't tell if the powerful front they present, with their eyes fixed on us, is meant to scare us away, or if the hippos are deciding which one of them should take out which one of us if we dare to come within striking distance.

Hippos keeping cool.

We watch, poised to snap pictures the moment a hippo stretches its jaw into an enormous yawn. Stanley tells us, "When a hippo gives birth, she goes to stay on an island. When the baby is two weeks old, the mother takes it back to the pod; but she must be careful. The pod may not want her and the baby."

Having been away, the mother must reestablish herself as well as introduce her newborn to the group. During the time spent on the island, the baby learns to identify its mother and the mother to recognize the constant, pulsating sound the baby emits. The sound lets its mother know where the baby is at all times; it also complicates reentry.

Hippos, with their sensitive ears and poor eyesight, are easily agitated. The sounds of the baby are enough to set the pod on edge. The mother, with the baby struggling to swim alongside her, must approach the pod slowly. If the hippos show signs of aggression, the mother and baby must make a dash to get outside the pod's territory. Trying to flee is difficult and exhausting for the newborn; but if it doesn't make it, it will be killed. They remain on the periphery of the marked territory until the pod settles down and accepts them, a process that can take several weeks.

"When the mother and her baby are allowed back, it is still a very dangerous time," explains Stanley. "The mother must watch her baby to make sure its curious relatives don't accidentally crush it. Sometimes the dominant male rejects the baby. If he does, the mother must fight him or he will snap the baby in two with his jaws."

Just then, the biggest hippo stretches his mouth and snaps it shut. I gulp.

It must take tremendous courage to fend off such a dangerous aggressor. I can understand how every nerve in a mother's body snaps into action when she senses danger to her child. But, having seen the size of the canines in the cavernous mouth of a hippo, I believe it would take more than an alerted nervous system to fend off an aggressor of that magnitude—perhaps the male aggressor's generosity or a gargantuan adrenaline rush that renders the mother a formidable opponent. I suspect the latter.

I sit quietly, awed by the courage of the mother as she re-enters the pod, pushing away images in my mind of babies being snapped in two. Fortunately, we move to another area along the bank where I can begin to bury the images.

Stanley sets up for our mid-morning snack. The three of us are quiet as we stand in the now-warm morning sun munching cookies and sipping coffee. A leisurely drive brings us back to the camp in time for lunch served at 11:30. We help ourselves to an array of fresh salads and then go back to our tent to shower. Although it's barely past morning, I feel as if I have had a full day's worth of experiences; but there is more to come.

Chapter 13
THE UNEXPECTED

The sun-warmed water runs down my back, relaxing every muscle. I could linger in the shower until the tank outside our room runs dry, but that would be unfair to Joel. He's napping, and, if he's left undisturbed, the tank could refill twice over before he would awaken. Unfortunately for him and me, we don't have much time left to get ready for the 3:30 game drive.

As I shower, ridding myself of the dust from the morning drive, I glance out the glass door at the claw-foot tub on our deck and think that maybe tomorrow I'll soak in it. I let the water run over my face and body one more time before turning it off and stepping out.

I wake Joel letting him know he has an hour to get ready. I trade our shade-drawn room for the openness of the lodge and the cooling breeze that blows through it. Settled into a comfortable chair, I sip a cup of tea, open my journal, hold my pen above a page as I formulate my thoughts on what to write. Before the pen meets the page, I'm attacked by mosquitoes. No amount of arm-swinging or swatting deters them from feeding on me. The eucalyptus DEET-free mosquito repellent I so carefully researched for effectiveness is in the tent. Annoyed that my quiet time has been eaten into, I march back to the tent to retrieve the repellent.

My determined stride takes me within a few feet of our door when I hear leaves rustling in the trees and shrubs that surround our tent. I look to the right expecting to see a bird. Instead, the massive head of a bull elephant, with ears flared, is rounding the tent with a rapid, bouncing stride. Startled, we both jump back. The jerk of his body mirrors mine. In that instant, the whole world collapses into just him and me. For a few breathless seconds, with no more than ten feet between us, we stare at each other. Every fiber of my body is frozen in place. He is just as still.

It's a standoff until he makes the first move. With slitted eyes fixed on me until the last moment, he snaps his head over his right shoulder as if to turn, and then swings it back, resuming the frozen stare. I haven't moved except to breathe, if I breathed at all. If he is testing me to see if I will take any action if he turns his back on me, he has nothing to fear. Apparently satisfied it is safe to retreat, he turns and heads back behind our tent.

I had my fright, and now I flee from the path and the tent. That's when I remember Joel. I gasp when I think he may be done showering and that, at any moment, he could walk out the door and into an elephant. I pick up my pace, now almost at a run, and search for a staff member, any member. I blurt out, "Elephant," and something incoherent about elephants and my husband to the first person I find, a man I haven't seen before. Just then, the rounded backs of a line of elephants becomes visible above the tents.

"Look," the man says pointing to the moving grey humps. "They're all leaving. It's okay."

"But . . ."

"It's okay. See? They're gone."

I take my doubts with me and head back alone to warn Joel. I find him seated on the bed in his underwear, cleaning the lens of his camera. I give him a still garbled, but better, version of what happened. He doesn't react. I become indignant.

"Ten feet from me. Ten feet from the door! A big bull!"

"I know," he says without lifting his eyes from the lens he is cleaning. "I saw four of them walking by our deck. I took pictures."

I want to tell Joel a bull elephant looks a lot bigger when you stand face-to-face with it on level ground, with nothing between you except a couple of scrawny trees; but I don't say anything more. He doesn't understand that being behind a wall and a camera with elephants walking past is not the same as being alone and exposed with an elephant walking toward you. Nevertheless, he took photos and, despite my indignation, I want to see them.

A smirk appears on his face and a glint of mischief flickers in his brown eyes.

"What?" I say, still pouting.

"I kept picturing you soaking in the tub when the elephants walked by."

"I bet one of them would have paused to take a drink," I add.

I half-close my eyes and envision sitting in the tub, watching an elephant sucking up the bath water and then catapulting me into the bush so it can slurp up the remaining drops.

Finally, Joel's nonplussed attitude yields to curiosity and he asks, "How did you know it was a bull?"

With one eyebrow raised, I respond, "Do I really need to tell you?"

He laughs. He understands I am referring to the bull's "private" anatomy. In truth, my eyes were too focused on the bull's head to notice much else. The head of a male elephant is more rounded, a female's more angular. The intense seconds of the encounter left an imprint of his rounded head held high tattooed on my brain.

When Stanley arrives to take us on the afternoon safari, I tell him about the elephant. Like Joel, he just smiles. A few steps beyond our door, I point to where the elephant halted his stroll. Shock registers across Joel's face, and surprise across Stanley's as they take in the nearness of the encounter. I feel vindicated.

We climb into the vehicle, Stanley in the driver's seat, Joel and I behind him. Always cheerful, always chatty, Stanley is even more so today. Joel and I do not have to say a word; we are completely entertained.

"Look, look," Stanley calls out. "There's a male kudu. Oh, and there's a female! See it? There, in the bush."

I'm half-watching Stanley in his excitement, and half-following where he's pointing. At least I know from previous sightings that I am looking for a large antelope. The light-colored male, with a hump at its shoulders and fringe of hair tapering down along the ridge of its back is easier to spot than the female. He is standing in the open, his long horns twist and turn from their thick base to their pointy tips. Thin, light-colored, parallel stripes run down its sides. Two motionless females stand partially hidden by wispy branches. Without the distraction of spiraling horns, their elliptical ears, the size of which would qualify for wings on a smaller animal, appear more prominent on the females. They, too, have stripes down their sides.

Kudu ram.

A few minutes later, Stanley stops the vehicle in the middle of the bush and tells us we're getting out. We have no idea what's happening until we see a small helicopter in a clearing ahead of us.

"We are going on a different safari this afternoon. We are going to search for animals from the air," he says.

Joel is good at keeping a blank face; but I can tell by the slight shift in his posture that he is as uncertain and surprised as I feel.

He turns to me and asks, "Is a helicopter ride included in our itinerary?"

"It's not," I reply; but I'm too excited to care if it's included or not. Prepaid or not, we are going!

Stanley tells us the flight is a gift to us from Cullen, the host at Linyanti Bush Camp. Cullen checks in with us frequently at the camp to make sure we're enjoying ourselves. We let him know we are in good hands with Stanley who's always upbeat and informative. Cullen need not worry; his staff makes us feel like we are part of a family, a very welcomed part of a family.

As Joel, Stanley, and I approach the clearing, we see that the landing skids of the helicopter rest on logs that are strapped together. Beneath the logs, extending well beyond their width and length, there's a black, portable mat. The pilot is ready for us; he has removed all four doors to make taking photos easier from the air. When I get closer, I see he is the man at camp who told me with great confidence that the elephants were gone. I hope he doesn't recognize me as the frazzled lady who latched onto him earlier.

Helicopter ride over the delta.

The only other helicopter ride I have been on was in Kauai. On that flight, I sat up front between Joel and the pilot. As the pilot was delivering a monologue about the Hawaiian island, I was watching the oncoming mountains. He kept talking, I kept watching. The mountains kept getting closer. I wasn't sure the pilot was paying attention, but I didn't dare interrupt his monologue. As the mountains got bigger, blotting out all else from my vision, I pressed farther into my seat. At the point where I was ready to brace for a crash, my right arm, independently of my mind, swung out and swatted the pilot.

Joel was aghast. "Louise! You didn't! You hit the pilot?"

"I'm sorry. I'm so sorry. I'm so sorry," was all my embarrassed self could say.

The pilot assured me no harm was done; he even managed a smile.

On today's ride, Joel makes it a point to keep me away from the pilot; he sits up front with the pilot. I sit in the back with Stanley. The pilot passes headphones with mikes to each of us so we can communicate above the roar of the rotor blades. Securely buckled, we rise and begin our sweep over the Linyanti Marshes where dark blue waters flow from the Chobe and Linyanti Rivers, winding their way through islands of lush greenery.

We fly high enough above the marsh for elephants to look like six-inch toys. At this height, our noise is less disturbing to animals below. As I look down, I feel I am peering into a spa for elephants and crocodiles. In a private pool created at one of the many bends in the river, I see elephants soaking in water half-way up their bodies. Another elephant rests up to its ears in the cool wetness surrounded by grasses. Crocodiles sun on a sandy beach hidden at ground view by a border of foliage. A small cluster of other elephants walks knee-deep through water in search of their own place to indulge in the comforts of the delta. Hippos' eyes, ears, and noses form repeated patterns of dark lumps in the water. Giraffes linger along a slender sandy beach at the edge of the delta.

The helicopter tilts from side-to-side and turns as the pilot searches for herds passing through. I am so enraptured by the beauty of what I am seeing that I don't give a second thought to the absence of doors.

Elephants wading in the Linyanti marshlands.

We don't find herds. The pilot is disappointed.

He tells us, "I wanted to show you herds. It's fantastic to see. There were so many yesterday. . . huge herds of elephants and buffalo."

I'm delighted by how excited game rangers are when they spot something even though spotting something is a daily occurrence. It attests to the endless variety of nature's offerings. I assure the pilot that what we are seeing is amazing. I silently add seeing large herds in the delta to my next-time list alongside hearing lions roar, something I missed in Sabi Sands.

We spend an hour in the air and then return to the bush. My mind is so full of images that I don't think I have room for any more today. Stanley takes us to a sandy beach by the river for a sundowner. There's just the three of us enjoying the quiet minutes before sunset. As the sun slowly sinks toward the horizon, the sky turns blood red. Bands of grass that stripe the water in daylight become strokes of feathered blackness. A semi-transparent layer of gold floats on the water turned red by the sunset. As the sun meets the horizon, its bottom flattens, altering its shape, making it look like an egg yolk dropping into a bowl.

It's almost dark when Stanley says, "It's time to go."

I want to stay longer taking in every bit of the sunset until it ends. He indulges me, and then nudges me; but, still, I am not ready to leave. He climbs into the vehicle, starts the engine and says, "Let's go." It's not like Stanley to rush us. Joel gives me a little shove and I give in.

Sunset near Linyanti Camp.

We're the only guests in the camp tonight. Cullen is waiting for us at the entrance. I barely greet him before a full description of today's experiences pours out of my mouth accompanied by a heavy dose of enthusiasm.

"I am glad you enjoyed yourself. I thought you would like the helicopter ride," he says with pride and pleasure written across his face. "I have another surprise for you."

This has already been such a generous day. I can't imagine what he has planned.

"I have arranged a special dinner for you at your tent."

I picture a table set up inside our tent. How nice!

Instead, Cullen leads us around to the side of our tent. Two chairs and a small table covered with bottles of wine and spirits are placed near a glowing fire. I feel my eyes widen like they do when I open presents; I'm so amazed he arranged this. Now I understand why Stanley was so eager to get us back to camp.

"Come," Cullen says and walks us along the path leading to the deck at the back of our tent. Flickering, golden light from candles lining both edges of the path, and dimly lit lanterns hung from branches, illuminate the way. On our deck, a table resplendent with tea candles trimming its edge, a white linen tablecloth, and champagne glasses awaits us.

We return to the fire where Joel and I are left to enjoy it alone. After a while, Cullen comes to let us know dinner is ready to be served. Glowing, almost giddy from the pleasure of this evening, we move with silent steps to the table. A woman appears and serves the first course, green lentil soup with a slice of cherry tomato floating in the center and homemade bread. She leaves us to enjoy our soup. Joel attempts to pop the cork on the champagne bottle and has no success. As he studies the situation for the next attempt, the server reappears, pops the cork, pours the champagne, and disappears as quietly as she had appeared. We toast to how good life has been to bring us here. We enjoy our soup and talk quietly, taking in the experience of dining alone, out in the air, at night, in a jungle.

Just as we are ready for the next course, the server appears with the course in hand; her timing is so good it seems as if we had rung a silent bell. She sets the steaming plates of beef steak in red wine reduction before us and takes leave. Delicious! Joel and I wear grins we can't contain. It feels as if we are on our honeymoon or celebrating a milestone anniversary.

To top off our meal, cake with whipped cream is served. Whipped cream is Joel's absolute favorite thing to eat. We linger over dessert not wanting the evening to end. Joel pours the last of the champagne. I sip mine and keep the cork for a souvenir.

Chapter 14
ON FOOT IN THE BUSH

We wake to the news that a female lion walked by the front of our tent this morning and then down the path into the camp. I survey my surroundings on this cool, grey start of day and consider whether I'm lucky I missed the lion or sorry I did. I'm leaning toward the latter.

It's nearing the end of August. We are already eleven days into our three-week adventure. We're well into the rhythm of getting up at six, donning one of three freshly washed outfits, having breakfast followed by a morning drive, lunch, a break, an evening drive, a sundowner, dinner, a night's sleep, and then waking up to start over again. Even though the day is structured, nothing is predictable about what it will bring. The vast hours of downtime with nothing to do that we had anticipated have not materialized.

We welcome the simplicity of our mission for this morning—find a lion and see giraffes. On our way to Chobe National Park, the largest park in Botswana, we spot three warthogs sniffing out slugs or other goodies in a grassy area. From a distance, their chubby bodies look adorable as they look up at us and then move around on tiny legs while grubbing for food. I borrow Joel's camera with the 800 mm optical lens so that I can get a closeup view. Small though they are, they have a menacing presence. They have the heft of a hippo, the sloping face of a hornless rhino, the tusks of an elephant, the tail of a giraffe, and skinny legs. In other words, they are the Edsels of the animal kingdom.

Warthog on our way to Chobe National Park.

We leave the warthogs with smiles on our faces and continue our drive to the national park where we enter through the Linyanti Gate. Unlike our other safari drives where we were permitted to plow through thorny bushes tracking animals, here, we are required to remain on the main trail. We drive around for a while and see no wildlife. I conclude that, while we have to stay on the main trail, animals stay off it. Thank heavens Stanley, with his jovial chatter, is a form of entertainment.

We pass primitive campsites that offer basic accommodations but no frills like lodges, safari vehicles, or game rangers. Stanley tells us he wants to open his own camp like one of these.

As we pass a fifteen-foot-high termite hill with a large, leafy tree growing at its peak, an old six-seater station wagon approaches from the opposite direction. Three passengers sit shoulder-to-shoulder in the front seat, three fill the back seat, and three lie on their stomachs on the top of the vehicle clinging by their fingertips to the roof above the front windshield. They are laughing up a storm as they fly past rocking side-to-side.

Stanley shakes his head. "That's how people get killed. They are not with anyone who knows the jungle ... They are crazy," he says.

I concur. For the sake of the passengers on top, I pray there will be no short stops. While animals are used to seeing humans, their comfort with us goes just so far. A sudden motion, like someone jumping or falling off the top of a car, could result in a startled animal attacking. The soft, sandy roads waggle vehicles and invite them to get stuck, especially if weighted down. I hope the station-wagon-riders come out of this unscathed with good stories to tell. They probably will; but according to Stanley, some don't.

We bounce along, eyes casually searching. It's pleasant being here even if no animal appears. We come upon another game vehicle with passengers parked along the edge of the road. Stanley pulls alongside and carries on an exchange with the ranger in a local language. The other vehicle leaves the road and plows into the bush. We follow. I raise my eyebrows at this flagrant violation of the rules but figure it must be for something worthwhile. Soon we stop. With pointing and prodding from Stanley, we get our first, close-up glimpse of giraffes.

A veil of leaves and shadows teases us with spotty views of the animals making it difficult to discern where one body begins and the other ends. The pattern of brown squares, diminishing in size as they travel from the giraffe's body to the top of its neck, blend into the leafy shadows—a perfect camouflage for an otherwise highly-visible, twenty-foot-tall animal. We bend and stretch, trying to see enough body parts to imagine a whole. All the while, the giraffes ignore us, snipping choice morsels from the foliage above and around them.

The other ranger starts his engine and moves to another small clearing. We follow. There, we can see nearly all of a giraffe at once. As the gangly animal begins to walk away, its neck moves in graceful undulations. I have noticed tall men move in a similar way as they duck under and through doorways too low to accommodate their height.

Giraffe at Chobe National Park, Botswana.

We return to the main road; the other ranger is in front of us, moving faster than we are. Within a few seconds, Stanley calls out, "Leopard!"

"Where? Where?" I ask as my eyes scan the ground, shrubs, and trees with no results.

"In the tree," he says. He steers the car toward a tree in the middle of an open space.

"I don't see it," I answer. Joel sits beside me casting his eyes in different directions, carrying on his own fruitless search.

While I'm still searching, Stanley starts the engine and flies off leaving me bewildered at the abrupt exit. He speeds along the road and begins beeping his horn as we approach the other ranger from behind. The ranger doesn't stop. Stanley shifts gears, thrusting the vehicle forward at an even greater speed. He pulls alongside the driver and shouts, "Leopard!"

A neck-snapping U-turn and we're headed back to the tree with the other vehicle close behind. Stanley positions our vehicle eight feet from the base of the tree, just outside its canopy, where we can't miss seeing the leopard. Except we still don't see it until Stanley verbally climbs the tree and creeps along the branches to the leopard. The male, sitting erect, casually looks at us, apparently not giving our presence a second thought. It must have figured out a long time ago that safari vehicles can't climb trees.

Cameras click every time the leopard blinks, flicks his tail, moves his head. He shifts from sitting to lying down, flattening his body along a branch. His long tail, curved at the tip, drapes over the tree limb. His head remains erect. The blank, steady gaze of his near-transparent yellow eyes makes it clear he is not to be trifled with.

Leopard reclining on a branch.

"We don't see leopards here often—maybe three times a year," Stanley tells us.

No wonder he radiates excitement! Impressed by his having spotted the leopard in the shade-filled tree, I ask, "How did you *ever* see it?

He shifts around, as if struggling with the answer. He starts and stops a couple of times and then says, "I just get a feeling and I know it is there."

We watch, mesmerized by the beauty of the cat. Its spots, so perfectly formed with brown centers and trimmed with black cloverleafs, look like miniature paw prints. He lies still, either having satisfied his hunger or gathering energy for a hunt.

"A leopard can run as fast thirty-five miles an hour," Stanley tells us. As if that doesn't impress us enough, he adds, "He can cover twenty feet in one leap. He is better than a basketball player; he can jump ten feet high!"

I pick a spot about twenty feet away and envision the leopard covering the distance between it and us in one powerful leap, and then, with little effort, jumping onto our terrorized-selves sitting stone-like in the vehicle. I decide I would rather stand up to an elephant than a leopard; I've done that already.

We leave the park and pass more elephants, warthogs, and kudus on our way to the river for our morning snack. I ask if the hump at a kudu's shoulder stores fat.

Stanley answers, "No. It is a muscle. It helps the kudu when it jumps."

By the riverbank, we are offered the usual wine and spirits; Joel and I stick with coffee and biscuits. We would not have made good drinking buddies for Ernest Hemmingway when he ventured into Africa.

Another ranger joins Stanley. They chat for a few minutes before Stanley brings us into the conversation. He tells us that, as part of his plan to open a safari camp, he has applied for and was accepted into a Walt Disney World work-study program to develop business skills.

"I will work and study at Disney World for three months. I am going to be a guide there." He pokes his chest with his index finger and says with a smile and a chuckle, "*I* will be the authority on Africa."

He pulls his friend over, and with an arm around his friend's shoulder and a giant smile on his face he says, "We are Bushmen!" and follows with bellowing laughter.

Stanley on the right with a fellow Bushman.

I join in the laughter and then realize that, though laughing, Stanley is telling the truth; he and his friend are Bushmen. I need to do a quick rewire of my brain to broaden my limited image of Bushmen as primitive hunter-gatherers. Stanley was probably laughing because he knows he and his friend are not what is expected when people from western cultures think of Bushmen. I make a mental note to learn more about them.

Stanley gets serious and says, "I will work very hard. I will study, study, study every day."

Thoughtlessly, I say, "But leave some time for fun." And then I realize what a special opportunity this is for him to gain business acumen. I should've shown appreciation for his plans to stay focused on learning rather than encourage him to play. I wonder if this sweet, jolly man is ready for the aggressive females he will encounter in Florida and the not-always-polite park visitors.

When we return to the camp for lunch, a table of salads, set buffet-style, awaits us on the deck. Potato salad trimmed with shredded purple cabbage; tomatoes mixed with feta cheese, red onion, and silky light-green lettuce leaves; and freshly baked rolls overfill my plate. I barely get to sit down in the dining area before I see a line of elephants passing just yards from the deck on which the buffet is set. Without a word, I spring from my chair to take a look; Joel keeps eating—his priorities are set differently from mine.

I'm cantilevered over the deck edge stretching left, trying to see where the train of elephants ends. But it doesn't. Hundreds of elephants gather in well-spaced clusters along the Linyanti riverbank. The elephants before me are at the head of the first herd stopping at waterholes that are barely visible through the grasses in front of the lodge.

Joel calls to me, "Are you coming back?"

"No! Come here! Grab my camera! You have to see this."

"I can see it from here."

"No you can't!"

Joel leaves his food and joins me on the deck. We look out across the grassy plain that extends to the horizon line. A constant slow and graceful flow of giants pass in front of us, pausing to drink at the waterholes. It's a breeding herd, females with babies in tow that travel in line behind their mothers. While adults circle the edges of the ponds filling up on water, little ones playfully weave in and around their mothers' legs.

No bulls are with the herd; they would be easy to spot with heads held high, rising head-and-shoulder above the females. According to a documentary on elephants I watched on television, males live alone or in bachelor groups except when they go into musth once a year, usually during rainy season; we are well into the dry season. When males are in musth, their testosterone levels soar to sixty times normal as does their aggression. Battles are fought for dominance but not to kill or maim. Although, accidents do happen. A puncture from a misplaced tusk or a misstep that leads to a broken leg can result in the death of an elephant.

When seeking females with which to mate, they prefer ones that are in estrus and not pregnant or nursing. Bulls will mate with as many females as they can while in musth; for old bulls, this could be for as long as half a year. Fortunately for them, females can be in estrus any time of year.

Elephants migrating past the lodge at Linyanti Bush Camp.

Joe, one of the game rangers, joins us on the deck. He tells us in a low, soft voice, "The matriarch is the grandmother. It is her job to lead her family to food and water in wet and dry seasons." He pauses and then adds, "She's responsible for their safety. She teaches them to avoid humans and poachers. She teaches them how to survive."

Joe tells us that the second elephant, the one walking behind the matriarch, is the next in line to become the matriarch. The third elephant is the third, the fourth the fourth, and so on. The females jockey for position. As Joe speaks, I'm busy taking pictures of the babies; they are amusing even standing still. They find a way to make anything a game, including a journey that covers hundreds of miles.

With his eyes surveying the herd, Joe tells us, "The babies are under a year old if they can pass beneath the mothers' bellies. A baby weans from the mother's milk when it is between three and six-years-old, sometimes later. If you see it is not nursing any longer, it is at least three-years-old."

I'm struck by the length of time the mother nurses. The gestation period of nearly two years plus the nursing period is quite a commitment. Having had children and nursed my own, I think "enduring patience" needs to be included in the description of a mother elephant.

Joe feeds us more information we eagerly take in. He tells us, "If someone is near the elephants, the mother will move the baby between her and another elephant, or she will nudge the baby to move to safety under her belly."

He turns our attention to the calves' trunks and tells us that, just as a human child doesn't have enough control of the muscles in its legs to walk until it is about a year old, a baby elephant doesn't have full control of its trunk until it reaches about the same age. Its trunk will flop around requiring persistence to compensate for the lack of control.

All of what he says plays out in front of us. Floppy trunks, calves small enough to fit under the bellies of cows, playfulness, and the orderly progression on a trek. The elephants are comfortable here; no babies are sandwiched between two grey walls for protection or under a belly supported by four sturdy pillars.

I ask Joe the size of adult elephants.

"Females are about nine-feet tall at the shoulder, males about eleven. They can be sixteen to twenty-four feet long."

I picture an elephant twenty-four feet long and eleven feet at the shoulder in my downstairs family room. It would fill the room end-to-end with its tusks piercing the outside wall and its head occupying a significant section of my upstairs living room.

Joe adds, "African bush elephants are the largest animals on land. Botswana has the largest concentration of elephants in the world." I realize how privileged I am to be here.

I'm not able to identify the matriarch until a female leaves the water and a single line begins to form behind her. As she leads her extended family onward, another family herd makes its way from the riverbank, across the grassy plain, and to the waterholes by Linyanti Bush Camp. Distinct clusters of other herds wait their turn, shifting positions along the riverbank, repeating the pattern of waiting, watering, and moving on. Each is led by its own matriarch.

I ask Joe where the elephants are heading; from the mass of them, it appears they are on a migration route. He tells us they may be on their way to Namibia, just beyond the horizon line. Recently, some fences that interrupted the elephant's migration path were taken down. Now elephants can migrate through Namibia and into Angola.

I toss around in my mind what Joe just told us. I know it is good for an animal's gene pool to have an expanded territory; but I also know that Botswana is better than Angola at protecting animals from poachers.

I return to my lunch. The elephants continue to stream by. I could watch their graceful, agile movements for hours, but there's not much time left before the afternoon walking safari. I barely manage to download photos onto the small computer I brought with me when it is time to meet Stanley at the entrance to Linyanti Bush Camp. Gathered with us are guests from nearby camps that are invisible to us except on occasions like this. We hide whatever apprehension we may have with easy chatter and light laughter. For Joel and me, this is the first time we will be leaving the security of a safari vehicle to walk on paths shared by wild animals.

Stanley, poised with a rifle in his hand, is leading the walking safari. He tells us he is using blunt bullets large enough to kill a charging elephant or lion.

"I have to shoot the elephant or lion between the eyes to kill it. If I just injure it, it would be worse."

For a lion, he must get down on one knee to shoot. He is trained for this and practices with targets—stationary for elephants, moving for lions. He gives us rules, the first being to remain silent except when we stop to hear what he has to say. We're to walk in a single line. Joe will walk at the back to lead us away from trouble while Stanley fends off danger.

Stanley leading the walking safari.

He snaps his fingers and says, "When I snap my fingers, there's danger. You stop whatever you are doing." He snaps his fingers again. The snap is strong and loud.

Armed with these rules, Joe at the back, and Stanley at the front, we head out for the walk. Joe is unarmed. I wonder about the advisability of leaving the armed ranger at the time of danger to follow the unarmed one. Perhaps the mass of eight screaming tourists, propelled into flight by adrenaline, would frighten or amuse any animal contemplating an attack.

I walk in front of Joel and make it a point to stay close in line to the guy with the gun. As we silently follow a narrow trail through the bush, my confidence in Stanley and the thrill of daring to be on foot replace any apprehension I may have had.

We arrive at our first stop, elephant poop. Stanley tells us it contains a lot of liquid. I already know from an adventure program on TV, that if you are desperate with thirst, you can squeeze elephant dung and drink the liquid that streams from it. Thank heavens the dung we are looking at is dry and we won't have to try squeezing it.

Stanley points to a small pod in the dung and says, "Insects feed on berries and other things that pass through the elephant's digestive system. They make their home in dung." He pauses to poke around the dung. "Elephant dung is even used to make coffee." He waits for a reaction from us and gets it as all eyes dart laser-like to the dung.

Stanley nods, reassuring us this is true. He adds with a smile, "The coffee beans are first fed to the elephants. When the beans pass through the elephant's stomach, enzymes, fruits, plants, and leaves in the elephant's belly give the coffee beans their flavor. The beans collected from the dung are cleaned. When they are roasted, they make a delicious coffee. It is smooth and less bitter than other coffees."

"Have you ever tasted it?" asks a guest.

"No. It is too expensive."

"What does it cost?" pipes up another guest.

"It costs five hundred dollars a pound."

Gasps and chuckles echo through our small group. Meanwhile, I'm eyeing the dung and wondering what it would take to set up a business here. Later, I check out the price of Black Ivory Coffee on the internet. Stanley was wrong. It's not five hundred dollars a pound; it's one thousand dollars!

I tune back into Stanley who is telling us you can tell how recently elephants passed through by how dry the dung is. He also tells us elephants are so large, they have no enemies to worry about other than man— poachers in particular.

"Botswana's policy on poaching is that you say to the poacher, 'Drop your weapon.' If he doesn't, you shoot to kill." The drama plays out in my mind. I decide that, although the policy is severe, it is necessary given how many rhinos and elephants are mutilated and killed for their horns or tusks.

The antipoaching policy has gone a long way toward rebuilding elephant populations in Botswana. Botswana's herd population, which had exceeded 100,000 in the 1800s, was decimated by trophy hunters and hunters for tusks. Herds were further diminished by a lethal virus epidemic that nearly caused eradication. Beginning in the early 1900s, attempts to reestablish the herds began. At that time, licenses to hunt became a requirement. But it wasn't until the Chobe Game Reserve was set up in 1960 that the elephants began to thrive. Under its protection, by 1968, the year the reserve became the Chobe National Park, the herds had returned to normal levels.

"How many elephants are there now?" Joel asks.

"About a hundred thirty thousand."

I only half-dare to ask, "Are elephants still being killed by poachers?"

"A few each year. But the number has increased in the last few years."

We move on to a lighter topic. Stanley points to a small fruit and tells us it is poisonous. He adds, "If you are lost in the jungle, you should follow baboons; they know what is safe to eat and what is poisonous. You can eat anything they can."

I note an exception—the sausage tree, the fruit of which has to be roasted to be eaten by humans without killing them.

As he is speaking, Stanley suddenly snaps his fingers—the sign there is danger. But he continues speaking. After the second snap, it becomes apparent there is no danger. My eyes ping-pong between his face and his fingers as the snaps come every two seconds. The firmness of his facial expression and the erectness of his posture tell me Stanley's enjoying being serious and having an audience; the finger-snapping must add to his sense of authority.

We move to another area where Stanley points to healthy-looking, low-growing trees with small dark leaves and says, "These are fish-eating trees."

That makes our ears perk up. He lets us cogitate on a tree eating fish before he explains that the tree exudes a substance that kills fish but is not harmful to humans. Fisherman used it to catch fish until that was outlawed and the use of nets replaced the practice.

He asks us what we notice about the tree and the trees around it. Someone volunteers, "They are all the same."

"Yes. They are all the same. The tree's leaves contain a chemical that is poisonous to other trees but not to them. When the leaves drop, the chemical seeps into the ground. It poisons any other species that tries to grow. That is how they eliminate competition."

Amazing! I don't know if comparing fish-eating trees to monopolies holds. For the latter, there are laws to control them. For the trees, there are no laws of nature to control what they do; in fact, what they do is designed by nature itself.

We continue walking, more relaxed and less silently. Soon we arrive at the river. Mekoros—the boats formerly made from carved-out tree trunks but now made from fiberglass—line up along the water's edge awaiting us. We slip on life jackets and, two-by two, head off to choose a boat. I choose the one that feels right for me. In reality, they are all the same.

A game ranger, wearing a broad-brimmed hat and holding a wooden pole, helps Joel and me climb into the mokoro. He will use the pole to glide the boat through the waters. Soon, we are quietly drifting among waterlilies as the sun begins its slow descent to the horizon. The pole barely disturbs the water or makes a sound.

Game ranger in a mokoro poling through the river.

As the sun gets closer to the horizon, a line of elephants, silhouetted by the sun, crosses the water along a land bridge available only when the water is low. I hold my breath at the sight of the sun setting, the darkened shapes that move in near-slow motion, the silence, and our peaceful glide through the water.

Elephants crossing a land bridge that spans the river.

The sun is low on the horizon as we pass a grove of grasses that shape a deeply set cul-de-sac in the water. There, a pod of hippos waits for total darkness to climb onto land to graze. It's time for us to leave.

We return to shore where several game vehicles are parked including ours. Long tables are set with snacks and drinks. A heated grill is alongside the end of one table. On it, chicken wings, doused in barbeque sauce, are grilled to bright red with black, charcoaled patches. Staff from multiple camps man the tables helping eager guests to drinks and snacks. I wander around chatting with others about what we've seen and done, exchanging tips about cameras, and sharing photos we've taken. I find myself back at the grill-end of the table. A staff member approaches and asks if I have had the chicken. I tell her I haven't but will later.

"You should have it now. It will be gone soon," she says.

"I will, soon," I reply.

She puts two wings on a plate and hands it to me. I smile and thank her. I'm not all that hungry, but I have the wings in my hands and have to do something with them; so, I take a bite. Oh, they...are...so...good! I half savor, half devour the sweet and smoky wings. I turn to reach for some for Joel who is busy talking. The wings are gone, just like the woman said they'd be, and there will be no more. Now I *am* hungry. Just about then, Stanley comes by with Joel in tow and another couple from our camp to take us back to the lodge for dinner. I spot the staff person who insisted I take the wings. I go over and thank her heartily.

The lights in the camp are a welcomed sight after a long day. Dinner is served on the back deck of the lodge from which we had watched elephants pass earlier; a fire glows on the lower deck. Four new guests have arrived at the camp, two of whom were part of the walk through the bush. The chef stands behind a long table proudly displaying a variety of vegetable dishes he's prepared along with white polenta and thin slices of kudu in a reddish-brown sauce. I'm too tired to inquire more deeply into the ingredients of each dish. I know that, like everything else we have had, the meal will be delicious.

Joel and I join others in convivial conversation until nine o'clock then excuse ourselves to retire early. There's packing to be done; tomorrow morning we travel to our next adventure.

Chapter 15
THE WAYS OF THE WATER

A slender pilot stands tall alongside a six-seater plane, the smallest we've flown in so far, He greets us with a smile made brighter by the darkness of his skin; his rolled-up sleeves attest to the day's building heat. As we settle into our seats, he announces there will be three stops to take us to three separate camps. That's way too many takeoffs and landings for me. As luck would have it, Joel and I will be the last of the six passengers to be dropped off.

From the air, we get an expansive view of the Okavango Delta in which Pele Camp, our next safari stop, is located. We included the Delta in our itinerary because it would be a "wet safari." We had no idea what that meant, but it sounded intriguing.

I gaze out the plane's window, thankful that on a small plane like this every seat is a window seat. Usually, I'm the one in the middle seat, stretching across a sleeping window-seat occupant, struggling to see out, not able to see down. As the plane buzzes along at a fraction of the height and speed of a jet, thousands of small islands covered with vegetation come into view. Meandering rivers narrow into streams that trickle into rivulets. Pockets of lagoons bulge where coves have been carved over time. Even though Joel, seated across the aisle from me, has his own window with views, I keep calling to him that he must look out my window to see what I'm seeing. Dutifully, as the plane banks, he stretches as far as his seatbelt allows, takes a quick look, and smiles in acknowledgement.

I reach for a travel booklet I acquired while waiting at the airport. From it, I learn that the Delta is fed by the Okavango River which has its origin in the highlands of Angola. From there, the river winds its way through Namibia's panhandle and into Botswana where it pushes up against the flat, dry Kalahari Desert. There, it splays across the landscape forming what looks like a giant vascular system, as it pours three trillion gallons of water into 2,300 to 5,800 square miles of the 350,000 square-mile desert. From there, the Okavango River has no place to go—no outlet to a sea, no outlet to an ocean. It terminates and evaporates in the Delta.

I read that the flood waters peak in July through August during Botswana's dry season. It's now the end of August. I think twice about the contradiction between dry season and concurrent peak flooding, but quickly realize how valuable the water's timing is for the wildlife of the Kalahari Desert. Their adaptation to a desert climate, in which the average annual rainfall is five inches, is nothing short of amazing. Just as the fraction of an inch of rainfall received each month reduces to zero in the desert, the life-saving waters that feed the Okavango Delta arrive.

It's hard for me to grasp that even the Kalahari, with its already near-insignificant annual rainfall, could have a drought; but it does. When rain fails to fall for months, even years, and traditional water sources deplete, enormous herds of ungulates traverse the desert in search of water. They use trails, the knowledge of which seems to have become implanted in their genetic makeup, to lead them to the Delta. Many thousands die along the way from dehydration and the absence of water-bearing vegetation.

I can't imagine how any lion or other large animal could possibly live in a climate with so little water. It's not until I later read *Cry of the Kalahari* by Mark and Delia Owens, that I learn that a major source of water needed to sustain an animal's life, especially in drought, comes from other animals it eats.

I read on and learn that the Delta is a UNESCO (United Nations Educational, Scientific, and Cultural Organization) World Heritage Site. It was granted that recognition in part because it is unspoiled by mining, poaching, or war. Inhabitants, indigenous and others, mostly settle along its fringes which aides in preserving the natural beauty and wildlife. Difficulty in accessing the Delta helps keep it pristine, its water crystal clear. In other words, its natural state, being difficult to navigate, helps protect it from humans. There are other protections that extend from the Delta into the rest of Botswana.

Wildlife throughout the Delta falls under the protection of the Moremi Game Reserve and private concessions. Concessions, originally set up for hunting safaris, were taken over by photographic safari companies as interest in hunting declined and photography gained in popularity in the 1980s and 1990s. Today's safaris are solely photographic. Leasing a concession in Botswana brings with it the requirement to protect the wildlife and the environment. Joel and I have experienced first-hand the entrenched protectiveness and respect for the animals at each camp in which we have stayed. That we are guests in the animals' world has become ingrained in us.

I am so engrossed in reading and thinking about the Delta, that I barely notice the first two takeoffs and landings. We are on our third leg. When our plane lands, I spot a guide with a Range Rover waiting for us alongside the edge of the dirt runway. I have come to expect having a driver ready to greet us. It hasn't gotten old; I still delight in seeing someone with a smile waiting for us. It reminds me of the excitement I used to feel when flying half-way across the United States to visit family knowing they would meet me the minute I stepped off the plane, waving and eager to give giant hugs. But the attacks of September 11, 2001 on the World Trade Center took that away—now family, no longer allowed in the arrival area, must wait in the baggage claim area where the business of plucking luggage from a conveyor belt shares the moment.

Our driver, with sunglasses propped on the top of his shaved head, delivers a warm greeting welcoming us to the Okavango Delta. With introductions made and bags loaded, Sam, a game ranger who will be our driver and guide for the next three days, settles in behind the wheel. We are his only passengers.

Sam, a game ranger and our guide in the Okavango Delta.

Open expanses of tall, dry grass line the dirt road on which we travel. Small, light brown antelope stop grazing at the first sign of our approach and flee as we get closer.

"They are red lechwe." Sam says their name quickly, fluidly running the two words together. I ask him to spell what he is saying before I understand it's composed of two words and I can repeat red lechwe (red lech' way) with confidence.

He slows when we come to the next herd grazing so that we can get a better look at these small, agile animals. The chestnut coloring of their upper body is the source of their name. Their pale white and beige necks and underbodies make them look as soft as suede. We pass several herds of red lechwe spread out over grassy areas. I begin to suspect, and Sam confirms, that like the impala in dryer areas, the red lechwe are the "plentiful food" of the wetlands. While in the swampy areas, lions are no match for the lechwe that are well-adapted to cavorting in water. On dry patches of the Delta, the tables turn and the lions prove quite adept at snagging their prey.

Red lechwe grazing in tall grasses in the Okavango Delta.

We drive through puddles and then deeper puddles until water in marshy areas is too deep to cross. There, we come to a bridge cleverly constructed to minimize the amount of wood used. Widely spaced logs connect vertical posts across from each other. Rough-hewn planks run the length of the bridge approximating where the wheels of a vehicle will roll. A gaping hole remains down the center. Showing no signs of slowing until we are inches from the bridge, Sam lines up the Range Rover perfectly with the planks and drives across.

Crossing marshy areas on bridges made of rough-hewn lumber.

With his eyes fixed straight ahead, Joel mutters to me, "Thank heavens you're not the one driving."

He's probably remembering the time an unfortunate turtle crossed the road while I was at the wheel. Attempting to save the turtle's life, I swerved to the right. I can still hear the crunch that followed and Joel saying in total disbelief, "Why did you do that?" Had I not tried to save it, the turtle would have passed safely under the center of the car instead of under my left tire.

We splash through more puddles, cross more bridges, and follow a stream as the air blowing through the open vehicle mitigates the heat from the African sun. Sam points out a baobab tree that commands the open space on the other side of a stream. Its expansive, leafless crown resembles a root system, that gives it the nickname "the upside-down tree." The massiveness of its trunk contrasts with the slender trunks of trees scattered nearby.

Sam stops the vehicle so we can take in the majestic site. He tells us, "The baobab has pockets that hold water. They serve as waterholes for birds in the dry seasons. Animals and humans drink the water as well. A lot of villages are built near baobab trees." He pauses and then adds with a dreamy smile, "It is sooo nice to sit under the baobab and drink the water."

He tells us the tree can grow to nearly one-hundred-fifty feet in circumference and over eighty feet tall. He explains that the tree is a succulent that stores water in its immense body during rainy season. The reserved water enables it to produce a fruit in dry season that provides nourishment for villagers as well as animals. Elephants eat the tree's bark for water, but that does not hurt the tree—the tree has an amazing capacity to regrow bark that has been stripped.

Water, shade, nutrition, it's the all-purpose tree!

I ask Sam the age of the tree across the river from us; he answers, "It is very old. Baobab can live for over a thousand years."

A cave-sized, hollowed-out section of the tree's trunk becomes clearly visible as I extend the telephoto lens of my camera.

"The trees hollow out as they age," Sam says. "The hollows are a good thing. Animals live in them. Sometimes humans live there, too." He pauses, his eyes fix on the tree. "There aren't many baobab trees around. Recently, many have died suddenly."

I ask if it was from disease.

"No. Scientists have found no sign of disease. No one has found the cause. They think it may be from climate change."

I think about how sad it must be to lose something that has a dramatic presence in the landscape and is integral to everyday life.

Baobab tree across the stream.

My thoughts are interrupted by something Sam says. "The trees are solitary; they do not grow near any others."

I scan the expansive spaces surrounding the tree we are viewing. There is not another baobab in sight. I wonder, if it is solitary, how does it reproduce?

When I ask Sam, he says, "No one knows."

Later, I check on Sam's answer and find he is correct. There is speculation, but mostly mystery, about the baobab's reproductive system.

Farther along, we come upon one of the many birds for which the Okavango Delta is renown. A pair of long-feathered, long-necked, long-legged birds, easily four feet tall, stand side-by-side in the grass. Their graceful tubular necks are white, their bodies mostly white with tan-fringed feathers leading down to a train of brown tail-feathers. A crown of grey caps their heads slipping into a red patch that leads from their eyes to their grey beaks. Like the lapels of a tuxedo, a narrow band of dark feathers wraps around the upper part of their bodies giving the impression the birds are dressed for a formal occasion. Their slender elegance is reminiscent of Erté's Art Deco sculptures of women.

Wattled cranes.

"They are wattled cranes," Sam tells us.

Their name, "wattled," made from poles interwoven with slender branches, does their elegance a disservice.

We have driven for about an hour when Sam parks the Range Rover under an open-sided shade structure. Branches laid across its top let light slip through painting zebra stripes across our faces. Sam leaves us in the shade as he carries our duffle bags and backpacks onto a dock where he awaits the boat that will take us to Pelo Camp. The camp, accessible by water only, is on a small, heart-shaped island. To get to it, we will travel as deep into the Delta as one can in a small, motorized boat. As described in a travel brochure, Pelo Camp is for the *adventurous traveler who desires a classic, rustic Delta experience*. It's the camp on our itinerary with a bucket shower.

Chapter 16
ON THE WATER

We wind our way through quiet waters that tie together nature's montage of islands. Our motorized boat seems to respect the tranquility; its sound is barely noticeable, its movement smooth. I spot a camp, nestled along the edge of an island, half-hidden by bushes and shaded by leafy trees. I turn my head expectantly toward Sam and ask if it is Pelo Camp. It's not. A short distance later, we begin to turn into a cove. The familiar sound of welcoming mingles with the warm air. Four women, handclapping and singing, stand on a wooden dock; three are in off-white uniforms, the fourth, in shorts and a sleeveless top.

The chanting ends with an ululation that pierces the air like a sonic laser causing my eyes to bulge and my heart to freeze. The sharp, pulsating sound ends as abruptly as it began, its shock softened by an endearingly shy giggle that tickles its way out of the singer who delivered the ululation.

Greeting upon arrival at Pelo Camp in the Okavango Delta.

Sam extends a hand to help me climb onto the dock; Joel, as usual, is on his own. I find myself in a place so lush with vegetation that it could have spawned Adam and Eve. Huge trees stretch their leafy, dark branches over ferns and palms saturating the island with shades of green from bright mint to quiet greenish grey.

Joel's tap on my arm brings me back into focus. A neatly rolled wet towel and a glass of chilled lemonade are being offered by the women at the dock. I accept both. Drinks in hand, we walk down a path and climb several steps onto a spacious wooden deck on which a few small structures sit. Carla, the woman in shorts who greeted us at the boat deck, introduces herself as the camp manager. She invites us into a lounge for orientation and to sign release forms.

Long, wide screens separated by foot-wide bands of canvas form the lounge walls. Canvas shades, neatly rolled up and fastened with Velcro, lay across the tops of the screens. A black leather sofa and upholstered chairs face a cloth-covered, wood coffee table on which fruits, biscuits, and a pitcher of ice water are set. As Carla hands release forms to us, she casually mentions that elephants roam through the camp. Usually, I don't think twice about signing a release form, but roaming elephants triggers a pause. I recover and sign the forms.

While we wait for two other couples to arrive, we chat with Carla about where we come from and where we have been in Africa. She tells us that she and her husband, Jeff, manage the camp—he is the business manager, she is the social manager. I had been wondering how she came to live on an island set so deeply into the Okavango Delta. Apparently, for this couple, who look like they are in their thirties, the camp is their family business.

Carla tells us she and Jeff have made improvements to the camp that will allow it to receive a higher comfort designation. One of the improvements is that they have added batteries to solar heating. I welcome this news. It means that, unlike our time at Linyanti Camp, we will not run out of hot water before the day's end. The good news is quickly drowned by the thought that this is the camp with the bucket shower. Never mind running out of hot water; my bigger concern is running out of any water.

Before I get lost in my thoughts, Carla adds, "We also have added plumbed showers to each room; but we kept the bucket shower outside each tent for anyone who wants to try it."

I exhale. My concern about using a bucket shower now turns into curiosity. It's amazing how quickly knowing I have a choice alters my attitude.

After telling us the tents are built on platforms and can easily be collapsed and transported to be reassembled elsewhere, Carla adds, "If you ever try to come to the lounge area for breakfast or dinner and an elephant is on the path, don't try to pass it! Go back to your tent. We'll see you are missing and come for you."

I don't want to think about "you are missing" and all the forms that can take.

Word comes that the other couples are delayed. Sam suggests we use the time to freshen up. He leads us along a path that's neither made of dirt nor stones. It has the texture of dry grass, but is soft, not crunchy. I ask what the surface is made from.

"Elephant dung," Sam replies.

I search his face to see if this man who sports a giant smile is teasing me. He's not. It's then that I notice that not all parts of the path are equally dry.

"Sometimes, we buy bags of dung if we run out," he continues. "But it is expensive, so we use of our own as much as we can."

I think about the marketability of dung and wonder how much dung an elephant produces. Sam seems to tap into my thoughts.

"An elephant eats about 300 pounds of food each day and leaves about 165 pounds of dung each day," Sam tells us.

A quick calculation reveals that if a herd of twenty lingers for a day, it leaves behind 3,300 pounds of poop. That's a lot of pathway material!

Sam continues, "If you take a deep breath of smoldering dung, it will cure your headache. It makes pain go away. Many of the leaves the elephant eats are the same ones medicine men use." He stops to poke the strands of dried dung on the path and says, "It is used to make paper, too."

I rethink the texture of the dried dung under my feet and consider its possibilities for creating hand-made-papers. As I ponder painting or writing on it, a sensation of paint or ink soaking into the fiber, softening the edges of colors and letters, tingles my fingers.

We approach our tent, the fourth in the string of five, each one offset from the main path by a narrower one. Sam places our bags inside the door and leaves us to unpack. I take in the view of the Delta from the wood-trimmed, glass sliding doors that open onto the front deck. Part water, part vegetation, the Delta is picture perfect, its stillness calming. A five-foot wide tree grows just off the front deck. Gnarly vines as thick as branches twist and braid their way up its trunk. It's hard to tell what is tree and what is vine.

Steps to the deck.

View looking out from inside.

The airy room, with its carefully made queen-size bed and plumped pillows, belies the description of Pelo Camp as providing a "rustic Delta experience." Two chairs and a small table create a cozy reading corner near the sliding doors. A wooden chest, half the width of the bed, sits at its foot. Shielded from view by the headboard is a private bathroom that stretches across the back of the tent. A plumbed shower occupies the right-rear corner, a commode with a curtain door the left. A rack for clothing hangs between the two. A counter with a generous-size copper sink in the middle is mounted to the rear of the bed's headboard. I marvel at the luxury of a large copper sink and remind myself that this is Botswana, a country rich in copper.

Everything other than plumbing and bedding is made of wood or canvas. The use of space is maximized, providing all that we need including space itself. I am amazed at what has been done with a basic tent.

Inside the tent.

A half-hour later, we are back at the lounge when the other couples arrive. One couple exudes excitement from traveling, the other fatigue. Joel and I are the picture of calm having had time to slip into the relaxing atmosphere. After introductions, the camp manager begins a tour. Just outside the lounge, there is a well-stocked bar. I note that it carries Compari, an aperitif frequently missing from the shelves of even some of the best bars. I mention it's my favorite before-dinner drink.

As we approach the steps to the deck, we spot a bull elephant grazing three feet across from the bottom step. Unlike the bull I encountered at Linyanti Camp, this elephant knows people are around, but shows no sign of retreating. He's preoccupied with something at the top of a palm tree easily twice his height, perhaps three. He elongates his body as he raises his cobra-like trunk, coiling it around the tree at a point well above his neck and head. With the tree firmly in his grasp, he delivers a tree-bending shake. Nothing happens and the tree recovers.

In our desire to capture the moment up close on camera, all of us have crept one incautious step after another toward the bottom of the stairs.

"Back up." The command, absent of any threat or alarm, comes from Carla.

It's not until I back up that I'm able to fit all of the elephant into the frame of my camera.

Jack, an old bull and frequent visitor to the camp.

"That's Jack," Carla says. "He's easy to spot with the broken left tusk. Jack's one of our regulars." She pauses and then adds, "Not all elephants that come through here are as nice as he is. We have a real grouchy one. But don't get too close to Jack; remember he's still wild."

Easing his front legs onto the tree trunk, Jack raises up on his column-like hind legs. He uses his new height to wrap his trunk farther up the palm tree. His trunk, a thick mass of 40,000 muscles, has the flexibility to coil around a tree. Two finger-like protrusions at the end of his trunk provide enough dexterity to pick up something as small as a berry. Not counting the trunk and the height gained by standing on his hind legs, Jack's length is between twenty and twenty-four feet. That means, when he stands on his hind legs, reaching up the tree the way he is now, his vertical height is a staggering two-stories!

He gives a second shake to the tree. This time, several brown balls, each three to four inches in diameter, fall to the ground.

"He's having his dessert," says Carla. "The fruit from the tree is like candy to elephants."

I wait to see the yield from the next shake and then turn my attention to Joel who is asking, "How old is Jack?"

A game ranger standing nearby says, "He is maybe forty or fifty."

"How can you tell?" I ask, returning my eyes to the elephant, trying to get a glimpse of the protrusions at the tip of his trunk.

"You can tell by the wrinkles on his face."

Damn wrinkles! They're even giveaways for elephants. I remind myself to use the tube of moisturizer I tucked into my travel bag; so far, the tube has not seen daylight.

We leave Jack to enjoy his dessert and follow Carla up a few steps into the dining room, a three-sided structure made from saplings and topped with a thatched roof. A serving shelf lines the wall between the dining room and kitchen. A rectangular, wood table that seats twelve occupies most of the room. Its seating capacity testifies to the fact that just ten guests can be in residence at any one time; the remaining two seats are for staff to join the guests at meals.

In Botswana, keeping the camps small is deliberate; keeping the rates high is deliberate also. The country decided it would rather have higher prices and fewer tourists impacting the environment than lower prices and more visitors.

Across the deck from the dining room, there's a plate-wide counter along the riverbank with a row of stools cut from tree trunks running its length. That's where we will sit at breakfast time, facing the water.

I don't bother to ask if there's a telephone, cell phone, or internet service. I already know the answer, there is none. I welcome the peace that comes with not having rings and buzzes that fracture moments of pleasure or excitement.

We are done with the tour, but Jack is not done with the tree. We give up waiting for him to clear the path and take an alternate route to the water. Eager to get on our way to our first wet safari, we don't wait for Sam to help us into the same aluminum motorboat that brought us here. Chatter among the guests begins the minute we settle into our bucket seats—Joel and I at the front, Mary and Larry from Scottsdale, Arizona by way of New Jersey behind us, and Jill and Seymour from Miami, Florida by way of South Africa at the back. Sam makes his way to the stern and starts the engine.

We travel through the shallow waters of the reed-filled Okavango Delta. Reeds lying underwater in clumps of flattened strands point to the direction in which the water flows. Lily pads float along the surface. I should be watching for birds, something for which the Delta is well-known, but I can't take my eyes off the reflections in the crystal-clear water. Slender reeds arch until their tips join their reflected bodies at the water's surface creating outlines of fish. The shoreline, lush with papyrus, doubles its beauty with its rippled, mirrored image. I could sit in one spot for hours sketching the simplicity of the reeds and the tangled complexity of the papyrus-filled shores.

Reeds reflecting in the water.

Papyrus lining the shores of islands in the Delta.

Sam's voice and the *Where? Where?* of my fellow travelers brings me back into the fold in time to see a bird by the shore. It's ample size, the brightness of its red bill, and the striking contrast between its iridescent white feathers and the black ones covering most of its body make the bird easy to spot in the golden grasses.

Sam tells us it's a saddle billed stork, its name derived from the wide, black band that straddles its bill.

"These are the tallest storks in the world," he adds. "The male can grow to five feet tall."

That means, if I were standing in the grasses with it, we'd be looking just about eye-to-eye.

We watch the stork slowly move along the tall grasses at the shoreline, stopping to jab at the water with its sharply pointed beak. With a beak more than a foot long, I wonder how it manages to fly. Later, I learn that it flies with its beak drooping.

Saddle-billed Stork

We cut short our evening safari so we can get back before dark when the hippos come on land. To save time, we have our sundowner in the boat; all the necessities were loaded on board before we left. Hearing that I like Compari, Sam made sure it was included. As we imbibe, chatter becomes livelier; but when the sun begins to set, things quiet down in anticipation of what's to come. The densely black silhouettes of trees and shrubs that stretch between the setting sun and land add drama to the magnificence of the sunset. The intensity and breadth of the reds and golds in the African skies is unmatched anywhere I've traveled.

It's still the grey-time of evening, but I know the vibrant colors of sunset will come soon. I hope we will still be on the water.

We are. And tonight, once again, the sunset does not disappoint.

Sunset on the Okavango Delta.

We arrive back at the camp in time for dinner at seven. Greeting us on the dock with chilled wash cloths and drinks, Carla tells us elephants have been hanging around the camp all day. After having met Jack, this does not set off any alarms for me. And then Carla says, "It's a breeding herd. They are the most dangerous. We have been watching them."

I don't dare ask what "watching" does and if there is another plan. I push the breeding herd from my mind and opt for oblivion. Temporary oblivion, something I'm well-practiced in, can be a good thing.

Dinner is served in the boma tonight. The boma is becoming a familiar site for us. Like the others in which we've dined, it is open to the sky and surrounded by a sapling fence. I notice that instead of being tied together, the saplings are secured in their upright position by their tangled bodies. I smile thinking of the clever use of a natural resource.

Long tables draped with white linen stand end-to-end. Wine glasses and silverware glisten in the candlelight. A fire glows in the center of the circular clearing. Chairs, set in a semi-circle, and cocktails await us. Soon voices can be heard. The staff, dressed in light khaki staff uniforms, enters singing traditional African songs and dancing to African rhythms.

They begin to form a circle moving to the rhythm of their songs. The circle widens and comes closer to us. Each staff member extends a hand inviting a guest to join him or her. I've already been moving my feet to the music, copying the movements of the circling dancers. When it's my turn, I eagerly accept the invitation.

The chants become a song about friendship sung in Tswana and then in English. Soon, everyone is on their feet, caught up in this magical moment under the stars. The chorus, "Hand-in-hand. Two-by-two," and the lyrics extoll friendship among all people.

We dance and sing our way to the dinner table where staff and guests sit side-by-side. Wine is poured and, table-by-table, the chef invites us to the buffet table where he has displayed the feast he prepared:

Corn Soup
Springbok Sausages
Grilled Kudu
Polenta
Vegetables in Red Sauce
Chocolate Pudding with Whipped Cream

Pride shapes the chef's eager smile; delight in knowing the dinner is topped off with chocolate shapes mine. For Joel, I'm sure it's the whipped cream. I think about trading my whipped cream for his pudding. He'd gladly accept my cream but would be unlikely to part with his pudding.

The mood is set. Spirited conversation flows. Time passes quickly. It's almost nine o'clock, time to head back to our tents. Guests must be escorted. As we are exiting the boma, I glance up at the sky and stop dead in my tracks. My mind races to understand what my eyes are seeing. There's something different and startlingly beautiful. The stars are more brilliant than any I have ever seen. It takes a moment for me to realize that the light emanating from the stars doesn't disperse into the air—it is condensed into a white ball of brilliance set into the darkest and densest of blacks imaginable. I still haven't caught my breath when Joel gives me a tug and tells me to keep up with the other guests. I don't want to move, but I do, sensing even then that I will regret it later.

We head to the tents; Sam warns us the elephants are nearby. We leave Mary and Larry off at their tent. So far, so good. We move on to the next tent and Jill and Seymour say their good-nights and head up their path. We are the only remaining couple—our tent is the farthest out. No more than a few steps later, Sam motions us to be still. We hear the unmistakable sound of a tree being shaken by an elephant.

We creep a few steps farther curving slightly to the right. From there, we can see an elephant's hind quarters firmly planted on the main path and the front of his body hidden by the foliage lining the path to our tent. The silhouette of a palm tree shaking, and the thuds from round fruits hitting the ground, confirm the elephant is not done with his dessert.

We wait.

He's not budging.

We wait longer.

Sam motions for us to remain still as he moves a few steps closer to our tent's pathway. By now, Jeff, Carla's husband, has joined us. He waits by our side.

Sam returns, "He's going to be there for a while."

At Jeff's suggestion, we head back to the lounge to wait for the path to clear. We wait. It's ten thirty. I'm starting to fade; the elephant isn't.

Sam looks at Jeff and says, "He might be there all night."

Jeff, looking as tired as I feel, offers a suggestion, "We could try going through the bushes around Tent Number 5."

He turns to Joel and me and says, "It's not bad; it's a path the elephants use."

What!!! Take an elephant path? Is he serious? I hope it's not in use.

We take the elephant route. Jeff, holding a flickering lantern—our only source of light—is out front, Sam behind us. I know I inhaled when I stepped onto the path, but I'm not sure I have exhaled yet. Every sound we make is magnified in the nighttime silence. Jeff moves at a quick pace. In the blinding darkness, I can't see where I'm going or what I'm stepping on.

"Keep up," I hear Sam stage-whisper.

Through a break in the shrubs, Sam sees that the elephant has moved. "We might be able to get through," he says.

The lantern I'm following reverses direction. I change with it. I brush past Joel and he falls in behind me. A few steps later, Sam calls back to us that the elephant has moved—he's blocking our path again. We turn around and continue in the original direction. We make it to our tent. I practically push Joel over the threshold and into the room. Sam and Jeff leave, and we lock our door. That night, we fall asleep to the sound of the elephant wrestling with the palm tree and wonder if he still will be there in the morning.

TOO CLOSE

The morning sun drenches me in light, nudging me to start the day. I open one eye and see it's 6:25; the alarm is about to go off. I flip onto my stomach and push my head farther into my pillow. That doesn't stop the alarm from endlessly repeating its siren-like sound.

Joel groans and slaps the clock a few times before he hits the right button. With sleep-slurred speech, I say to him, "The elephant must be gone; I don't hear any rattling."

Joel, the one with mother's ears, the one who got up in the middle of the night to bring my infant daughters to me to nurse when I hadn't heard them cry, says, "The elephant shook the tree until three in the morning. It's probably sleeping now, which is what I should be doing."

I drag myself to the bathroom, splash water on my face, and stare at the over-sized Ziploc bags, each with nearly identical outfits sealed within. "One to wear. One to wash. One just in case," resounds in my mind. I'm thankful, once again, that a friend suggested this packing system; it helps both Joel and me to get our slothful bodies out the door in ten minutes. The clarity and coolness of the morning air soon adds a lightness to our steps as we head to the lodge. We are relieved to see the elephant is no longer chowing down at the bottom of our path.

With images of a warm breakfast swirling in by mind, I barely feel Joel grasp my shoulder, stopping me in my tracks as we turn onto the main path. I turn to him. He says, "Elephant."

No more than ten feet away, the broad side of an elephant is in full view along the edge of the path; its head is buried in the foliage it's feeding on.

"Let's go," Joel says pointing down the path.

"What? Are you crazy?"

He starts walking.

"Joel, stop," I call with a tensed jaw and semi-paralyzed vocal cords. "If we're missing at breakfast, a ranger will come for us."

My utterance falls on deaf ears—his and, fortunately, the elephant's, too. With a desperate sound barely above a whisper, I squeeze out another "Stop!"

All I see is Joel's back as he moves with an easy stride inches from the elephant's belly.

Over the more than fifty years of marriage, I have followed Joel through every danger. I even followed him trekking in the Himalayas, pushing back my fear of heights and lack of sure-footedness. But this time is different—he's not beside me or reaching out a hand to help. His back is toward me. He's walking away.

My eyes shift from Joel to the elephant. Its head remains buried in the rustling bushes as foraging continues. My upper body juts forward in attempt to follow Joel, but my feet do not yield ground. I'm standing at the proverbial edge of a chasm debating whether to plunge. Like a child testing the cold waters of the Atlantic Ocean in summer, I muster enough courage to move the toes of one foot forward with the slowness of a snail. The elephant whips its head, the size of a boulder, toward me. This time, I don't freeze; I about-face.

Ten paces later, Sam explodes out of the shrubs. Ordinarily that would scare the life out of me, but it registers zero on the Richter scale after the elephant encounter.

"You are too close! These are wild animals!" Sam says.

"You should tell that to Joel!" I reply as I process that Sam thinks I'm too close now; he should have seen me ten paces ago.

Encounter on the way to breakfast.

"Where is Joel?" Sam asks, his eyes scanning the area.

With all my anger at Joel's recklessness flexing in my index finger, I point down the path and say, "He walked past that elephant!"

Sam says nothing, but his body registers a gulp. He then leads me on a broad arc that circumvents the tree-fringed meadow where the elephant continues to forage. When we arrive at the breakfast location, I can barely speak to Joel, but I'm glad he's alive.

"You left me alone!" I mutter as I brush past him.

"I told you to come. It was safe."

"Safe for you! The elephant saw me as soon as I lifted my foot a quarter-inch off the ground!"

Joel says no more, not even a "poor baby," let alone make an apology or statement of regret.

I wonder how he gets away with things for which I get in trouble.

It takes hot cereal, fresh fruit, strong coffee, and sitting by the counter facing the unrippled waters of the Okavango Delta to settle my nerves and wave away the fear-borne anger I was harboring. Joel doesn't balk when, after breakfast, Sam says he'll escort us to our tent. In silence, we retrace the route Sam and I had taken earlier in the morning and then follow the elephant path we had crept along the night before. He waits outside our tent to escort us back to the lounge after we grab hats and jackets. I suspect he doesn't trust leaving us alone.

Three mekoro line a small patch of riverbank near the deck where we had breakfast, one for each couple. Mary and Larry, and Jill and Seymour are engaged in conversation as they await our arrival.

"We are going to spend the morning on the water," Sam tells everyone. "Choose whichever mokoro you would like."

I'm a little confused over *mekoro* and *mokoro* and ask Sam which one is correct.

"*Mekoro* is the plural, *mokoro* the singular."

Unlike the fiberglass mekoro we used at Linyanti Camp, these are hollowed-out tree trunks. We climb into the mokoro nearest us. Galexy introduces himself. "I will be your poler." He is tall, meticulously dressed in the staff uniform of light khaki shirts and long pants as are the other polers. His voice is soft, his smile gentle.

We travel slower, quieter than we did last evening. We pause more and listen carefully. There's hardly a sound as we slip through the reeds. Birds are nowhere in sight; they may be keeping cool in the tall grasses.

We leave the open waters and glide through clear water channels. The channels are lanes opened among the reeds by elephants and hippos passing through. For the animals, the lanes are like highways between islands. From the air, these intricate trails are easily visible. We stop at a pool to watch two female elephants with their calves splash their way through the grasses along the bank, their babies protectively tucked between them as they walk head-to-tail.

Protective mothers.

We round a bend into a shade-darkened cove. A huge tree drapes over the bank; its broad leaves contribute to the darkness. The mekoro that had been well-spaced, now converge, crowding into the cove's arc. An air of expectation is palpable, but nothing has been said. Seemingly out of respect for the silence, my eyes roam rather than dart from limb to limb in search of something, but I don't know what I'm looking for.

Galexy points and, in a whisper, says, "Look."

I see leaves with bits of light filtering through.

"No, look up," Galexy verbally directs us to a space between treetops where the owl, its wings forming a "V" above its head, can be seen preparing to land. Within seconds, a speckled brown and white owl sits tall on a broad tree branch. The owl's fluffy feathers make it look cuddly even though it is quite large.

"That is a Pel's fishing owl," Galexy says. "It is just an adolescent. The first time I saw it, it was a baby. It was ten inches tall! It looked funny standing up in the nest."

I sink back into the mokoro, imagining a ten-inch-tall hatchling, its body extending well above the nest's edge. I comment on the owl's size and Galexy responds,

"Adults are twenty to twenty-five inches tall. This one is already almost that tall."

Perched upright, close to the tree's trunk, the Pel's fishing owl watches us as we watch it. The owl's calm, casual viewing of us takes on an almost-human quality. It's shiny, near-black eyes appear perfectly round like giant marbles; yet the outline of each socket is a horizontal almond shape tipped upward at the outside edges.

Galexy, Joel, and me watching a Pel's fishing owl landing (arrow).

Adolescent Pel's fishing owl.

I turn my thoughts back to Galexy and hear him say how rare it is to
see these owls. Not being a birder, I don't fully appreciate what he says
until I later learn that the owls are masters of camouflage. They choose
trees with bark that best match the color and pattern of their plumage.
Perching near a tree trunk, where their body shape and verticality mimic
an offshoot of the trunk, they maximize the effect of their camouflage.
Even though the Okavango Delta is one of the best places to come to see
Pel's fishing owls, finding one of the 100 pairs believed to be spread over
the area the size of the state of New Jersey is a challenge.

We watch the owl; it doesn't move, we don't move either.

"They are nocturnal," Galexy tells us in a near whisper. "They fish
for food at night. They use their sharp talons to snatch fish from the surface
of the water. They can dive if they want to; but they don't like to get wet."

He adds that the owls prefer to roost in trees that overhang water. Hollows in thick branches form nests that need no further enhancements. Monogamous pairs breed in the dry season when the water level is low. At that time, fish crowd into smaller spaces making them easier to spot.

"Sometimes, two eggs are laid; usually only one will be raised," Galexy continues.

I ask why. He responds, "Maybe they raise only the strongest."

I ponder what he says and think perhaps it's too hard to keep two large, hungry offspring fed.

While the male provides food, the female guards the nest. At the first sign of an approaching predator, she distracts the intruder from her brood by feigning injury and carrying on with piercing cries of pain. Dropping to the ground and feigning a broken wing is a favorite, convincingly-carried-out routine. If a predator, such as an African fish eagle, comes too close to the owl's nest, the wing suddenly repairs itself and the mother attacks.

I chuckle picturing a broken wing enactment and turn back to the adolescent sitting alone. I ask if it's been left on its own. It's big, but it looks shy and vulnerable.

"It is on his own except that sometimes his mother calls to him in the evening. He will go to her and they will spend the night together."

I can't help but utter an *oh-that-is-so-sweet*.

We leave the cove and drift for a while in an open area. I dip my hand into the pleasantly cool water and withdraw it quickly—I've seen too many crocodiles to prolong the pleasure. I glance at Joel who looks completely relaxed. I envy him; even in a state of relaxation my mind races on to a multitude of the next things to do. For now, I entertain myself photographing water lilies and reeds gracefully reflected in the water. I snap a picture of a frog, no larger than my thumb, that rests on a bent reed. Thick brown strokes trace floral-like patterns onto his pale green body. Like so many things I have seen on this trip, the frog is there and then gone in an instant. I'm glad I captured a photo of it; without one, I would not have had time to admire its light green and brown painted body.

Frog on a reed.

Each mokoro is well-spaced from the others giving us privacy while enjoying the Delta. The sun feels good on this still-chilly morning. We linger for a long while, barely moving in the calm waters. I glance at Galexy and see that his nimble fingers are busy weaving what he calls "Delta jewelry." From a water lily stem, he weaves a long necklace for me; the lily at the end of the stem becomes the pendant. As a gift to Joel, he makes a coiled medal on a string from the fiber inside a reed.

"When I was a child," Galexy says, "I would use the stem of the water lily as a straw to drink water directly from the Delta." A broad smile appears on his face as he adds, "I had to; I couldn't lean over the boat to drink. There were too many crocodiles."

We relax awhile longer in a near-meditative silence. As if given an unseen signal, the three mekoro begin to glide through the water. Hidden from us on one of the many small islands, the camp staff has set up a table with coffee, tea, and cookies. They greet us as if we are long-awaited family come for a visit. Each of us shows off our newly acquired Delta jewelry to the smiles and compliments of the staff. We share conversation and laughter and then head back to the lodge for lunch.

Mid-morning snack on an island in the Delta.
Sam is on the left, Galexy on the right.

It's 11:30 when we arrive at Pelo camp for a lunch buffet of colorful fruits and salads made from leafy vegetables, roots, and grains. The camp director and a game ranger join us in conversation at the table. Sam is missing; I suspect he is taking time off to flirt with one of the kitchen staff; he seems to have his eye on the youngest one. Whenever we run into her, Sam says, "This is my wife." She shakes her head in denial, casts her eyes down, and offers a timid smile as her cheeks flush.

Following lunch, we have two hours to ourselves. I journal, Joel snoozes. It's 100^0. I strip down to my underwear, seek a breeze and some shade on our deck, and hope that I really am in a very private place.

It takes me an hour to catch up on my journaling. To celebrate and cool off, I decide to try the outdoor bucket shower. I drop my journal off inside, wrap myself in a towel, and take the wooden slatted steps down to the shower. I look up wondering if there is something I should pull slowly (a cord? a chain?) so the water doesn't dump out all at once. There's no cord or chain. I look down and see a hot-water faucet demarcated as such by tiny red beads, a cold-water faucet by blue beads. I step in.

Just as I get soaped up, I hear thrashing. *Oh no* flashes through my mind. The shower is alongside the old elephant path. More thrashing. My heart stops. Feeling more vulnerable than I have ever felt, I stand still, certain elephants won't want me, hoping they don't want the water! And then, I hear men's voices just behind the three-sided shower stall. Elephants or men? I don't know which is worse.

They pass; the thrashing follows them. I dump water on myself, grab my towel, go back up the slatted steps, and into the tent. I doubt I'll try that again. Meanwhile, Joel sleeps.

At 3:30, we gather for high tea. The camp's tradition is to serve coffee and spirits, something warm (spinach quiche or pizza squares), and something sweet (cookies or cake squares with squiggles of icing on top) along with tea. It's a lovely way to refresh. Although I knew about high tea, I hadn't realized that, at home, I break for teatime at about the same time of day. But, instead of tea and cake, I have an espresso and a piece of chocolate to relax and recharge me.

A new couple joins us. She's about eighty, tiny, and spritely; he's about fifty, tall, slim, and very protective of her. She is full of humor. He is quiet but quick to find fault with what she says. She brushes it off with levity. He backs down, but remains attentive to her, anticipating her every need. It's hard to make out their relationship. Mother and son? A paid travel companion?

We don't have to wait long to find out the answer. After the couple leaves to go on their evening excursion, Mary, who is one of those joyful, engaging persons capable of extracting secrets you wouldn't dare share even with your spouse, tells us that she had taken a dip in the swimming pool earlier. Two monkeys joined her along with the woman we just met. Casually, in between dodging monkeys, the woman told Mary, "He's my Boy Toy."

I look down the path and see that, as the couple retreats, they are holding hands. I feel a smile spread across my face and hear the words *Good for her* echo in my mind.

After high tea, the six of us, Mary, Larry, Jill, Seymour, Joel, and I, share a motorboat with Sam at the helm. Seated in swivel seats, we talk, laugh and keep things light—we have no desire to engage in anything heavy, we're on vacation. Jill and I discover we both paint portraits—she with humor and flamboyance, I with realism and a focus on portraying inner strength and beauty. It feels good to talk about the stirrings within when faced with an idea and a blank canvas, the physical act of mixing colors, and the satisfaction felt from a well-placed, single stroke of a brush.

Mary asks Sam if we're going to see hippos. He tells her we are headed in that direction. When we arrive at the location he has in mind, there are no hippos in sight.

"We *have to* see hippos!" Mary says in jest. And then, mustering a stern expression that would accompany foot-stamping if we were on land, she says, "We have to see hippos. I'm not leaving until we do."

"Maybe you will have to stay here all night," Sam replies.

We burst out laughing at Sam's response which he managed to deliver with a straight face.

We follow channels no wider than an elephant's body. Sam reminds us that any extremities we wish to keep should remain inside the boat. He credits the hippos with creating the channels by walking and running along the bottom; their buoyancy underwater enables them to travel quickly and with ease. He points out that, as the water pours into the Delta from Angola and Namibia to the north, it spreads out along these channels giving new life to scorched vegetation. In effect, in the process of creating highways between islands, hippos create a vast irrigation system. New vegetation spreads outward from the channels fed by the water and nutrients it carries.

Hippos travel along the channels enjoying the rich vegetation and the cooling wetness they require to survive. As the Delta waters evaporate, grasses turn to straw, and fires break out across the land, the hippos move northward following the channels seeking the last of the vegetation on which to graze and the remaining water in which to soothe their skin. They cling desperately to life, even sharing dwindling pools of water crowded with other pods of hippos, until the waters begin their return in March.

We move from island to island along the channels. Sam tells us that the islands are formed by currents pushing sand into a pile. As the pile continues to grow, the water reaches a point where it cannot get over the pile and an island begins to form. He also tells us that termite mounds, for which Botswana is well-known, contribute to the formation of the islands.

"Their excretions build up, forming a mound. Mounds can grow so big that they grow together making a bigger island," he tells us.

Termite mound—the beginnings of an island.

As we look at the monolithic mound before us, wondering how many termites live in it, Sam tells us, "Termites don't live in the mound. They live under it. Nobody knows what the mound is for. Maybe for ventilation or to keep where they live underground cool."

As with bees, there is a queen, and the job of her court is to keep her fed and protected; her job is to procreate.

He turns into another channel and says, "Maybe there are hippos around the other side."

I don't see them at first, but, sure enough, hippos are in the next cove. Silently, dark eyes and ears appear above water, disappear below the surface, and reappear at random times in random places making it impossible to count. I turn toward Sam and ask how many he thinks are swimming around.

"Hippos can't swim," he replies. "In deep water, they push off the bottom to get their heads above water so they can take a breath."

That helps explain the popping up and down of heads that makes the pond resemble an amusement park game where you hammer down a head in one place and another one emerges elsewhere only to be hammered down as well.

Seymour asks how long hippos can stay under water.

"They can stay five minutes or more," Sam replies. "They like to eat the nutrient-rich plants that grow at the bottom. They can even sleep underwater."

"Do they breathe while they are sleeping?" I ask wondering if they go into some form of hibernation or if they are limited to five-minute naps.

"When they are asleep, their bodies automatically push up to the surface. They take a breath of air and then they sink down again. They do not wake up when they do this."

I keep my eye on the bobbing heads. While they are still closer to the other side of the cove, they seem, as a group, to be inching up on us. The unpredictability of where they'll appear next, and knowing they don't fear humans, makes me feel uncomfortable in this small boat, in this small cove.

A second boats joins us. We watch the disappearing and reappearing heads until content. The second boat takes off, shoots across the water, and runs behind the hippos buzzing them. I'm ready to be out of here.

We retreat down the channel from which we came, and head back to the lodge arriving as the setting sun slips below the horizon. I leave Joel near the bar, laughing and talking with the others, and take time to sit by the water, away from the chatter. Alone, I enjoy the dwindling light painting bands of purple and orange across the sky behind silhouettes of trees. A narrow river, turned pink, reflects the shadowy silhouettes.

Sam comes to sit beside me. He's worried that something is wrong. I explain that I enjoy being alone. I decide not to add that I need a break from socializing, that I prefer to spend most of my waking time engaged in solitary activities: painting, writing, reading. Since we arrived almost two weeks ago, the balance has tipped; I now spend most of my waking hours in social situations. I have enjoyed every bit of my time with others, but this evening, the innermost me says, "That's enough."

I chat with Sam for a while, mostly about the beauty of the area and the lingering sunset giving way to evening stars. I carry the peace from the respite with me to dinner and then to my room. There, a goodnight story, left by the staff, is on our turned-down bed.

The Giraffe in the Sky

An ancient Bushman Story

At the very beginning of time, say the Bushmen, the Sun did not know its way around the heavens. Giraffe had a habit of staring curiously at everything and so the Creator thought it would be a good idea to give giraffe the task of watching over the Sun, so that it didn't go astray.

Giraffe took his job very seriously. (Indeed, he was so good at it that the Sun never again took a wrong turn.) The Creator was very proud of Giraffe, and He decided to honour him. He rearranged a few stars so that they made a giraffe shape in the sky, and you can still see it to this day. The Bushmen call the pattern Tutwa (giraffe) and use it to guide them when they travel at night. English speaking people call Tutwa the Southern Cross, and use it as a guide, too.

Chapter 18
JUST US

We're up, breakfasted, and ready to go when Sam puts the kibosh on our enthusiasm with, "We don't usually have anyone stay a third day. What would you like to do?"

Joel and I turn to each other in bewilderment, but neither of us speaks. We can't. The camp has no plans for us, and we have no ideas.

Sam looks at me for a response and then turns toward Joel. Assessing the giant voids in our minds, he says, "Come with me."

Hearing those words, I feel my brain resume activity; now I begin to second guess our plan to stay an extra day. Any regrets that begin to surface soon fade as we skim the Delta waters and head in a direction we haven't traveled. A boyish energy radiates from Sam's body. I sense we are entering his playground.

The morning air, cooler than it has been, gently blows a smile onto my face. Birds flit back and forth, dive for fish, and strut in the grasses. They, too, appear to be enjoying the crispness of the morning.

Sam slows the boat to a crawl. "See that bird?" He points to a small reddish-brown bird with a white neck and spindly legs. "That is a Jesus bird."

Before I get a chance to consider the origin of the name, Sam says with a chuckle, "It walks on water."

As the bird, an African jacana, steps from lily pad to lily pad, its super-long toes spread out dispersing its weight over a five to eight-inch area. The lily pads barely slip below the surface giving the illusion the bird is strolling across the water on twig-like legs.

Jesus Bird (African jacana) walking on water.

"They are good at swimming and diving, but not so good at flying. That is why they walk so much," Sam smiles.

He goes on to explain that African jacanas build their nests on floating plants. The female mates with several males in a season, spreading out her nests over a large area. Taking care of multiple nests of eggs is of no concern to her; it's the males' job to tend to them. The males tuck the eggs, and later the hatchlings, under their wings to keep them warm and safe. If the nest is endangered, the male carries his charges under his wings to safety. If eggs are destroyed, the female returns and mates with the male again. If another female comes by, tempting the nesting male, the egg-laying female returns to chase the intruder away.

As I travel through Africa, I try to associate the animal behavior I observe with human behavior. I need to bend my imagination considerably with the jacana male-female relationship. At first blush, what I see is a free-spirited, promiscuous female with a slew of adoring males. Hmmm, that sounds promising! And then I realize she is not as free of responsibility as it appears at first glance. She is the one that lays the eggs and then oversees a landscape of nests and nesters. The male gets to care for the little ones, protect them, teach them to swim, and watch them grow. As a mother, I realize how privileged that experience is.

As we travel through the waters, we trace the flight of birds with their expansive wings spread to catch the wind. We stop to watch other birds with brightly-patterned feathers perch in trees. We drift close to a Goliath heron standing tall in the grasses, stately with its slender body and subdued colorings. We follow the coastline; the boat's engine barely makes a sound. Sam's keen eyes anticipate where birds are and what they will be doing. I'm enjoying having Sam all to ourselves. The conversation changes from spirited to quiet, allowing us to sink into the tranquility of the Okavango Delta.

Goliath heron taking flight.

Goliath heron in the grasses.

Pied kingfisher.

The boat slides partway onto a grassy shore. A crocodile, asleep with one eye open, stretches out on a narrow sandy bank less than ten feet away; a small pond, barely bigger than a puddle, is all that separates us. We let it sleep and move around to a more open area where several crocodiles sun on small sandbars and swim among the lily pads. We drift for a while, soaking in the sun along with them.

Crocodile sunning nearby.

Leaving the open area, Sam maneuvers the boat into the far end of a small, protected cove. He brought us here to see a nesting colony in a tree. The tree, silhouetted against the sky, is crowded with nests of different bird species. Chicks, with outstretched necks and open beaks, express their urgency to be fed with rapid chirps. Parents tuck food into the young ones' mouths. The constant comings and goings, along with the density of birds and nests, creates the avian equivalent of a bustling city.

Nesting colony in a tree. *(Photo by Joel)*

With glossy black feathers and long chestnut-colored necks, the African darter is by far the dominant species in the nesting colony. The bright white of a fellow nester, an African egret, strikes a sharp contrast. The darter gets its nickname, snakebird, from the way it swims. Its body remains under water while its neck and head slither along the surface like a snake. Its webbed feet propel it toward its prey. With its sharp beak, it spears its catch, flips it into the air, catches it, and swallows.

We see none of the hunter-prey activity, just the caring family part.

Nesting African darter.

Sam reaches into a canvas basket for a thermos of coffee and prepares to serve us. Joel accepts, but I pass, content to watch the birds as I try to preserve the moment with photographs. It's easy to see that Joel, who is much more adept at relaxing than I am, is having an idyllic day. He and Sam are seated in the bow of the boat, watching birds, exchanging comments, sharing laughter. I'm enjoying the comfortable relationship that I see developing between them. I get the feeling they could stay here, in this spot, forever. Sam slips me a smile.

Sam and Joel at the nesting colony.

It's funny how time drifts by on the water, not too fast, not too slow. When Sam turns on the motor, we shift from a state of stillness to a state of motion; our senses sharpen, seeking the next surprise. An elephant's head pushes through tall grasses along the bank; an egret takes flight, a crocodile slips into the water.

We arrive at the camp in time for lunch. Local women sit on the deck displaying baskets they have woven from reeds and other plants. Each person's work has the weaver's handprint on it by virtue of the materials and colors chosen and patterns woven. I'm so concerned about the lack of space in my luggage, that I don't buy anything. Foolish me.

While we were on the waters this morning, the two couples with which we spent the past couple of days were preparing to leave. Sam excuses himself to take them to the airport. Like all game rangers, once assigned to guests, Sam is responsible for them until they are safely on their way. He will not take on new guests until the old ones have left. So, not only do we have Sam all to ourselves, but he has just us until we too leave.

He returns in time for the evening safari. It's August, the end of winter is approaching. Average mid-afternoon temperatures reach the upper seventies—five degrees higher than in July and eight degrees lower than they will be in September. Coming from the Houston, Texas area—the land of high temperatures and high humidity—any dry place with temperature below ninety is heaven. Being on the waters of the Okavango Delta, with a breeze blowing, is just that kind of place.

Throughout the safari, we have been seeing African fish eagles—at first a novelty, and then a common occurrence, but always spectacular to view. Today, as before, they are present in abundance, sometimes alone and sometimes perched in trees in small groups of two or three. Near my home in Texas, there are a pair of nesting American bald eagles, cousins to the fish eagle. In two years, I've seen only one circle the lake by our house. Even at that, I considered myself lucky.

I pause to take in the fact that I'm watching these magnificent birds perched on branches instead of quickly soaring in and out of sight. Their hefty, dark-chocolate bodies, crowned with brilliant white plumage and punctuated by bright yellow beaks, exude power. There is no doubt that they are the ruling predators among waterfowl. Though well-equipped to snatch fish from the river, if they decide to get food the easy way, a fish eagle will harass even a five-foot tall Goliath heron to the point where it abandons the meal it worked hard to get.

Lost in my own thoughts, it barely registers that Sam is talking. I tune in as he is saying that the fish eagle is extremely territorial; it allows only family members to share the tree it occupies.

I turn my attention to a nearby tree that extends its outstretched branches through cloudless blue sky. Two eagles perch well-spaced from each other. A small bird, either of no consequence to the eagles or not noticed by them, perches higher up. Like stars commanding a stage, the fish eagles draw focus to themselves by virtue of their confident posture. There's no flittering as seen with small birds—just a stillness that comes with having no fear of being attacked, the benefit of being top predator.

Their only enemies are deforestation, and water pollution. In the protected areas of the Delta, the eagles are thriving. If their numbers were to decline, it would signal substantial ecological problems.

Fish eagles.

One-by-one, the eagles take flight. We continue down the river and come to a swampy area where red lechwe are romping. We watch as they leap between islands of grass. One gets a running start, leaps and misses its target splashing into the water. Seemingly unphased, it leaps and misses again. It gives up and chooses to lope through water instead. Sam lets out with an "Oh! Oh! Oh!" and a hardy laugh as he watches the mishaps unfold. His laughter is more hilarious than the blundering red lechwe.

Red lechwe about to miss its target.

We hug the bank. Sam grows silent. He senses something.

"There!" he says, pointing into thick reeds. Joel and I crane our necks, but we can't find what Sam's seeing.

"Look in the reeds," he says. "It is a sitatunga. They are very shy."

We look, don't know what we are looking for, and don't see anything.

Joel asks, "What is a sitatunga? What are we looking for?"

"It's an antelope. It likes to hide in the swamp. It is safer there. It is very fast in the water but not so good on land." Sam explains that the sitatunga has elongated, splayed feet that allow it to move quickly through marshy areas and even walk on floating vegetation without sinking. But the size of its hooves is a hinderance on land.

Sam interrupts the silence that follows with, "If a sitatunga is frightened, it can hide underwater with only its nostrils showing."

Now I don't know whether to look up or down in search of the sitatunga.

Sam, determined not to let us miss the opportunity for a rare siting, starts up the motor to startle the sitatunga into moving. It works. I see one eye, an ear, and wavy horns as its head snaps up. It's still difficult to discern among the reeds. How Sam spotted it is beyond me.

We wait for the sitatunga to rise or run away so we can see more of it. No dice; the engine runs, but the sitatunga doesn't. Sam drives the boat farther into the reeds. No movement. I take a quick glance at how far into the tangle of growth we have advanced. I picture engine blades strangled by reeds and wonder if we'll get out. Finally, Sam drives the boat so far in, I am convinced we'll be stuck here until the Delta waters evaporate. The sitatunga assesses the situation and must decide it doesn't have a chance against Sam's determination. It bounds through the reeds, creating as much space as it can between us and it. I'm surprised at the heft of its compact body. Joel is quick to get a video of the sitatunga leaping through the reeds; my shutter finger is too slow to get a shot.

"You are lucky to see this one," Sam says. People travel here just to see the sitatunga. They do not always get to see one."

Sitatunga hidden in the reeds.

Sitatunga taking flight. *(Frame from Joel's video)*

The sitatunga was probably keeping cool in the heat of the day, resting on a platform it had made in the swamp by circling around and around, stomping on reeds. I'm sorry we disturbed it; but in the balance of things, seeing the sitatunga, at least for me, outweighs disturbing it. Hopefully, it will make its way back to the platform and not have to build another. Given that we have seen no one else as we traveled through the waters the last two days, perhaps the sitatunga won't be disturbed again. The realization that we've not seen anyone else on the waters causes me to wonder if, while Sam was telling us how rare it is to see a sitatunga, the sitatunga was telling its herd about the rare siting it had had of us.

We follow wherever the water takes us, watching for birds, pointing out crocodiles, enjoying waterlilies. Nothing is new; but nothing is the same. We sip sundowners while watching the sun make its slow descent; its reflection paints a lantern-like image on the rippled waters. It's time to head back to see what awaits us.

Sunset on the Okavango Delta.

Chapter 19
SWEET OBLIVION

For the last two weeks we have been living in a bubble of comfort and adventure. Every need is anticipated and satisfied. Every day unfolds, surprising us with something new. With the absence of TVs, phones, and internet, there is no news from the outside world to interrupt the sweet oblivion into which we have willingly slipped. Our trip to Africa is the most relaxing we have ever had, and yet it is adventurous as well. Tonight, I expect it to be no different.

Joel and I join two new guests and staff at the buffet table and survey the offerings. There is no need to be strategic; I am going to take a little bit of everything. Soon, fresh vegetables, polenta, lamb, and fruits abut each other on my overflowing plate; a steaming, fresh-baked roll is wedged in between. I head to the dining room table looking like I needed a platter instead of a plate.

Dave, a new guest, tells us that he and his son just arrived from Chicago. He asks us where we're from—a typical question for new encounters.

Between bites Joel replies, "Houston."

"You mean what's left of it!"

I can't grasp what Dave is saying. I try to shake my mind out of its confused state. "What do you mean *what's left of it?*" I ask.

"A hurricane is slamming into it."

Joel is stony silent. I wait for Dave to say more, but he's on pause.

Not able to wait any longer, I ask, "When did it hit?"

"It's happening now! Hurricane Harvey has been sitting on top of Houston since yesterday, lashing it with rains. Last I heard, Harvey is expected to dump thirty inches on the city. It's already dumped over twenty."

Images of overflowing bayous and fender-deep waters surface from my memory. I've been through a storm that dropped seventeen inches in two days. It was disastrous even without hurricane-force winds. With high winds, hurricanes spinning into Texas from the Gulf of Mexico create storm surges with enough power to push walls of Gulf water up against rivers, halting their flow out to sea. With nowhere to go, the rivers back up and overflow. They, in turn, push up against streams and their tributaries, causing them to splay out across the region. Being thirty miles upstream from Houston, but not thirty miles from its vast network of rivers and tributaries, leaves our community and surrounding areas vulnerable to severe flood damage even if we don't encounter the full force of the storm.

I cut short my thinking when I hear Joel ask, "What category is it?"

"It's a Category 4." Like a good doctor would do after dropping a bomb on his patients, Dave rephrases what he has just told us, "Its winds exceed 130 miles per hour."

I feel my ribs collapse into my chest. During ordinary storms, the lake, a half-block from our house, fills to the brim and a stiff breeze blows choppy waves across its surface, splashing water onto the shore. The space between our townhouse and the ones next door acts like a wind tunnel; it's an unobstructed path straight to the lake. I realize we may not have a home to return to. There is no way of getting information on what is happening until we leave Botswana tomorrow and reach the airport in Johannesburg where we will have access to Wi-Fi.

The other guests have moved on to another topic. Joel and I turn to each other. He breaks the stunned silence between us and says, "There's nothing we can do about it from here." He sees me nod and then adds, "We may as well continue to enjoy what we are doing. We would not be able to get home even we wanted to."

We rejoin the conversation, which has moved on, and dig into our dinner, which is waiting. Nothing ever interferes with our appetites.

The next morning, we motorboat across the Delta to dry land, drive over strategically placed planks on bridges, and stand in an open, sandy field watching the arrival of our airplane at the airstrip. Our three flights will zigzag across the continent, first south to Maun, then southeast to Johannesburg, and finally back northwest to Windhoek, the capital of Namibia, where we will spend the night. At our first stop, I have just enough time to text my daughter, Jessica, to ask if she could find out about the hurricane.

Her reply is quick, "I'm on it."

When I see her words, I feel a shudder of relief travel through my body. Jessica grew up in The Woodlands, our town, but now lives half a continent away from our home and the storm. I can see her fingers flying across the keypad of her cell phone, poking out inquiries and requests. I smile picturing her calm but serious face as she manages surveillance from afar.

We leave Botswana and ninety minutes later arrive at Johannesburg. We thread our way through the airport terminal to an information center where we get instructions on how to connect to the internet. After multiple attempts at different seat locations, Joel gets a connection on his phone. For the first time, he sees the text messages Jessica sent out yesterday, Sunday, August 27:

> *Jessica:* I dropped a note to your property manager last Friday before the storm hit asking the plan for checking on your house. It appears there is no plan. I can't ask her to go out in this unless we know there is a need. Do you have your neighbor Paul's number? I'll call him. Cell number is best so I can text. I am sure phone lines are inundated. (8:52 AM)

> Update (Sunday midday)- I reached out to the property manager again and she responded. She is unable to leave her subdivision. I have emailed Paul (I found his address in one of your group forwards) to see how things look in your neighborhood. I asked him to let me know if things become serious re: flooding. Does anyone have a key to your house? Thinking about your cars and a couple of pieces of art on your ground floor.

I can't think of anything else truly valuable that's not off the ground floor. (12:58 PM)

Jennifer said she will do a drive by if it is safe to leave her children. Hughes Landing [on the opposite side of the lake from our townhouse] is quite flooded. Hillary and Shanti have offered, too. Such good friends! (1:22 PM)

Update (Sunday 11:30 PM) Still no word from anyone. 21-22" rain over last 24-36 hours and continuing heavily. You are missing a catastrophic rain. Houston is a mess! (10:40 PM)

Jessica: Update (Monday midday): Jennifer drove by your house today and took pics of the outside. All looks good. No standing water (2:07 PM)

Looking over Joel's shoulder, I breathe a sigh of relief as does he. I leave to search for snacks; we haven't eaten since breakfast. Joel remains seated in the midst of shops selling food, drinks, and every souvenir you wish you had bought, focused solely on the internet. He, unlike me, isn't tempted by anything going on around him. He doesn't dare move or disconnect from the Wi-Fi, not trusting he will get on again.

Jessica: BTW . . . the rain let up for a while but is back. (3:09 PM)

I'm keeping the weather channel on. Looks like downtown Houston may become part of the Gulf of Mexico if this keeps up. I called Jennifer to find out if the roads are still that bad there and she said that it depends on where you are coming from. I contacted your property manager and said we would like to get someone out to your house as soon as it's possible. She doesn't think she'll be able to get out of her house until the end of the week. At this point I am focused on making sure there are no roof leaks. (4:10 PM)

We spend the afternoon waiting for more news. None comes. We board the plane and fly to Windhoek. It's after 9:00 p.m. when we arrive. We've been traveling for eleven hours. I surrender my pen to Joel who patiently fills out the customs forms. Our half-hour drive on two-lane paved highway turns into a mini evening safari. Jackals, something we haven't seen yet, crisscross the road on their nighttime hunt for food.

We arrive at the Olive Lodge in the dark and are led up unlighted steps, first stone then metal, feeling our way with the barest of ambient light. I swear the man leading us is part cat the way he negotiates the darkness. I'm certain I'm going to wind up on all fours before this is over. It's only when we're just outside our room that the man flicks on a light he holds in his hand. I look at him as if to say, "Why didn't you do this sooner?"

The room has a grey-on-grey motif with painted concrete floors, a concrete wall-to-wall-floor-to-ceiling unit of shelves, and a massive concrete headboard reaching almost to the ceiling. The theme is carried into the bathroom with a concrete tub, a separate concrete shower, and two concrete counter and sink areas. The only things that are not concrete are the mattress, the commode, and the faucets that look like pipes sticking out of uncaulked holes. Overall, the effect is contemporary and surprisingly pleasing—at least it is to my tired eyes.

I turn to Joel who is standing behind me and say, "This looks like the ideal home you can clean in a flash by turning a hose on everything."

He laughs but points out that it is actually quite clever and pleasing.

Bathtub, part of the grey-on-grey concrete motif.

I leave Joel to wrap up the texting with Jessica as I close my eyes, too weary to even think about the next day. He reads to me what he has written . . .

> We are at a hotel for the night and have Wi-Fi. Thanks for all you are doing. You are doing all the right things. Please let Jennifer know we appreciate her checking on our house. Knowing you are on top of things gives us great comfort.
> Love ya.
> Mom and Dad

and then kisses me goodnight. I go out like a light and remain blank until morning.

Chapter 20
URBAN INTERLUDE

While Joel showers, I search the web for news, hoping the hurricane has passed. I scroll past sites and images that may exaggerate the effects of the storm and turn to an update on weather.gov/Houston, a site I know I can trust to give just the facts:

> Catastrophic flooding is ongoing with flash flood emergencies remaining in effect. The threat for continued additional catastrophic, unprecedented, and life-threatening flooding continues today and into next week.

CATASTROPHIC? INTO THE NEXT WEEK? I search multiple news station websites to find more specific details of what is happening now. I sink back into my pillow. What Dave said last night about the hurricane sitting on Houston was no exaggeration. Pushing against other atmospheric conditions, Harvey moved at a snail's pace of two miles an hour as its eye traveled across Houston. Corralled by weak winds in the upper atmosphere unable to steer Harvey east, a tropical disturbance along the Atlantic blocking the storm's exit to the Gulf of Mexico, and a high pressures system from the north pushing it back toward the Gulf, Harvey couldn't move.

With one foot in the Gulf and one foot set on land, the hurricane whipped trillions of gallons of water into its winds and then dumped them on Texas' coastal areas. This morning, the storm finally moved into the Gulf, but it looks as if it will make landfall again. Meanwhile the rain continues.

I search Click2Houston.com, a local television channel's website. Parts of Houston have had over fifty inches of rain between August 25 and today, August 29. Montgomery County, the county I live in, has had over thirty inches.

I find photos online, each amazing, each with a layer of horror underpinning it. I know from previous hurricanes that people are stranded on top floors of their homes, on roofs, clinging to branches, washed away. Pictures are vivid in my mind of rescuers dangling from ropes hung from helicopters, extracting people from rushing waters, neighbors and strangers steering their boats along what had been streets to check on others and lend help wherever they can. From past experiences, I know that no matter how destructive the winds may be, it's the flooding that is the most devastating. This storm, and its ruin, will be with us for a long, long time. Our potential leaky roof means little to nothing now; at least I know my house is still standing and not washed away like so many others.

Hurricane Harvey flooded Houston ...
houstonchronicle.com

Incredible photos as Hurricane Harvey ...
houston.culturemap.com

Houston hit by 'catastrophic flooding ...
kalb.com

Website images of hurricane Harvey flooding Houston.

I update Joel before heading to breakfast. We choose a table on the deck and inhale the sweet cool air as the sun shines through clear skies. We agree to let the hurricane go and wholeheartedly slip back into our adventure; there is so much left to enjoy and nothing we can do about our home except worry.

We turn our attention to the breakfast menu and see that it offers Namibian, English, Italian, Canadian, French, Scottish, and International fares. In silence, we study it, curious to see the foods ascribed to each.

"Which one did you pick?" I ask Joel. I always ask him his choice before I order because he seems to have a knack for picking the most interesting, and delicious, item.

"I'm not telling you," he teases me.

He forces me to commit to my choice before he reveals his. The Namibian breakfast, with game sausage along with eggs, bacon, mushrooms, onions and peppers, is the one we each have settled on.

Namibian
Two eggs (fried, scrambled, boiled or poached), bacon, game sausage, fried mushrooms, onions & peppers.
Served with white or brown bread toast.

English
Two eggs (fried, scrambled, boiled or poached). Served with free range game sausage and white or brown bread toast.

Italian
Fried eggs on toast, with basil pesto and mozzarella cheese.

Canadian
Four mini-pancakes served with maple syrup- bananas and mixed berries.

French
Two slices of French toast, served with honey and grated cheese.

Scottish
Steaming bowl of oat meal porridge, served with honey, brown sugar and a tot of single malt scotch on the side.

International
Two egg omelette with a choice of fillings: Cheese, tomato, ham, onions, green peppers and mushrooms served with white or brown toast.

Olive Grove breakfast menu.

We enjoy a second cup of coffee before returning to our room to finish packing. Our guide, Audy, is waiting at the checkout desk. His grey, stubbly beard matches his short-trimmed, black and grey speckled hair; dark eyebrows accentuate his coffee-colored skin. We load our luggage into his car and set out for a tour of Windhoek before heading to the airport to catch a flight later in the day.

I have lost the lens cap for my camera and ask Audy if there is a camera store nearby.

"We'll make that our first stop," he says.

On our way to the downtown area, I notice that many streets have German names.

"Namibia was a German colony," Audy tells us.

Unlike other guides, Audy is somewhat quiet and appears less likely to volunteer personal information. I don't inquire about his life as I have with others.

At the downtown shopping area, low-rise buildings let sunlight wash the spotless streets with light. There is a youthfulness and an energy to the people walking along the sidewalks lined with window displays and outdoor cafes. Cars flow through the multilane main street; traffic lights halt vehicles so pedestrians can cross.

Audy slips his car into a parking spot across the street from the camera store. I make use of the much-needed corner traffic light to cross. Once across, I can't resist taking time to peek into store windows even though Joel and Audy sit in the car waiting for me. Wecke & Voigts, a department store, advertises that it is 100% Namibian, established in 1892, and carries full lines of Namibian-made products. One look at the colorfully patterned women's clothing and bathing suits—some modest, most revealing— and the summer hats with ribbons of color laced through them and I want to start and end the tour here. I doubt I could get Joel to agree to that. I drag myself away.

A few doors down, I come to a men's clothing store; the full width of its storefront is open to passersby. Two salesmen, dressed in the casual contemporary style of the store's merchandise, smile welcomingly. I smile back picturing Joel in slim-cut pants and T-shirts. He'd look good.

Men's clothing store in downtown Windhoek.

An outdoor café, populated with staff laughing and talking with customers and each other, fills a patio just outside the camera store. I take a moment to people watch, admiring the gaiety of voices, the gracefulness of movements, and the variety of dress combining the traditional with the current. I love the energy of this area and must discipline myself not to linger. I step inside the camera store and order the lens cap. Audy and Joel are polite when I rejoin them; they don't comment on my extended absence. Perhaps Audy is used to delays. Perhaps Joel is enjoying the street activity or, more likely, has been looking at architectural details and asking questions.

Sidewalk café by the camera store.

I comment on the Wecke & Voigts store. Audy tells me the store has quite a history. He doesn't elaborate, but he has said enough to stir my curiosity. I look up Wecke & Voigts online to find out more about it. From the store's history chronicled on its website, a story unfolds revealing the indominable strength of early colonists and the family that cradled the stores existence through over 100 years of good times and upheavals. What follows is a condensed version of the history as it appears on the website:

> *1890* – Albert Voigts arrives in South Africa from Germany and becomes Fritz Wecke's assistant. Wecke owns a trading station. Gustav Voigts follows younger brother two years later.
>
> *1892* – The brothers establish the Wecke & Voigts company.
>
> The goods are easily sold to the Herero [Bantu speaking people of Namibia] and traded for oxen. The demand for even the most primitive goods, such as spades, buckets, cooking pots is incredibly big. The first trip to Johannesburg

with 500 oxen has to be undertaken within a few weeks of setting up the firm.

1897 – Business based largely on oxen badly disrupted by Rinderpest [cattle plague]

1898 – January 1 – W&V own stock . . . [that] consists of furniture, skins, stationery, horseshoes, wagon spares, shoes, building material, tinned goods, liquor, flour, jackal skins, saddles, trowels, schnapps-glasses, tinned onions, cocoa in tins, stirrup leathers, butcher knives, corsets for ladies.

1904 – 1907 – Herero Uprising – Everything is lost except buildings in Windhoek and Swakopmund. The buildings at Okahandja, Otjozonjati, Otjosazu and Waterberg are looted and burned to the ground, all the cattle and sheep are stolen, the farmhouses are devastated and almost 20 workers and assistants are brutally killed. W&V faces financial ruin.

1908 – Trading business is very quiet in all places . . . cash money is very scarce.

1914 – While Gustav Voigts is on holiday in Germany with his family, WWI breaks out and they are stuck there till after the war.

1920 – Gustav Voigts is finally able to return to SWA [South West Africa, former name of Namibia] after the WWI.

After the war, recession and depression lasting 14 years sets in. W&V loses unpaid debts due to deportations of German nationals by the South African Government, who bought mainly on credit during the war years. The Firm is also forced to sell mostly on credit as most customers do not have any means of paying immediately. Farmers try to pay in kind, offering skins, boerseep [bar soap made from animal fat], everything except cash.

1925 – May – "You are twice overstocked and what you sell, you sell entirely on credit. You are helping the public and your brother too much." A letter written by the bank to the firm.

"But we are simply compelled to provide our farmers with foodstuff." Gustav Voigts writes in reply.

1932 – The Great Depression causes W&V to reduce their employees to half the original number. Firm sells no cattle in this year.

"As a matter of fact, the only fact in the whole balance sheet is the item debts. These we must pay." Gustav Voigts in a letter to the bank.

1934 – Gustav Voigts dies at the age of 68 years. His widow Frida Voigts assisted by his sons Gerhard and Harald takes over the management of the Windhoek firm.

1973 – The New shopping centre and W&V is completed. The new W&V store is the first in Windhoek to be fully air-conditioned.

1987 – July 16 – A bomb explodes in the parking garage of the Gustav Voigts Centre. No one is hurt in the explosion.

1992 – W&V is one century old.

A parallel story is wrapped up in the Voigts' personal story. The colonization of Namibia, then called German South West Africa or just South West Africa, began six years before the Voigts brothers arrived. What followed was confiscation of lands and the institution of laws and policies destructive to indigenous people. The Herero nation, a mainly pastoral people who bred cattle and traded with Wecke & Voigts, were economically and socially more powerful than the colonizing Germans. They were able to push back against the changes until 1897 when the Rinderpest (cattle plague) struck. It almost destroyed Wecke & Voigts, but it ravished the Herero. The plague killed nearly ninety percent of the Herero herds thereby eliminating their source of wealth, ruining their economy, and weakening them physically by destroying their source of protein.

In 1904, the Herero rebelled against an oppressive German rule and, in their weakened state, were easily defeated. Recognizing that their defeat was certain, the Herero sought to negotiate terms for ending the war. The Germans, however, were set on a policy of extinction and refused to negotiate. By the end, eighty percent of the Herero population was wiped out. About 12,000 indigenous people were forced into concentration camps where a lack of food, water, and sanitation led to rampant diseases and daily deaths. Female prisoners were forced to scrape, and boil clean, the skulls of their relatives and other dead Herero to send to Germany for research into theories of racial inferiority and German superiority. Male prisoners were used as slave labor to build railways and buildings. Many Herero that evaded capture, escaped into the desert where they faced thirst and starvation. With the Herrero defeated, the Nama people rose up in 1905 carrying on the war for the next two years during which the Germans experienced humiliating defeats. With pressure from the populace tired of war, and pressure from world organizations, the governor finally declared the war officially over in 1907.

We drive a short distance from the downtown shopping area when Audy pulls into a parking lot and gets out of the car. We follow. He points to the Independence Memorial Museum, an architecturally stunning, contemporary building, and tells us the museum focuses on the anti-colonial movement and the struggle for independence. He asks if we would like to go inside. It's tempting, but if we choose the museum, we will not have time to see any more of Windhoek. We opt for an overview of the city instead but ask about the statue at the museum's entrance of a man with his right hand held high. The statue is as grand as the building itself.

"That is Sam Nujoma," Audy answers, "the first president of Namibia after we gained our independence in 1990. He was a freedom fighter." He then adds, "He's credited with having won the country's independence."

"What is he holding in his right hand?" I ask.

"It is a copy of the Constitution of the Republic of Namibia."

"How is Namibia doing since becoming independent?" I ask knowing how hard the transition has been, and still is, for South Africa.

Audy keeps his expression neutral as he says, "The government is undergoing growing pains as it learns to govern and refine its new government. Apartheid left most of the people unprepared to govern. The country is doing a lot to remedy the problem. The government is working hard to raise the quality of education. Blacks are now allowed to attend what had been white-only schools. A lot of money is going into teacher preparation." He pauses and then says with an affirming nod, "It is a slow process, but we will be fine."

As Joel asks about the architecture and Audy tells him the museum was designed and built by a Korean firm, I'm still questioning in my mind if I heard right. Apartheid? Apartheid in Namibia? The question spills out of my mouth, "How did Namibia come to have an apartheid policy?"

Audy tells me that after WWI, German colonies were divvied up among European nations. South Africa, itself a colony under British rule, lobbied hard to get Namibia declared its territory—the discovery of diamond-rich fields 1909, and a booming copper industry, made Namibia highly desirable. South Africa got its wish. The League of Nations mandated German West Africa to South Africa thereby placing it under South African protection.

Under the mandate, reinforced in 1946 by the United Nations as the successor to the League of Nations, South Africa was to safeguard the rights and interests of the indigenous people. Two years later, after securing the continuation of the mandate, South Africa imposed the apartheid policy on Namibians.

In the 1950s, Sam Nujoma was driven to activism by the crippling restrictions placed on his people. Particularly devastating was the issuance of passports to limit indigenous people's movement within the country. By 1964, the South West Africa People's Organization (SWAPO) was formed. Led by Nujoma, Namibia's struggle for independence bore a similarity to South Africa's ongoing experience—demonstrations, petitions for change, demands met with brutality, imprisonment, terrorist acts, atrocities, international pressure, and finally a general population weary of war leading to an agreement to hold and honor a democratic election.

In 1990, The Republic of Namibia was born, independent and free of apartheid, a freedom not attained in South Africa until 1994.

Independence Memorial Museum

We turn our attention across the parking lot to where Christ Church stands. Its pinkish, frilly façade stands in contrast to the sleek lines of the museum. Its architecture resembles curvy-edged eyelet, its white-trimmed windows mimicking the embroidered holes that cover the fabric. The church, built from quartz sandstone, has a portico made from Carrara marble imported from Italy and three bronze bells shipped from Germany. The bells are inscribed in German with *Glory to God in the Highest, Peace on Earth,* and *Good Will Toward Men.* It was built between 1907 and 1910 while Namibia was still German South West Africa.

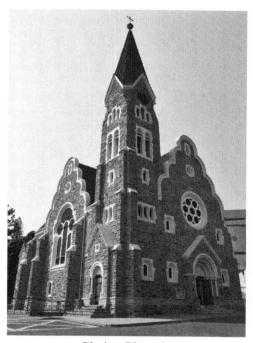

Christ Church.

We head to the Ink Palace, Tintenpalast in German, Namibia's parliamentary building named for the quantity of ink used for paperwork produced within. We explore its gardens filled with round-trimmed shrubs, thick-leafed topical plants, and massive trees in a variety of shapes and shades of green. Nestled among delicate ferns and leafy palms, bronze sculptures of people dressed in their Sunday best, bathe in the sunlight. There are no sculptures of armed soldiers, no rearing steeds, no cannons, just calm. I want to spend time seated next to the bronze man with a dignified hat and a crumply suit. I know I could learn so much history from the silent conversation carried out through his eyes fixed in memories, and the words that fill his rumpled cheeks set in an iron jaw.

Who he was didn't mean much to me while I stood beside the sculpture feeling, without knowing, the wellspring of its power. As I learned more about the struggle for independence, what I had been feeling came into focus. The seated bronze man was Chief Hosea Kutako, leader of the Herero people and one of the founders of SWAPO. The sculptor had captured suffering, strength, determination, pride, and contentment all in one masterful piece.

Chief Hosea Kutako, leader of the Herero people.

We move on, continuing our drive through Windhoek. Audy points out historic landmarks; Joel is fully engaged. I'm casually listening until I spot an art museum and request that we stop. I burst from the car ahead of everyone, eagerly climb the steps to the front door, open the door, and barely get one foot inside when a woman says, "Sorry. We are closed." All the excitement I had felt washes out of me. I'm well-versed in art that is prized by American and European museums but know nothing about art considered important enough to be displayed by African countries in their art museums. I didn't plan time for a museum visit and am feeling the pangs of regret.

It's still morning when we drive away from the center of the city and head to the Windhoek Train Station. The charming one-story, white stationhouse was built in 1912. It looks like a museum but is an active station. Joel busies himself examining and taking pictures of a German-built engine that ran until 1939 and other rail equipment in the station's outdoor museum. I browse, too, but not as intently as he does. What does catch my eye is a small, white building across the street—the Happy Hair Salon. It looks like a freestanding, one-car garage. Drawings of a pick comb, scissors, and hair dryer on the narrow wall to the right of its turquoise door make clear its purpose. The salon looks so cheerful and welcoming, I'd love to peek inside; but its overhead door is pulled down.

Joel at Windhoek Station.

Happy Hair Salon across from the train station.

Audy and I are ready to leave, Joel, still taking pictures, reluctantly joins us. We travel to the outskirts of the city where informal settlements rise and fall with the contours of the undulating landscape. Here, as in Johannesburg where we began our travels, anyone can raise a piecemeal house on any patch of land.

We approach an informal settlement from a rise in the road that affords a semi-birds-eye view. There appears to be more space between dwellings than in the Johannesburg settlements. The structures, made from pieces of corrugated metal, appear more carefully built. Posts strung with wires measure off small yards providing more private space for properties. There's a smattering of vehicles, some under carports attached to houses. The community, neat and clean, appears to be a permanent settlement rather than one overwhelmed with new arrivals to the point of chaos. I marvel at the ingenuity of the people that managed to convert what is, in essence, living in a tin can into a habitable environment. Yet, by any measure, the living conditions, with no electricity, no plumbing, and no insulation from heat or cold barely meet the standard of habitable.

When we drive alongside the periphery of the informal settlement, the view changes. The spaces between structures are smaller, the structures less carefully built.

Audy, in a voice more animated than I have heard from him, says, "Any census taken underestimates the true population of Namibia. The census figures are meaningless; they don't match the number of houses crowded together." Driving, with one hand on the steering wheel, the other raised in a sweeping motion, he adds, "Look at this! How can you count it?"

I bring my camera up to take pictures of the settlement; Audy tells me not to. People don't like it. I promise him I won't include people, but people are what interests me most. I can't *not* photograph people. They are an important part of what is Africa. I want to record how they look, how they move, how they greet each other. Just as a writer makes note of words, phrases, or statements she hears that can be used to develop characters in a novel, I take photos to help me when I paint people to recreate feelings expressed by faces and body language. The images become part of my painting vocabulary.

I push aside a lurking feeling of guilt and sneak photos that include people. Audy probably suspects what I'm doing but says nothing more about the matter.

Viewing the top of an informal settlement from a rise in the road.

The informal settlement viewed at its lower level.

As we continue along the perimeter of the informal settlement, we pass a stand cobbled together from pieces of wood. Foot-high pyramids of onions and oranges, and small bunches of carrots and mushrooms form an enticing display. A striped canvas strung above the stand shades the produce. A woman sits tucked into the shadows of the canvas. I don't see her until after the photo is snapped.

A few blocks away, we come to a neighborhood shopping area lined with small, single story businesses. Corrugated-walled shops fill in the gaps between brick and stucco buildings; a hair salon, made of patched-together corrugated metal with the ribs carelessly laid in random directions, sits among them. Its workmanship is so raw that I picture getting lacerations just opening the window—a blank space covered by a cut panel. I need to remind myself that whatever the informal settlers have here is better than the terror of unstable governments and wars they left behind. I hope there is a measure of joy and comfort in their lives.

We stop at a large, canopied open market. A well-braced network of metal beams connects slender poles that support an array of canopies. Sunlight streams through all four open sides; the poles, gayly painted yellow, lavender, and orange, lend a festive feeling. Underneath the canopy are rows of stands forming mini concessions, each with a variety of products set atop unique combinations of tables and display stands.

The market is inviting, colorful, delicious! I ask if it is okay to take pictures; Audy says, "Yes, but not of the people."

I photograph grains and beans, white, brown, and red. I photograph cans of vegetables and fruits. I photograph fresh red meat lying in the open on a butcher table. It kills me that I can't photograph the people seated with inquiring eyes and inviting smiles among their products. I greet them and wish I were here to shop for groceries instead of just to look.

"People used to set up anywhere to sell goods. They don't have jobs. They need to find some way to make money," Audy tells us. "The government set up an area for them to gather. This helps them."

Even though it has permanent structures, the marketplace is called an "informal market." It resembles the parking-lot farmers markets at home, but much bigger and more colorful.

Canopied informal market.

Butcher shop at the informal market.

We leave the informal market and move to the "formal market," a three-story building with an open floorplan. Racks of colorful Namibian-made clothing and cases of wood carvings, pottery, woven baskets, and jewelry separate spacious concessions. Audy leaves us on our own to shop and have lunch.

We almost make it to the third-floor restaurant without my lusting over something to buy. No more than ten paces into the third-floor shopping area and I'm standing at a counter, fingering ivory-colored necklaces made from six strands of quarter-inch round pieces of ostrich eggshells strung together. The strands are twisted into different-length necklaces. Each lightly and gracefully drapes over my hand as I pick up one at a time to admire them.

Joel, watching me return to a particular necklace multiple times, says. "Try it on." He smiles as I look in a handheld mirror, moving the mirror from left to right admiring the necklace hugging the base of my neck. He unlatches the necklace and hands it to the proud artisan to purchase.

While he is reaching for his wallet, I slip a set of three delicately carved bracelets cut from PVC pipe onto the counter; they look like they are carved from ivory. "They'll go well with the necklace," I say.

The open-air dining area on a balcony overlooks the parking lot. Our driver will pick us up at one o'clock to take us to the airport. We order fire-roasted lasagna made with beef and wild game. It is even more delicious than it sounds. Joel has a beer; I stick with water. My digestive system has been engaged in a battle. I've narrowed down the culprit to coffee with milk from containers that are sold on shelves and claim they require no refrigeration—my intestines seem to take exception to that.

Audy appears promptly at one o'clock to shuttle us to the airport. We are happy to find that the Wilderness Safari, the company handling this leg of our trip, has a lounge area at the airport where we can sit. The lounge, which is about half the size of a standard living room and has seating for eight, opens to the terminal; a rope strung, across its front, keeps uninvited guests out. An elderly woman with the demeanor of a bag lady, drags her wheeled suitcase up to the lounge, undoes the rope and invites herself in closing the rope behind her. The hostess, after polite, but firm, conversation, unhooks the rope and invites the woman out.

Joel and I watch the encounter weary eyed. Exhausted, after only five hours of sleep, we try to stay awake, embarrassed at the thought of sleeping and possibly snoring while on display. We check our phones to see if our daughter has sent more news about the hurricane and our house. There is a text, but it is not what we are expecting.

> August 29
> *Jessica*: You may want to consider flying straight here [Massachusetts, where she lives]. The water is still rising in Houston. They expect Aug 31 and Sept 7 to be bad days because of water moving down the rivers and streams from the north. I bet the airports are going to be a mess for a handful of weeks. This is said to be the largest natural disaster in our country's history. (3:50 PM)

Weeks? We're due to fly into Houston on September 6! I close my eyes; I don't care if I snore. I can't deal with the possibility of not being able to get home. I'll let the hostess wake us up when our flight is ready to leave.

Chapter 21
Kulala Desert Lodge

I feel as if I have just fallen asleep when the airport lounge hostess says, "Your flight is ready to board." It takes me a minute to clear the fuzzies from my head before I understand what she's saying. I don't dare ask if I was snoring, but I slowly canvas the faces of fellow travelers to see if any are giving a knowing look. They aren't. They, too, are in various states of somnolence.

Our pilot, Andy, dressed in a crisp, white short-sleeve shirt and khaki shorts, leads us onto the tarmac and to our plane. With its sleek body and its pilot's seat window flipped up, it looks like a Lamborghini with wings. We fly over desolate land that has pale hues of blue and pink peeking out from greys. Patches of mountains poke up from the sands. From the plane I see no movement, no meandering waters, no animals. It's beautiful in a quiet way.

We land on an airstrip in the middle of the Namib Desert. Namib, in the Nama language, means "area where there is nothing." I have learned from having spent a good deal of time in New Mexico that where there seems to be nothing, you need to take the time to look more carefully to uncover the visual treasures.

A driver and jeep are waiting to take us to Kulala Desert Lodge. He introduces us to another man in khaki shorts and shirt standing by a second jeep. Tall, slim, suntanned, dark-haired and dark-eyed, the man looks like he stepped out of an adventure issue of GQ Magazine.

I stop staring and join the conversation about where we have been and how long we plan to stay in Namibia. The tanned man tells us he runs a ballooning business and asks if we might be interested in taking a balloon ride over the dunes.

I'm ready to jump in with a "yes," but Joel beats me to it with "we might be."

"I would recommend doing it on Wednesday morning," the balloonist tells us. "It looks like strong winds are coming in on Thursday and Friday. We may not be able to fly then."

I am so disconnected to a calendar and time that I need to ask what day this is.

"It's Tuesday," he says.

"What time would you take off Wednesday morning?"

"Five-thirty. We have to leave early to catch the sunrise."

Any interest I had in ballooning hitches a ride on the desert breeze when I hear five-thirty in the morning. I am desperate for sleep. Joel, on the other hand, looks alert and interested.

"How much does it cost?" he asks.

"Five-hundred dollars."

"For the two of us?"

"For one."

My fatigued mind snaps to attention and slams the door shut on any possibility Joel's interest may have awakened. The balloon owner must notice Joel's body stiffen along with mine as we hear the cost is per person. We have never spent that much on entertainment of any sort. The owner holds steady his gaze at us but takes in a slightly deep but inaudible breath. We thank him. He smiles, shakes our hand and gives us his business card.

On our way to Kulala Desert Lodge, we drive through mostly flat land that is both sandy and rocky. Brown and yellow vegetation appears in clumps along the ground; some pale green is visible on scraggly bushes. Dark-colored remnants of undersea mountains rise to the right and left of the broad expanses of open land. Instead of herds, we see solitary animals or groups of two or three. With sightings miles apart, it seems as if every living thing is spotlighted on its own stage.

An oryx grazing on the way to Kulala Desert Lodge.

At the end of the forty-five minute-drive, we arrive at the Kulala Desert Lodge met by a hostess and Obbie, our guide for our three-day stay. We welcome wet, cooling washcloths and chilled drinks made with ginger.

I leave Joel to begin exploring on his own and follow Obbie to our tent, a raised structure with a wood deck and thatched roof. Unlike the front of the tent, which is made of canvas and wood, the back is built with stucco. Its reddish-brown color and rounded corners are reminiscent of the adobe architecture of New Mexico. Completing the effect are wooden rain spouts poking out of the walls casting deep cylindrical shadows beneath them, and a ladder climbing to a flat area of the roof—both typical of structures in Taos and other parts of the Southwest. I notice that on a rack next to each tent there is a large barrel lying on its side soaking up the sun. I make note that, if it is our hot water source, we will have to be frugal with its use.

Obbie, our guide, at the front of Kulala Desert Lodge.

Our canvas and stucco tent.

I leave the unpacking for later and freshen up quickly before returning to meet Joel for dinner. I find him already making friends with the staff. Four men, laughing and posing for pictures, tease each other and then crowd around Joel's camera, eager to assess the outcome on the camera's screen. More laughter and teasing ensue.

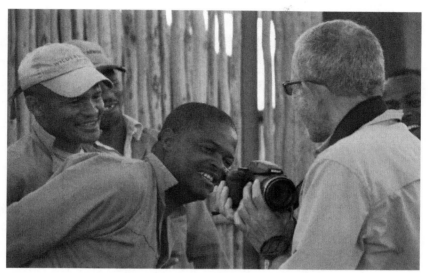

Joel making friends with the staff.

We head inside the lodge and take a few minutes to stroll through the lounge area with its roughly textured sandstone walls and an exposed, high, conical, thatched roof. Casual sofas and chairs, covered in light-colored fabric and chocolate-brown leather, nestle in clusters among wooden support beams. A lamp gracefully arches over a sofa in one of the seating areas. Niches carved into walls create spaces to display pottery and small sculptures; a bookcase makes a sitting area invitingly cozy. Nearby, several books lie haphazardly on a coffee table, abandoned by readers. One entitled *Picturing Bushmen* catches my attention. It's subtitled "The Denver African Expedition of 1929." The expedition took place not long after German control over Namibia was mandated to South Africa.

I flip through the pictures of men, women, and children, many posed, and turn to the introduction by the author, Dr. Robert Gordon, an anthropologist who was born and grew up in Namibia. He published

Picturing Bushmen in 1997 after researching the lasting impact of images from the Denver Expedition had on the Western perception of Bushmen.

According to the book, the Denver African Expedition set out to conduct scientific research using the latest technology in photography and cinematography. Its purpose was to document the existence of a then little-known group of semi-nomadic Bushmen that inhabited parts of Namibia, Angola, Botswana, and South Africa for over 20,000 years. The head of the expedition, Dr. C. Ernest Cadle, believed the people were a missing link in the development of humans. He planned to bring back to Denver with him a live man and woman from the tribe for further study and scientific research. Part of the plan was to market the compilation of photographic and cinematographic material to the public.

To put together the story of the expedition, the author of *Picturing Bushmen* searched museum, university, and art gallery collections around the world for photos and written materials. No evidence surfaced that findings from the expedition made their way into any scientific arena; however, an abundance of marketing material, from postcards to film, was discovered. The most valuable find was a detailed journal kept by the photographer for the nine-month expedition. The carefully catalogued photographs and film revealed the interest and intent of the images taken.

With an eye toward marketing to the public, several photos in the collection were composed to satisfy Westerners' expectations and to reinforce pre-existing ideas about the Bushmen. One of the most popular photographs in the collection is of two hunters dressed in ostrich feathers to disguise themselves while hunting. However, the Bushmen they photographed had never hunted wearing ostrich feathers; they were bribed with a gift of tobacco to dress in feathers for the photo. The cinematography tended to over-dramatize events in order to appeal to the public's expectation of danger. The overall effect of the popularized images was to romanticize the Bushmen that roamed Namibia as hunter/gatherers showing them as living in close touch with the earth in a pristine environment. Unintended consequences were a heightened interest in tourism and a self-serving affirmation of Western superiority.

I see Joel getting impatient, he's returned twice to the same spot in the lobby to check on me. I signal that I need just a couple of minutes longer. He tells me he is going to check out the pool area. I'm about to put the book down when a last glance takes me to the following passage:

> *". . . romanticization . . . does not necessarily help or promote indigenous interests. On the contrary, such activities have a long history and are quite compatible with state policies of simultaneously grinding indigenous groups down. Could it be . . . that such glamorization and romanticization is a psychological dodge to prevent ourselves from listening to unsettling voices? . . . Could it be that anthropologists, by ignoring contextual history, are complicit in the act of killing the people they study with kindness?"*

I pause to take in what I just read and then continue on, wanting to understand more:

> *"Sue Hubbard . . . developed a three-stage model of colonial plunder. The first stage is physical plunder, when 'artifacts' and 'curiosities' are ferried back to the metropole; and the second stage entails the appropriation of Third World images by the artistic avant-garde. The third phase is more elusive: 'We are killing with kindness: making icons of people whom we see as more 'organic' and 'in touch with the earth.' . . ."*

I re-read the passage, struggling in my own mind to weigh what it says. By romanticizing a people and its culture, are our expectations shoehorning them into a period in time? Are we preserving images we hold, and pushing back against their evolving as the world changes around them? Is that what apartheid did? Are we, even now, romanticizing a people into stagnation or annihilation?

I don't like being where my mind is taking me; it's disturbing. I welcome Joel's asking me to meet him on the deck. I take a picture of the book's cover so I can order it when I return home; I want more time with it.

I head outside. What I see takes me back into a world of beauty. The spacious deck, with quiet places to sit, overlooks a sea of subtle colors. Pink sand, speckled with small grey rocks and spotted with tufts of dry grass, lies just beyond the deck. Short, stalky trees lend vertical contrast to the flatness. A thick horizontal band of bluish grey separates the expansive sandy area from low rising mountains, grey in the distance. I am looking at a painting I would like to have hanging on my living room wall.

View from the deck.

I turn to Joel wondering if he's thinking what I'm thinking. We give each other a cat-with-a-canary grin. I break the silence with, "Shall we do it?" He agrees. This land is too special to miss a balloon ride.

It's getting late. People are drifting into the dining room for dinner. We join them. We ask the hostess to arrange for a balloon ride for tomorrow morning. She's happy to do so. She invites us to take any table set for two. A quick scan of the room set for fifty tells us everything is counted out according to the size of each party. There is an efficiency about the way the lodge and the dining room are run that may reflect the time spent under German rule. We choose a seat by the window overlooking the deck, order a glass of wine, and continue to gaze at the view as the sky changes from grey to black.

Chapter 22
SAND AND SURVIVAL

We gave ourselves the gift of an extra fifteen minutes to sleep and now must hurry to get to the balloon launch. It's still dark when we climb into the jeep, but the sun is threatening to rise above the horizon. Just as the jeep pops into first gear, Joel checks his back pocket and realizes he has left his wallet in the room. Barely waiting for the vehicle to stop, he jumps out and runs to our tent.

Muscles in his right calf balk at being forced into action so early on a cold morning. We watch Joel as he makes his way back; his gait resembles a lopsided gallop. Something is obviously wrong, but when he climbs into the jeep he assures us he's fine. I eye him, searching for a clue as to how *fine* he is. He avoids my eyes and fixes his gaze forward. I know him. He would not admit to a broken ankle if he had one. Under no circumstances would he miss a flight over the dunes.

The darkness lightens to charcoal grey, still robbing the land of full color. This is the time of day when the Namib Desert Beetle collects morning dew on its back and then tilts the rear of its body upward, letting droplets of water ripple down into its mouth. The bit of moisture it gets will allow it to survive the coming heat. I learn this as my curiosity about survival in the desert drives me to the internet searching for answers.

We approach the launch area. The balloon has the landscape all to itself. Easily eighty feet in length, the mostly grey envelope is decorated with silhouettes of warriors and dancers. It lies on its side partially inflated. The gondola in which we'll ride is attached to it by ropes and rods.

We see a handful of workmen dressed in warm jackets tugging at lines. Others are watching as the balloon comes to life, taking in breaths of heated air fed to it by fiery blast shot from fuel tanks. As the balloon strains to lift off the ground, a rope tethered to its top keeps it earthbound. At the end of the rope is a very strong man pulling hard.

Hot air balloon being inflated.

We join fellow passengers eager to begin the hour-long flight. The pilot, a leather-jacketed, grey-haired man with a bulbous nose, pale jowly face, and an eager laugh, looks as if he could be an off-season carnival operator. He tells us his name is Jerome and then introduces us to the others: a French couple that is about retirement age; a Yale University student working with talented Namibian students helping them apply to Yale; and a ten-year-old village girl with her father. The girl's father, a tall, dark-skinned man with eyes that light up as his infectious smile stretches across his face, is part of the launch team. There is extra room on the balloon today. As a rare treat, he gets to take a ride and bring his daughter along. In her pink hoodie, with "MY ROOM IS FOR DANCING" printed across the front, the girl nestles up against her father. Her eyes, wide with excitement, leave no doubt that this is her first balloon ride. His eyes, telegraphing pride, leave no doubt as to his joy in making this experience possible for her.

I peek inside the nearly chest-high woven basket and think about the ungraceful entrances I have made into other gondolas. The quickest way for me to deal with an entry is to throw myself in and get it over with. Even with that, I will need a boost from Joel.

The balloon rights itself and it's time to climb in. With a generous heave from Joel, one of my short legs makes it over the top followed by the second leg and an inelegant drop onto the gondola's floor. I regain my dignity and turn to face the others, all upright, and in their places.

The square gondola is divided into four corner compartments plus an area in the center for the pilot. From there, he will blast fire into the cavernous skin of the balloon to keep the air heated and the balloon afloat. As we settle into the compartments, each with enough room to shift about, the pilot gives us not-to-be-forgotten safety instructions—"Don't lean over the sides" and "When I say drop, drop to the floor of the gondola." Thank heavens there were no bail out instructions.

Our apprehension is barely concealed by nervous smiles and involuntary chuckles as the gondola wobbles while lifting off the ground. What we feel is more openly expressed by the little girl who presses herself firmly into her father, her eyes turned upward, fixed on the rising balloon. Soon, we float above the landscape as the sun begins to show its face.

Periodic sharp and then billowy blasts from the propane tank interrupt the silence that envelops us. Soon the recurring sound slips into oblivion; I become entranced by the play of light on the land as the pinks slowly slide over the greys.

We rise higher and travel farther. Patches of orange appear on what looks like low mountains rising to the west. Within minutes, the land morphs from rocks to sand, from grey to orange. A road, like a slender, black snake, stretches across the land. A small cluster of buildings, like tokens on a Monopoly board, are tightly wrapped in a circle on one side of the road.

"That's a road maintenance site," Jerome tells us. "There's no nearby place for crews to stay. They have to build temporary quarters." As he speaks, we can see a small, white rectangle move along the otherwise empty road. Perhaps it is a supply or maintenance truck.

We drift farther south and west as the sun continues to rise. Small dunes appear in waves. They are barchan dunes, crescent-shaped dunes with a gently sloping side facing the wind and steep side facing away from it. They form abstract, curvilinear shapes as they grow and migrate across open spaces. A group of barchans push up against a grove of acacia trees creating a landscape unlike any other I have seen.

Barchan dunes forming in the Namib Desert.

Barchan dunes migrating toward a grove of acacia trees.

I look to the south and see that what earlier had looked like low mountains with patches of orange, were the sand dunes for which Namibia is known worldwide. Soon, we are floating parallel to them.

As the sun rises, it sends horizontal beams into the giant dunes, blazing one side red-orange, leaving the other in darkness. A gently curved line, as sharp as a knife's edge, traverses the ridge at which brightness drops into blackness. The dramatic delineation creates a stunning effect much photographed in nature and travel magazines.

Despite having promised myself I would see the dunes with my eyes rather than through the lens of my camera, I snap away. Between gasps at the beauty, I call, "Look! Look!" to Joel, who is photographing his own discovered treasures.

Sand dune at sunrise.

Too soon, the sun rises high enough to dull the contrast between light and dark. But there is still great beauty to view from other vantage points. The balloon begins its descent to a place where a surprise awaits us. I watch the crisply delineated shadow of the balloon envelope slip along the sand. The chase team in a pickup truck is in sight, racing toward the area to which the wind is carrying us for the landing. The chase team's job is to hold down the balloon, still alive with movement, as it hits the ground.

The landing is as swift and as soft as any balloon-landing I have experienced; but this is the first time I'm in a gondola that falls on its side. We need to crawl out instead of climbing out. I don't know which is less graceful; but, at least, this exit is accomplished with much humor by all.

Joel and I upon landing.

We upright ourselves and board the vehicles leaving the crew to squeeze the last of the air out of the 200-pound envelope and wrestle it into its container. I did that once in New Mexico, joining a line of balloonists along the length of the envelope, lifting and squeezing the air from the top ever forward toward the opening at the bottom. It's hard, heavy work not meant for anyone with laughable biceps like me.

Shortly, we arrive at yet another vast, unoccupied space. Bright white sunlight bleaches the sand, turning it to light orange. I step out of the jeep and need to pause to savor what I am seeing.

In the middle of this boundless place, where absence creates an undisturbed presence, there are long tables covered with white linens set with china and silverware. A champagne breakfast awaits with thinly sliced sausages and cheeses, gently folded crepes, parfaits, and fresh fruit and vegetable salads. Like other moments we have had during the last almost-three-weeks, being in this moment comprises a full vacation's worth of pleasure. When we leave, the wind will cover our footprints as if the land had never been disturbed.

Joel and fellow balloon passengers at breakfast in the desert.

After indulging in conversation and food to our fill, Joel and I board our ride back to Kulala Desert Lodge. We are dreamy and the driver is talkative. He asks where we're from. When he hears just north of Houston, he says, "Houston! . . . The hurricane is really bad there."

Through my champagne-foggy head, I say, "It's getting better. The hurricane has moved offshore."

To which he responds, "It moved offshore, but it came back."

Oh no! I hope he misunderstood. He didn't. As we learned later, Hurricane Harvey blew on shore four times before it was done.

The first thing we do when we get back to the tent is check our text messages.

> *Jessica:* The storm is moving now but the
> rain is not done. People who were fine

through the heaviest parts of the storm have
found themselves suddenly flooded. What a
mess! It is impossible to comprehend what
is going on down there. It is widespread,
too. The whole metropolitan area from
Galveston to North of Houston (and east
and west) looks like a series of rivers. There
are so many boats in places that are roads.
And this is waist-deep flooding and worse
everywhere! (8:17 AM)

And then a later text:

Jessica: Your property manager went to
your house and said the house is "healthy
and well." (1:15 PM)

A sigh of relieve can be heard in our giant exhales. With the worry
we had pushed down inside gone, Joel takes time to nurse his sore calf
muscle and then settles in for a nap. I let him know I'm going to the lodge
to ask for a mattress to be placed on the flat roof at the rear of our tent so
that we can sleep under the stars tonight.

"I'm not sleeping on a roof!" Joel says with his sleep slurred voice.

"It will be beautiful."

"It will be cold."

"We'll bring blankets. I don't want to miss seeing the stars." By now
Joel is asleep and I am on my way to the lodge. The lodge staff is on my
side; my will prevails. But I may be sleeping alone tonight.

We manage to sneak in a quick lunch before leaving at 3:30 on a
nature drive with Obbie. Not far from the lodge, he stops the jeep along
the roadside and we walk a few feet into the dry grasses. The broad-
rimmed safari hat I'm wearing beats back the glare and heat from the
uninterrupted rays of the afternoon sun. Joel hates his hat, a man's version
of mine, but I see he's wearing it anyway.

Obbie stops at one of many light green, thorny bushes.

"This a ___. It's a succulent plant."

The plant's name is short and quick and I can't make it out. I ask Obbie to repeat the plant's name. After the third try, he realizes I'm still not getting it, so he spells it *nra*. The *n* is made by a clicking sound and the *r* trilled like a Spanish *r*.

Obbie tells us, "A nra gets its moisture from the fog. The stems have tiny holes in them. You cannot see them. You need a microscope. They open to let moisture in, and then close to keep it in."

As he speaks, I lean in closer and closer, as if trying to see the invisible holes.

Obbie pointing out a source of food and water.

He continues, "The fruit from this plant is the size of a melon. Animals eat it. You can eat it. You can eat the black pits; but if you get a bitter one, spit it out right away. It is poison."

I make a mental note, if I am ever lost in the desert, don't eat black pits.

The blossoms are tiny. It's hard to picture large melons emerging from them. Obbie assures us they do. The fog is dense and the dew is heavy; that feeds the plant's fleshy body. In the Namib Desert, where the annual rainfall is one-half to two inches and sometimes zero, dew is more important than rain for many plants.

We settle back into the jeep and Obbie tells us, "The Namib Desert is over fifty million years old—the oldest on earth. It is also one of the driest." Without stopping for a breath, he adds, "Now, we go to the riverbed."

We park the jeep and walk a short distance to acacia trees growing along a dry riverbed. Given the absence of appreciable rainfall, the absence of water does not surprise me. What does surprise me is the tangle of green trees, each over ten feet tall with above-ground roots climbing over each other as they spread out in every direction.

Acacia trees.

"When they are young, they have lots of thorns to protect them from being eaten by the animals. When they get older, they don't have so many."

As Obbie talks about the acacia trees, I sense from his voice that this land and its plants are part of his soul.

"When an acacia tree senses danger," he continues "it produces poison in its leaves. The poison is strong. It can kill an animal. Animals don't like the taste. They won't eat much." He continues with, "The tree will warn the other trees about the danger."

I'm looking at the trees and wondering how they communicate a warning. I know that mushrooms in a forest form communication links between trees alerting them to conditions among other trees; but there are no fungi here. Before my imagination gets carried away with trees sending ultrasonic messages or blasts of oxygen, Obbie provides the answer.

"The poison gives off a gas. The gas travels to the other trees and warns them to start making their own poison."

Obbie isn't done amazing us with the biological adaptivity of the acacia tree. He tells us, "The tree's bark lets air in to cool the tree." I barely have time to think about letting hot air in to cool a tree when he adds, "They have a tap root that grows ninety to a hundred feet deep or more." He adds, "The trees can live for hundreds of years."

I'm impressed with their determination to reach water; but I am stuck on the hot air acting as a cooling agent. Perhaps it is like a breeze feels in the hot, humid summers where I live. Hot though it may be, the breeze feels good.

We turn and walk no more than twenty feet along the dry riverbed when we spot an oryx under the leafy canopy of an acacia tree. Until now, we have seen this large antelope grazing only from a distance. From afar, it looks placid and beautiful; up close, it is magnificent. If there had been a contest to design the handsomest, hoofed animal, this antelope would have won hands down.

Obbie tells us it is a gemsbok, the largest antelope in the oryx family. It stands four feet tall at the shoulder of its mostly light tan body. A delicate, black line traces the ridge of its back flowing down to its slender black tail. The line broadens into a thick band as it crosses the tops of the gemsbok's legs and follows the curves of its underbelly completing an outline around its body. The effect reminds me of a child's coloring or a

Cezanne painting, where outlining colored objects in black helps the colors pop.

The oryx looks right at us but shows no concern for our presence. Its face is a mask of white with a ribbon of black running down from each eye melding into a broad, black band across its muzzle. Two long, pointy, cylindrical horns sweep up like a wishbone from its narrow head; two ears flare out creating balance. All markings follow lines of impeccable symmetry.

Gemsbok, the largest antelope in the oryx family.

I hear Obbie say, "Oryx like the shade under acacia trees when it is hot."

I'm glad it is content to stand there, giving me time to delight in its beauty.

I wonder how herbivores that size can extract enough food and water from the desert to survive. I find out that they live off roots, tubers, wild cucumbers, and tsamma melon (a type of watermelon). All are water-rich. They also have an amazing capacity to digest dry, stalky grasses. It is still hard to imagine finding enough water to meet the needs of such a large body when a scan of the land shows not a melon in sight. But then again, there is a vast amount of unoccupied land with a single oryx usually the sole vegetarian in view.

We move on. Obbie stops at a small bush and says, "Smell this."

It smells like an herb I might cook with.

"It is wild sage," he says.

"Do you cook with it?" I ask.

"No, it would make you sick. Our people use it when you get very sick. When you have the flu." Gesturing with his hands, he mimics grinding and says, "You grind it and add oil. Then you put it on your chest. You get better. We can cure a lot of things with plants. We can even cure broken bones."

He reaches down and picks up a flat reddish rock with a rough surface.

"I use this on my feet. It keeps them nice and soft." A smile slowly spreads across Obbie's face as if he is recalling the touch of smooth, soft skin.

He picks up a black stone. Passing it to us, he says, "When a woman is pregnant, and about to give birth, she puts six or seven of these in a fire. When they get red hot, she drops them in a pot of water, puts a towel over head, and leans over the pot. This cleanses her. Makes her ready to give birth."

There are other rocks around, granite, and quartz among them. Obbie tells us which mountains in the distance they came from. "This was an ocean once," he says. "The mountains were under the ocean."

"Were they part of the Atlantic Ocean or an inland sea?" Joel asks.

"Part of the Atlantic."

We move into a shady grove. Up ahead there's an acacia tree with branches gracefully twisting as they grow out from, and over, each other. Its stringy bark becomes noticeable now that we are closer and not focused on a gemsbok. Sprawled across the arms of the tree is an ovoid, hairy-looking mass the same medium brown color of the bark. We take photos even before we know what it is.

"Do you know what this is," Obbie asks pointing to the mass.

Joel answers, "It looks like a huge bird nest."

"It is. It is a sociable weaver nest. Hundreds of birds live in there. Lots of mothers, fathers, the babies and grandparents."

"A condominium for birds," I say. Obbie laughs, but I'm not sure he knows what a condominium is.

"See the holes in the bottom? That is how they get in and out. They make it that way so a snake can't get in. If the holes were on the top or the side, a snake could crawl in easily."

Sociable weaver nest.

The nest is huge, but Obbie tells us there are ones that are much bigger. He also tells us that chambers inside the nest provide cooling shade. At the very core of the nest, there's a chamber that retains heat and provides the birds protection from the cold desert nights.

My eyes search the branches and the sky for a sociable weaver, but none is flitting around. Obbie assures me he will point out a sociable weaver before our visit is over. With that, we go back to the jeep and head out for the sundowner. We snack on dried springbok and fruits, sip wine and toast to the sunset. The potato chips and popcorn take flight as the wind picks up and the sun goes down. We leave when the sky turns from bright yellow and red to grey.

By now, Joel's sore calf has him in agony. Riding in a jeep and slow walking on the afternoon nature drive, made it possible until now for him to tolerate the injury he received running back to the room this morning.

I suggest we find a massage therapist for his calf.

He declines.

I suggest more strongly.

He refuses.

I insist.

He says, "Go do what you want," and limps off to the restroom grimacing.

I speak to Obbie. He tells me there is a massage therapist at one of the nearby camps. He calls, but it's too late in the day and the person has left.

I update Joel as we sit down to dinner. We're so tired from having gotten up at five o'clock in the morning that we hardly pay attention to the food. We eat quickly and head back to the room. On the way, I remind Joel we ordered mattresses put on the rear roof of the tent so we can sleep under the stars tonight.

"*You*, not *we* ordered mattresses," he reminds me. I can tell this is not going well.

"Just try three steps up the ladder and three steps down," I implore.

He consents, but keeps his body aimed toward the path leading to the front door. I decide to check to make sure the mattresses are on the roof before I subject Joel to the climb.

"No mattresses!" I call down to Joel.

I'm relieved, but not as much as he must be. When I descend the ladder, I realize the strain on calf muscles is greater on the descent than on the ascent. If Joel had made it up, there is no way the pain would have let him come down. Tomorrow is a busy walking day. I hope Joel can manage it.

Chapter 23

THE SAND SEA

The pain he feels walking from the tent to the lodge blinds Joel to the beauty of the fog-bathed morning. For him, every step is a lightning strike. The coldness of the air aggravates the strained muscle. After breakfast, we meet Obbie at the front of the lodge. He watches us as we approach, shaking his head at the sight of Joel's hobbling. He hands Joel a walking stick he fashioned from a dowel, the top of which is wrapped with multiple layers of tape to cushion Joel's grip. Joel accepts the thoughtful gift with eagerness.

"We will be riding in the jeep most of the morning," Obbie says.

Joel gives a *thank-heavens* roll of the eyes. Dosed with Ibuprofen and carrying more to spare, he climbs into the hard-top jeep sealed from the morning chill, and we head out. It's a forty-five-minute drive to the sand dunes and I'm sure Joel is thankful for every minute of it. It's a good thing he has a powerful telephoto lens; he may be shooting from his seat in the jeep today.

We head to Namib-Naukluft National Park where we will view the dunes from ground level. The park runs most of the length of the Atlantic coast from Angola to South Africa and includes the Naukluft Mountains to the northeast. UNESCO (United Nations Educational, Scientific and Cultural Organization) selected the Namib-Naukluft National Park to be a World Heritage Site in 2013 in part for its being the world's only extensive dune system in a coastal fog desert; in part for its exceptional beauty; and in part for the very rare adaptation of its animals to the extreme conditions of the Namib Desert, the driest desert in the world.

Shortly after we enter the National Park, we come to Dune1. I recognize the pattern of curve made where the dark side meets the light. It was amazing to view from the hot air balloon and it is thrilling to be standing by it now. I take photos that capture the dune from multiple angles; but I'm aware I cannot capture the fullness of the moment. To do so, I would have to capture the cool clarity of the air, the gentle breeze, and the blueness of the sky that envelop the sand dune and me, wrapping us together in the scene; I'd be the little dark speck near the base of the dune.

Sand Dune 1.

I realize Joel has been standing near me taking pictures. I'm happy to see he can move about.

Obbie starts the jeep's engine and calls to us. "We are going to Dune 47 next."

There's a big gap in numbers between Dune 1 and Dune 47! I wonder what we are missing. My concern dissipates when Obbie tells us the sand dunes are named for their distance from the park entrance. He adds, "Not all are given names. Maybe just the important ones."

We pass several dunes barely slowing down. Most are set well back from the road. Obbie tells us the sand dunes we see to our left and right are star dunes. Unlike crescent-shaped Barchan dunes that are formed by winds blowing from one direction and have a single crest, star dunes are formed by winds blowing from multiple directions and have multiple crests. Viewed from the top, their ridges spin out like arms. The shadows between ridges form geometric shapes, some look like giant prehistoric birds in flight. As we are passing a dune I find intriguing, I ask Obbie if we can stop the car so I can get out and walk closer. He tells me distances are deceptive; it would take two hours to walk to the dune. I take a second look and think about how clarity of air plays tricks on your senses. Distant objects appear sharp, making them appear closer.

Joel asks about a rocky mountain jutting out from the top of a sand dune.

"Some dunes have mountains under them, but most are just sand," Obbie replies.

He tells us that the dunes have their origin in the mountains of South Africa. Streams flowing down the mountains gather iron-rich sediment that they deposit in the Orange River. The river, which flows between the southern border of Namibia and the northwest border of South Africa, empties into the Atlantic Ocean. Strong ocean currents drive the sediment onto the Namibian coast. High winds coming off the ocean blow sand inland, over time forming dunes. The sand dunes we are looking at are five million years old. The ferrous oxide in the sediment carried by the river gives them their eye-popping, orange color. The Orange River is where diamonds were first discovered in Namibia. It remains a protected area today, but management of the land will be turned over to the National Park once mining for diamonds ends. I think about how the dunes will still be here long after diamonds, and perhaps even the interest in diamonds, are gone.

From the road, what we see are the profiles of the sand dunes. Their bodies stretch inland, some for miles. Viewed from above, their narrow, meandering crests form waves that resemble a sea during a storm. I keep asking Obbie to pull over; there are so many pictures I want to take of sand dunes in the morning light and the abstract shapes created by the play of light on their contours. It's breathtaking.

I notice a band of bluish-grey color that looks as if fog has settled in at the base of a dune in the distance. When I ask Obbie about it, he tells me, "That is metallic sand. It is too heavy for the wind to push up the dune. It remains at the bottom."

We arrive at Dune 47, hundreds of feet high. It commands the view with its majesty. Full grown acacia trees, nestled into the shadow at the foot of this giant, look no larger than bouquets. The slow, curving shadow outlining its crest winds down to the base where the boot of a giant is shaped by the light cutting into the dark. I have found my favorite dune.

Curved crest of Dune 47 divides sunlit side from shaded side.

When Joel and I are ready to leave, Obbie says, "We are going to Dune 45, another famous dune." The inflection in his voice and twinkle in his eye betray something special is ahead.

When we arrive, we see that Dune 45 is close to the road and that several cars are parked nearby. A quick glance upward explains its popularity. Footprints follow a crest of the dune to its top 600 feet from its base. This dune is too busy for me; there are too many people. I figure we won't stay long. We'll take a couple of pictures and leave.

I turn and see that Joel, with his dowel walking stick in hand, is already out of the jeep. I catch up with him and ask how he's doing.

"This little stick is amazing," he tells me. "I'm doing fine." And then he says, "Let's go!"

Pulled muscle and all, he brushes past me and heads toward the trail of footsteps leading up the dune. Obbie follows close behind him. I check out the steepness of the slope and decide to remain behind. I could climb it, but the urge to go up is not strong enough to override the image of toppling down.

I watch as they make the climb. Obbie remains close to Joel. They are past half-way and Joel's leg seems to be holding up. They have almost reached the top when they turn around and head down.

"How come you didn't go all the way to the top?" I ask Joel when reaches me.

"It doesn't look it from here, but at the top the path gets narrow. Only one person can get by. I made the mistake of looking down; both sides have steep drop-offs." He pauses and looks as if he's reliving the moment. And then he says, "I got an attack of vertigo. I had to come down."

I glance up and now get curious about what it looks like at the top. But even as I stand thinking about it, my fear of heights makes the earth wobble under my feet.

Obbie with Joel climbing Dune 45.

I continue to enjoy the visual games the shadows play as we drive to Sossusvlei, a salt and clay pan within the National Park. Its name is derived from *sossus*, the Nama word for dead or the place of no return, and *vlei*, the Afrikaans word for marsh. The area acts like a pan collecting water during the rare-occurring rainfalls. The water evaporates leaving behind salt and other minerals. The bit of water the pan does receive makes Sossusvlei less arid than surrounding areas and, thereby, able to sustain vegetation. But, it is still very much a desert with an abundance of orange sand and wind-swept dunes.

I feel different being here from what I felt along the dune-lined road we drove. Although the sand dunes are closer, and the open spaces smaller, somehow it feels more open and simultaneously more intimate. At Sossusvlei, I walk through sand from dune to tree, leaving footprints behind that will be erased by the wind. The light alters my depth perception; the reflected colors change my skin to turquoise. Just as I alter the landscape with my footprints, it alters me. Both are temporary except, perhaps, for the images of color and form I am trying to imprint upon my mind.

Dunes and acacia trees at Sossusvlei.

Obie takes the dowel he has given Joel and draws a map in the sand showing the Namib Desert stretching along Namibia's western coast. He uses the sand drawing to tell us pictorially what he had told us before about the dunes having the origin in South Africa's mountains. I watch him as he draws; the light is so sharp that his shallow lines become brown shadows in the sand. He tells us it is time to move on.

We barely drive a few yards when I spot a shadow on a dune that looks like a three-dimensional sculpture of a bird's wing. A two-dimensional photo might flatten the black area and make it easier for me to see the contours of the dune's surface that give shape to the wing. Obbie stops the car. I take a picture. But, when I review the image in my camera, nothing changes; I still see a three-dimensional wing anchored to, but rising above, the dune.

Wing shadow.

We leave Sossusvlei and head to Dead Vlei, a salt pan within the National Park. We park under the shade of one of the plentiful acacia trees and see a sign that lets us know Dead Vlei is a one kilometer (.6 miles) walk to the pan. It cautions us to take water. I notice that Joel is leaning more heavily on his cane than he had been before climbing the sand dune and ask if he is up to the half-mile walk. "*I'm fine*," he says. The curt response tells me he's not and that I should not ask further questions. We grab our water bottles and are off.

Within a few steps we are out of the tree area, completely exposed to the sun as we hike over white sand, hardened clay, and rock. It is still morning and, thankfully, the air is cool. I am sure the land we are traversing, on average, is flat, yet my body lets me know that I am constantly heading up only to drop down and then up and down again. The point-six miles must be as the crow flies and five miles if the rises in the land are flattened. Watching Joel, his posture revealing how hard he is concentrating just to walk, makes me realize that as fatiguing as the hike is for me, it must be totally exhausting for him.

We pause when we arrive at our destination to take in the strangeness that we see.

The circular salt pan, edged with towering sand dunes, is dotted with the skeletons of dead acacia trees. Clustered in twos and threes, standing alone or lying down, their blackened trunks and ragged branches contrast sharply with the pure whiteness of the salt pan. Each tree is like a sculpture displayed in a contemporary art museum.

The clarity of the air deceives the visual senses, as it did in Sossusvlei. The first clue that the pan is considerably larger than the eye perceives is that people moving about in it look like droplets of ink. Unlike Sossusvlei, Dead Vlei has no waters nourishing it or anything within in it that is struggling to grow.

Nine hundred years ago, the climate dried up and dunes blocked Dead Vlei from even a meager source of water. It was too dry for the trees to decompose! Scorched by the sun, they blackened into sculptures. The Salsola shrubs and Nara melon that manage to survive on the salt pan's perimeter do so by subsisting on the morning mist.

We step onto Dead Vlei and into what looks like a Salvador Dali painting. The starkness commands respectful silence. The only sound besides the wind is an occasional laughter-mixed scream from someone sliding down one of the surrounding dunes. The stark beauty of each form in the pan is so engrossing that it reduces the sound of the laughter to nothing more than a fleeting bird call.

My eyes are drawn to a set of trees, isolating them from everything else in view. Bare, ragged limbs of a mature tree spread protectively over two young ones, telling the story of death being indiscriminate. Crisp shadows blacken the ground beneath them creating a sculptural pedestal. How can death be so beautiful?

Nine-hundred-year-old trees at Dead Vlei.

Two hours pass without our realizing it. Obbie, who has made himself comfortable on one of the fallen trees, summons us to leave. It's close to noon and he must be hungry. As we leave, I take one last look at Dead Vlei and wonder if Salvador Dali had ever been here.

Obbie seated on a fallen tree.

We backtrack across the ups and downs of the sand and clay area between Dead Vlei and our jeep. Obbie leads us to a tree-shaded picnic table made from a concrete slab set on top of a steel barrel. A set of stools made from chunks of reclaimed concrete beams encircles the table. Obbie covers the tabletop with a cloth and lays out our lunch—apples, sandwiches stuffed with cheese and vegetables and cut into triangles, poppy seed biscuits, cold drinks, and tea. He tosses breadcrumbs to small brown birds with speckled wings and black bands under their beaks and tells us they are sociable weavers—the birds that build large, condominium-like nests. He made good on his promise to show us the birds before we leave.

Joel at the picnic table.

Completely relaxed, enjoying the easy exchange of banter with Obbie, we can barely coax our bodies into moving, but we must head back to the lodge for some time to rest; we still have an evening safari ahead of us. What could it possibly add to this day?

Chapter 24
SESRIEM CANYON

It's four in the afternoon and Obbie is ready to head out. Joel, still groggy from his nap, clutches his walking stick and makes his way to the jeep. Not having recovered from the walk across the sun-baked land to Dead Vlei this morning, I slouch into the back seat of the jeep, mindlessly watching desert scenery stream by. My moment of quietude is interrupted by a sharp jerk right and the sound of tires kicking up sand as the vehicle comes to standstill.

"Wildebeests!" Obbie calls.

I fumble for my camera, now lying on the floor. I'm not seeing what Obbie sees. Giving up on my naked eyes, I extend my camera's lens, aiming it where Obbie points. There are four wildebeests lying among bushes under the shade of dry-looking trees. Without the telephoto, they look like four clumps of black dirt. How Obbie saw them while driving is beyond me.

I'm out of the jeep, taking pictures with my lens fully extended, but can't see clearly if I am capturing any detail. I look at Joel snapping away with his 2,000 mm optical lens, seven times the power of mine, and lens envy sets in. He probably is capturing the smile on a wildebeest's face as it decides to stand and give us a profile, and then a full-face, view.

I enlarge the wildebeest photos on my camera's screen and am surprised at how much detail I got. With curvy short horns, rippled skin, droopy faces, and hairy heads, this is the first animal I have seen that I would describe as being something only its child could love.

Shortly, we arrive at the main entrance to the Namib-Naukluft National Park, a different entrance from the one we used to see the dunes. Obbie stops at an engraved granite sign that stands taller than he does. He lingers by it, making sure we have plenty of time to read what it says.

The inscription on the stone, honoring this area as a designated UNESCO World Heritage Site, reads in part as follows:

THE NAMIB SAND SEA
Inscribed on 21 June 2013 in Phnom Penh, Kingdom of
Cambodia, under all
natural criteria for World Heritage

(vii)   Superlative   natural   phenomena   and
outstanding natural beauty
(viii)   Exceptional example of on-going geological
biological processes
(ix)   Globally significant on-going ecological and
biological processes
(x)   In-situ conservation of species of outstanding
universal value

Officially inaugurated by the President of the Republic
of Namibia,
His Excellency Hifkepunye Pohamba

The sign reminds me of how privileged we have been to balloon ride
over, drive through, and walk in such an incredible place. Understanding
more about the exceptionality of it raises my experience to yet another
level.

Obbie at Sesriem entrance to Namib-Naukluft National Park.

Before leaving the monument at the park entrance, I point out to Joel that the engraved stone was donated by Phnom Penh, Cambodia. We have been to Cambodia. It is such a poor country, yet it is interested enough in Namibia to present to its people a monument that evokes pride in the country's importance and beauty. I have not seen any public manifestation of friendship expressed by United States anywhere I've traveled in Africa. In fact, before coming to Africa, apart from its music, which I love, much of what I heard about Africa in recent years involved violence and disease. There is so much more that can be said about Africa—the warmth and ingenuity of its people, the beauty of its land and wildlife, and the valuable role it can play as a partner in world economy and ecology.

We move on to our primary objective within the National Park, Sesriem Canyon. Its name means "six belts" referring to six lengths of hide, usually oryx hide, used to make rope long enough to lower a water bucket into the canyon one hundred feet deep in places. Some of the deeper hollows hold water all year round and are life-saving for animals.

Varying in width from three to ten feet, the canyon is no more than a slit in the earth's crust that is easy to miss if you don't know where to find it. As we stand along the edge of the canyon, I see forms that take the shape of people and birds in the shadows among the rocks. Beyond the shadows, I have little interest in the canyon. I have had a long, wonderful day and am ready to wrap it up when Obbie says, "Come, we're going down."

Going down! I don't have my hiking stick, my security pole, that prevents my many near-falls from becoming a reality.

I eye Joel's walking stick and am tempted to ask for it. I don't dare; I know he would give it to me. I try to get out of descending into this slit by using Joel's sore leg as an excuse; but Joel pipes in with, "My leg is much better. Let's go."

Before beginning our descent, Obie points to conglomerate rock. I think back to my one and only geology course in college where I learned about conglomerates. I had held a rock in my hand made of pebbles of different origins held together by a mixture of sand and minerals. Unlike the rock, so small it fit in my palm, Sesriem Canyon is a whole canyon of conglomerate rocks held together by pressure and nature's cement. Pebbles, well-rounded by the Tsauchab River as it cut its way through shaping the canyon, are visible in every rock formation. The size of the pebbles tells part of the history of the river. In periods when it flowed forcefully, the river polished stones into smaller sizes than it did when its power was reduced to practically nothing by multiple years of drought.

We begin our hike into the canyon on a fairly level dirt path. According to Obbie, baboons spend the night here. I scan the canyon walls an arm's reach away and am more disappointed than relieved that I don't see any sign of animals climbing about.

The path yields to irregular stone steps that twist down a short but steep rocky slope. I take a deep breath before I plot my descent. I want to close my eyes but settle on steadying them into a stare. Down I go on shaky knees. This is reminiscent of the trek I took with Joel in the Himalayas, only, thankfully, here it's not rainy and the stones are not slippery.

When I reach the bottom, I turn back to look at Joel who is ordinarily like a mountain goat traversing rocky surfaces. It's clear that he is straining with his stick and his still-sore calf. But, even at that, he makes it down in half the time it took me. Fortunately, the floor of the canyon levels off making it easier for Joel to walk and allowing me to spend more time looking at formations than at my feet.

Joel hiking into Sesriem Canyon.

What was dark and shadowy from the top, becomes a stunning clash of sun-brightened rocks glowing gold and shadowed shapes. The clarity of the air heightens the interplay of brilliance and darkness. Streaks of gold and silver spill down the edges of towering vertical rock formations through which we pass, trimming the edges of what looks like the earth's jewelry box.

I look at the gold ring on my finger. It's miniscule in size and drama compared with the extravagance of the sun's rays hitting masses of stone. I could argue that my ring is more valuable because it is constantly there. But, just as the canyon's gold disappears into darkness at night, my ring disappears into a dark corner. Like the canyon, my ring relies on the return of light to dazzle again.

It doesn't take long for me to find another marvel of light and dark. At my eye level, the sun has found its way to a white conglomerate rock resting in the pitch-black hollow of a porous oval rock. The white rock looks like a museum-displayed gem, set on black velvet with a beam of light focused on its beauty. The porous rock, wrapped around the blackened opening, glows bright orange.

Rock displayed like a gem.

We venture farther into the canyon. A swimming hole lies beyond a wide, arched entrance to a dimly lit cave. We peek in, but only see rocks, some large enough to sit or lie on. We'll have to take Obbie's word about the pool.

It's turning into evening. Time for a sundowner. On the way to a spot Obbie has chosen, nature serves up one more delight—a lone ostrich ambles across the otherwise unoccupied landscape. This is our last sundowner. The sun makes sure we will never forget what it looks like in the desert. Uninterrupted bands of reds and golds stretch across the width of the desert's western sky silhouetting the rounded mountain tops. Tomorrow everything changes for us; we're leaving the wilderness. I'm not sure I'm ready for it.

Ostrich at evening.

Chapter 25
Beaches, Expeditions, and Surprise Settlers

As we have done so many times on this three-week journey, this morning we will fly a zigzag path to our next destination. We board our first flight, the tenth since we arrived in Africa. It will take us north to Windhoek, another will take us south to Cape Town.

At our final destination, the airplane begins its descent as the sun slips below the horizon. A band of intense colors—red, indigo, gold, and orange—separates the darkening sky from the city below with its galaxy of lights aligned in rectangular grids and concentric circles. I want the plane to continue circling so that I may continue gazing at where the earth, sun, and sky meet.

A driver, with our name printed on a handheld sign, greets us as we leave the security zone. Our first view of Cape Town is from a highway. It looks like any big city with cars speeding along roads that slice through the least attractive parts of the city. The driver talks, but I'm too tired to listen until he points to an area of corrugated tin homes mixed with government-built stucco houses. Streetlights add enough illumination to the twilight for us to see grey, rectangular forms along the sides of the highway. We have seen them before, homes for uninvited settlers who are attached to, but not a part of, South Africa.

The driver tells us, "The government tries to help the people who come here from Zimbabwe, Somalia, Nigeria and other places hoping to find work. But they can't find work; they don't have the skills needed." His voice raises an octave when he adds, "It's too crowded in the informal settlements. We can't even get in to collect garbage! The government keeps building houses, but it's impossible to keep up."

It's not until three days later when we pass this stretch of the highway again that I see it is not just one settlement, but several massive ones spreading outward from the freeway. Rows of side-by-side portable toilets line the settlement border nearest the road, strategically placed to allow easy access for maintenance.

The driver adds, "Places for showers are also provided."

I choose not to linger on that thought.

Seeing the vast, and spreading, crowded informal settlements by daylight, I find it hard to believe that they began their existence in the 1990s, less than thirty years ago. I picture the informal zones expanding until they push up against the sprawling city as it presses outward. The occupants of informal settlements are uninvited, yet the government needs to provide health care, sanitation, education, and jobs for the masses of people. To do so encourages more people to come; not doing so is inhumane and leads to increasing health and economic problems that cannot be ignored.

I often have opinions on what can be done, where to begin; but, honestly, with South Africa's informal settlements, I am stumped. It's like trying to use a sponge to mop up a spill from a breached dam.

Heading to An African Villa, the boutique hotel at which we will spend three nights, we drive through streets that look like the ones I where I grew up in Brooklyn, New York. Streets with small businesses at street level and apartments above turn into streets with fewer businesses, fewer people, and more houses than apartments. As we approach the hotel, we drive through upscale neighborhoods with increasingly grand, light-colored stucco homes. Tall plantings branch out above privacy walls. Security gates offer glimpses of lush landscaping inside the walls. An occasional person strolls down a sidewalk.

We arrive at a two-story townhouse that could easily be on 5th Avenue in Manhattan. We enter what looks more like someone's home than a hotel. The entry foyer opens into a living room decorated with museum quality African sculpture, masks, and pottery. Our fresh-from-the-bush clothing does not fit in, but it doesn't matter; we are made to feel at home.

Living room at An African Villa.

The hostess tells us that Cape Town is experiencing a severe water shortage; this is the third year of drought. She asks us to collect, in a bucket, water we let run while waiting for the shower to warm. She explains that housekeepers use it to clean the rooms and water plants. She takes us on a tour of the townhouse that begins with a cozy sitting area with a fireplace and culminates in a stainless steel kitchen that would be the envy of many small restaurants.

I'm not hungry, even though we haven't had dinner; but I'm always up for something sweet. As the hostess tells us about the swimming pool in the back garden, which is not is use due to the drought, my eyes work like a divining rod, searching the kitchen for dessert. They fix on a sliced tea loaf set out for guests. We wait until our bags are brought to our room, and then Joel and I eye each other, smile, and head for the kitchen. We each take a slice of cinnamon ginger tea bread and bring it to the living room with the fireplace. On a table next to it, a decanter of Port wine set out for guests awaits to accompany our deliciously satisfying "dinner."

Peter, our guide for the next two days, arrives early the next morning. We gobble down our eggs, sausage, and biscuits and join him at 9:00 a.m.

to begin a tour along the Cape Town waterfront. People ride bikes, stroll, and push baby carriages along an elevated promenade while white caps from the South Atlantic splash onto the shore below them. Dressed in shorts and short-sleeved tops, the strollers are welcoming the end of winter. A sidewalk lined with palm trees separates the promenade from the traffic. Across the lanes of traffic, mid-rise hotels and apartments, in shades of white and beige, line the street. Behind them, white buildings climb up the mountains paralleling the shore.

I ride up front with Peter. Not being used to traveling on the left side of the road, I wince and slam my foot down on a non-existent brake pedal as we head into traffic, expecting a head-on collision at any moment. Right turns cause my eyes to bulge. I'm grateful that traffic lights are easy to spot among the cacophony of cars, buses, and people all in motion set against a backdrop of buildings, trees, hills, and curves. What sets traffic lights apart from the visual clutter is a white, reflective boarder that trims each stack of red, green, and yellow lights. Manhattan would be a good place to try using this device.

Cape Town traffic along the shore.

We leave the busy area and continue along the coast to Maiden's Cove, a tidal pool in Camps Bay with teal blue waters that wash onto a white sand beach. Homes, nestled at the foot of a string of mountain peaks, slope down toward the cove. We spend too little time soaking in its beauty and wish we had planned to allow time to dip in the water. Our desire chills down quickly when Peter mentions that the waters feeding the cove come from the Antarctic.

As we drive along the road between beach and homes, we pass small restaurants, cafes, and shops, most with European names. Peter tells us, "About thirty to forty percent of the homes are foreign owned, mostly by Germans. About eighty thousand foreigners live here full-time."

I look at the bay and think I'd like to make it eighty thousand and two.

We continue following the road south with the ocean on our right and mountains to our left. Peter points to eucalyptus trees planted on granite slopes alongside the road.

"They were brought in by Australians to bind the crumbling granite," Peter says.

The trees' roots run along the rock surface like long, slender fingers holding the granite in place. The same trees preventing the collapse of granite onto the road, pose dire problems for drought-prone Cape Town. Eucalyptus trees are invasive and much thirstier than native trees. If allowed to grow, as they have, in natural landscape where rain waters collect, they reduce the amount of runoff into reservoirs, shrinking the water supply to the city. Working with the Nature Conservancy to create a means of providing a more secure supply of water for Cape Town, the city has agreed to remove non-native trees from its catchments.

I gulp when I learn that acacia trees, too, are invasive, and their removal is included in the water conservation plan. In Cape Town, they threaten life; in Namibia, they provide shade that protects life. Their exceptionally long tap roots ensure their survival in deserts; here, their adaptation sucks out a disproportionate amount of ground water adding to the scarcity during droughts. I consider the difficulty of mixing and balancing nature when an element in an ecosystem can play opposing roles under different circumstance. It occurs to me, that mankind, as it populates dry places bringing with it swimming pools, landscaping, and other water-demanding features, may fall within the definition of invasive species.

I turn my attention back to the road as bike riders in yellow, blue, and black jerseys and matching helmets ride ahead of us. A team in orange, preparing for a seventy-mile race, is among those pumping their way up the mountain.

We pass an ostrich farm and Peter asks if I would like to ride an ostrich. I decline, maybe another time. What looks elegant in the desert looks gangly here. I picture myself perched on one's back, flopping around like its feathers do as it trots. Its beak, at the end of a long, skinny neck, would probably pluck me off as soon as it sensed my fear.

Soon, we pass through the entrance gate to Table Mountain National Park, a protected area that includes the Cape of Good Hope. The Cape, often thought to be the southernmost tip of Africa, actually is ninety miles west of Cape Agulhas, the southernmost tip.

The road down to the Cape is spotted with busses and cars; in season, they would be back-to-back. When we arrive at the open parking lot closest to the Cape, it is crowded with vehicles and people. A line of eager tourists, mostly Germans mixed with other Europeans, bulges with families eager to take a picture behind a three-foot high wooden sign for the Cape. To reduce the tensions that accompany long wait times, a second sign has been erected. Still, impatient tourists shift their weight and scan the area around them, watching for anyone who dares to cut in.

After several minutes at the back of the line and not having moved more than an inch, I decide I can live without a picture of myself standing behind the sign. As I leave the line and walk along its side, eyes start to follow me. Conversations stop. The moment the people in line most fear arrives when I raise my camera. I'm standing at a distance from the line and the sign, but that doesn't stop the angry shouts. For the first time, I hear an American voice; it rises above the others. My voice is drowned out by crashing waves as I try to explain with gestures that I'm just taking a picture of the sign, not of a person with the sign. I give up, snap a picture, and move away. Maybe having let off steam makes the line people feel better; maybe not.

I turn to face the promontory, a towering, ragged rock formation with a flat top. Its storm-beaten face drops straight down to a ledge over which sprays of explosive waves wash. Water from the promontory's ledge cascades into the sea forming a mist where they meet. Rocks and boulders, tossed by the violent waters, lie piled on the shore, their edges long ago softened by the pounding surf. Gulls peck for food in small pools in spaces between rocks. Birds fly in V-formations, low over the waves close to the shore. The sound of crashing waves clashes with the serenity of the birds in silent flight.

Cape of Good Hope.

Gulls feeding on fish trapped in pools.

The same scene that mesmerizes me has been treacherous to others. The Cape of Good Hope was first rounded in 1488 by Bartolomeo Dias, a Portuguese navigator, who named it Cape of Storms, more descriptively in Portuguese, Cabos das Tormentas. The tip of the African continent, between Cape of Good Hope and Cape Agulhas to the east, is where two of the largest currents in the world clash—the Benguela Current, fed by the cold Antarctic waters in the South Atlantic, and the Agulhas Current, fed by the warm waters of the Indian Ocean. Where they collide, each turns back on itself. The Benguela, pushed by the more powerful Agulhas, turns north. It travels along the coasts of South Africa and Namibia then west toward Brazil. The Agulhas reverses its westward flow, turning back into the Indian Ocean.

The collision point gives rise to enormous swells, tides, and whirlpools mixing and crashing with each other as if inside a mountainous washing machine. Rogue waves ninety-eight feet high have damaged or destroyed large ships as recently as the late twentieth century. The force from the Agulhas Current switching direction spawns eddies, the remnants of which can be detected as far away as Brazil. Heading to Brazil, it turns out, was the secret to successfully rounding the Capes and creating a trade route to India by water.

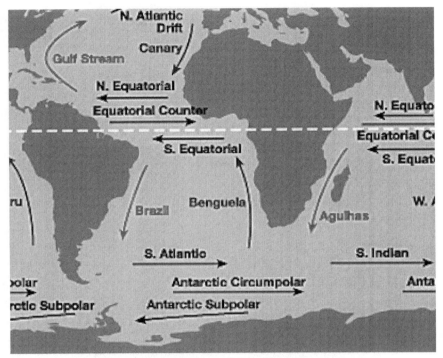

Map of Benguela and Agulhas Currents.

Vasco da Gama, a Portuguese explorer, came up with a plan that was nothing short of genius, given the tools of the day. In July 1497, he sailed south from Lisbon, Spain, around the bulge of West Africa, past Senegal, Guinea, and Sierra Leone. Instead of hugging the coast along Angola and Namibia, fighting the treacherous north-flowing waters of the Benguela Current that had doomed countless prior expeditions, da Gama turned west. He continued west, almost to Brazil. From there, he turned southeast, toward Africa staying away from the southern tip of the continent and its tumultuous waters. Five months later, da Gama successfully cleared the dangerous waters and traveled up the east side of Africa heading toward India.

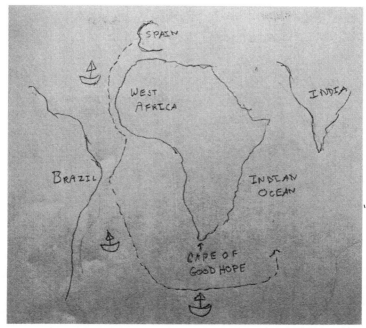

My drawing approximating da Gama's route (dotted line).

As I picture being on a small wooden ship, vintage 1498, being tossed around and slammed by waves washing over the deck, I can't help but marvel at the daring of the explorers and the deadly risks crews were willing to take. In the 1490s, their sailing adventures must have been the equivalent of space travel today, maybe a bit rougher.

I turn back to the rounded rocks, the birds flying over waves, and the waves asserting their power with vast inhalations followed by thunderous crashes. Peter signals it's time to move on to Cape Point where an historic lighthouse, painted bright white with a bright red circular roof, is perched at the highest point of the promontory. It was built to warn boats of the danger of being destroyed by barely submerged reefs near the shore.

After the lighthouse was put into service, boat wrecks continued at alarming rates. The problem came from ocean winds blowing a mixture of cold air from the South Atlantic and warm air from the Indian Ocean up to the top of the rocky promontory. Dense layers of clouds covered the top, obliterating the lighthouse, and swallowing the light from its beacon. The useless lighthouse was taken out of service and a new one constructed lower down.

As we approach the park exit, we pass a grassy area with families of baboons romping around and grooming each other. A sign issues a warning to tourists.

Another sign should be posted alongside it:

Fortunately, we are about to remedy that situation.

We travel up the east side of the Cape Peninsula to Simon's Town, a quaint town nestled between mountains and the shore. White, century-old two and three-story stucco and wood-balconied buildings, with shops and cafes at street level, line both sides of its main street. Simon's Town is a place for recreational boating and swimming, and the home of a small, but still active, 100-year-old naval base.

Navy vessel on right behind recreational boats on False Bay.

Peter points us to a restaurant in a small shopping mall built on a dock and then leaves us on our own. Our table overlooks False Bay where a naval vessel is moored. I order kingklip fish, a fish I have never heard of, and enjoy every flaky, white morsel of it! After our leisurely lunch, we take the remaining time before rejoining Peter to stroll down the main street, peeking into shops. I don't look too closely at the clothing, gifts, and wood and stone carvings. We have limited ourselves to a duffle bag and backpack and I'm sticking to it. However, my stomach is expandable. We don't make it past a pastry shop without stopping to have cappuccino and a yummy, custardy pastry.

Refreshed by our time alone together, and recharged with coffee, we meet Peter back at the car for a short ride to Boulders Beach. Homeowners long enjoyed swimming at their private, white-sand beach protected from the wind and large waves by giant granite rocks. But things changed when new neighbors moved in.

A pair of African Penguins left their homes on Dyer Island and set out on an expedition. They found a new world, Boulder Beach, settled in and colonized the area. That was in 1982. Cute at first, the penguins soon became a nuisance to the original residents as more of the penguins' families and friends moved to the new territory. Breeding in the lush, dark green foliage lining parts of the beach, the colony grew from two to 2,200 by 2017.

The new colony attracted thousands of human tourists eager to watch the penguins frolic among the rocks and in the water. With tourism, came artisans selling their wares from stalls lining the road to the beach and filling what had been a quiet neighborhood park. The original residents gave up their beach, footsteps from their homes, and took to packing their towels and blankets and driving to public beaches.

Penguin at Boulders Beach.

We spend an hour laughing at the tuxedoed-munchkins-turned-nuns when they turn their backs on the sea and waddle into the greenery, their nesting ground. Raising the young is a joint venture. Parents mate for life and take turns incubating their eggs, feeding, and protecting their young.

Penguins heading into the nesting area.

On the sandy beach, chicks, covered in fluffy brown feathers, snuggle against their mothers and cluster with other babies. Unable to swim until they shed their baby down, they remain on shore. Not until they reach adulthood will they acquire the black-speckled white front and black tuxedo coloring. The uniquely speckled pattern on their breasts is like a fingerprint.

Mom with chick.

I notice that a pink area above the penguins' eyes is more pronounced on some that others. Peter, who has been standing nearby, seeming to enjoy the penguins as much as we are, tells us, "The pink gland above each eye acts like an air conditioner; the hotter it gets, the more blood is passed through the glands to be cooled by the outside air."

I watch three penguins cavorting in the water close to the shore. Like children, the three of them splash, swim, get knocked down by waves, and run in and out of the water together. I could stay until sunset enjoying the colony, but Peter has a clock built into him that says it is time to return to our hotel. Tomorrow, our adventure continues as we explore the wine country.

Friends splashing about.

Enjoying the penguins at Boulders Beach.

Chapter 26
Vineyards and Chocolates

It's Sunday morning, our last full day in Cape Town. Peter is in the lobby waiting to begin our tour of the wine region. We leave the city and drive through small towns, passing women on their way to church wearing brightly colored dresses with geometric shapes that fearlessly mix fuchsia with periwinkle, yellow, and orange. Matching headwraps swirl the geometric shapes into endless convoluted patterns where they intersect and overlap. Would I dare wear something so outstanding? With my uneventful medium brown hair, medium brown eyes, and medium skin coloring, would I disappear into the garments becoming a mere conveyance for something strikingly beautiful?

I slip back into my seat and turn my attention to the architecture and lush hills. Lovely as they are, I find myself wishing I could hold on to the feeling of ease and belonging I had while in the bush. I loved stepping out of the canvas-walled tents that barely separated us from the outside shrubs, grasses, and fresh air. I loved the daily surprise of a wild animal slipping past our tent in the early morning. I loved being in a different world, one where the land and the animals could be enjoyed, but not disturbed, where the adaptation to each other's presence had to be made by us, not them. I loved the intimacy of the camps, being treated as if we were family by hosts, rangers, and chefs. I loved the shared banter, laughter, and excitement. I never felt like a tourist skimming the surface, passing through.

Here, I am a tourist being led around. I can't complain—it was my choosing. I wanted to maximize what I'd see during the three-day stay. I chose to see a lot superficially rather than anything in depth. Had I known better, I would have saved Cape Town for when I could enjoy its laid-back feeling, its beaches, its restaurants, and be enticed into savoring its beauty at length. Maybe another time; but for now, I need to push aside the longing to be back in the bush and refocus on what is here.

Vineyards near Stellenbosch.

A panoramic view of the landscape stretches in front of me from the front seat of the car. We enter a mountainous area with sloping valleys patchworked with bright green strawberry fields and rows of grapevines supported by posts. Soon we arrive at Stellenbosch, a town at the foot of Stellenbosch Mountains. We leave the car and enter 18th Century Dutch colonial South Africa. The scale of the historic buildings on the tree-lined streets is invitingly intimate. Curvy gables decorate rooftops; their ornateness lies in contrast with the simplicity of the structures they adorn. Dark-trimmed windows, subdivided into twelve or more segments by a grid of muntin bars, accent the whiteness of the lime-washed walls. Sharply defined shadows of the still-bare tree limbs cast graceful lines onto the white canvases. As spring arrives, leaves will sprout filling out the shadow sketches across the faces of buildings.

Woman outside an historic building in Stellenbosch.

Curvy gable and windows with muntin bars.

We walk to a residential area, also tree-lined and unmistakably Dutch in architecture. Some historic homes have thick, thatched roofs typical of the Cape Dutch architecture dating back to the 1700s. The depth and softness of the roofs' rounded edges radiate warmth. If I lived in Stellenbosch, I would want to have a home with a thatched roof.

Peter must surmise what I'm thinking from the gleam that undoubtedly is in my eyes. He says, "The roofs are high maintenance. And expensive. Owners must keep the roofs in good repair at their own expense; they are not allowed to replace them with any other kind of roof."

House with a thatched roof.

As we leave Stellenbosch, heading to Franschhoek and wine tasting, Peter tells us that Huguenots came to the Cape to escape persecution in France. When King Henry IV converted to Catholicism in 1589, he issued the Edict of Nantes that guaranteed religious tolerance. Over time, Huguenots, a Calvinist sect, became the largest Protestant group in France. As they grew, they gained influence and displayed their beliefs increasingly openly. One of the basic tenets of their belief, that no person—not a king, bishop, nor anyone else—could demand their ultimate loyalty, was in direct conflict with the throne and the papacy. By 1685 religious tolerance ended with the revocation of the Nantes Edict. Within two years, French Huguenots emigrated to Franschhoek, the English translation for which is *French Corner*.

French Huguenots brought with them knowledge of and skill in, wine production and were welcomed by the Afrikaners. Many refugees had their passages paid by Afrikaners in exchange for agreeing to a ten-year obligation to work at developing the fledgling South Africa wine industry. The plan worked. The wine improved greatly, and, today, the wine region is recognized as being a producer of quality wines.

The town of Franschhoek developed into a progressive area perhaps because its early settlers had been persecuted in their homeland. According to Peter, when informal settlements began to grow at its doorstep, the mayor and the town council decided to see to it that the newcomers would be "skilled up and working." The mayor, Frank Arendse, elected in 1992 by a racially mixed council made up of members from Franschhoek and surrounding Black/Colored townships, was the first non-white person to head the government of a white town in South Africa. Although plans were underway to do away with apartheid by the early 1990s, it wasn't formally ended until 1994, two years after Mr. Arendse was elected.

The council's plan has met with successes. While unemployment still exists, the shanty towns have changed from scraps of corrugated metal to brick and cement government-built housing. Land for gardens has been provided by the town and the settlers taught to farm. Whatever the settlers produce, they keep for their own use.

Peter tells us that the council gave a large plot of land to six women from the informal settlement in 1994. They planted vegetables and herbs and began selling them to local restaurants, hotels, and Bed and Breakfasts. Before long, the women built up a thriving business and are continuing to do quite well.

It feels good to hear a success story. I hope the influx of new immigrants continues at a pace Franschhoek can manage.

It's lunchtime. We walk through an area with boutique shops displaying artwork, gifts, and clothing that could be both gifts and artwork. With our stomachs on empty, we make sure our path takes us directly to a two-story bistro, *French Connection*. We enter at the second level. At the back, stairs descend into a tree-shaded garden with tables set for lunch. We opt to eat inside where dark wood-trimmed windows accent white walls and tablecloths, extending the outside architectural theme into the inside atmosphere.

I don't hesitate for a second when I see what's on the menu. I order the kingklip. I'm ecstatic at having another chance to taste this delicately delicious fish. Joel does the same. Even though we will be sampling wines after lunch, we decide this fish deserves a glass of chilled white wine of its own.

As I sip my wine, I notice the bistro's specialties listed on a chalkboard; kingklip is at the top. Below its name, in nicely scripted handwriting, it says that kingklip is a member of the cusk eel family. Had I known it was eel, I might not have been adventurous enough to try it yesterday. Sometimes, ignorance has value.

After lunch, we have time to stroll before rejoining Peter. We pass shop after tempting shop resisting the urge to go inside. Our resistance shatters when we come to a windowfront with a display of abstracted and detailed animal sculptures. I remind Joel that we are at the end of our trip and have bought trinkets for our two daughters and our granddaughter but nothing for our two sons-in-law and two grandsons. That realization opens the door and pushes us over the threshold.

The sculptures we purchase of hippos and an elephant are small. The five hippos, four for the men and boys plus one for me, are only six inches long and the elephant for Joel is only seven inches high. As the gifts are being wrapped, Joel raises an eyebrow and says, "Who's going to carry these?"

The sculptures, each a little different in color from the other, are made from dense, black stone beautifully veined with greys or greens. I don't know how far I can press Joel's strength. The already overstuffed duffle bags, into which these will be squeezed, have no wheels. To spare my sometimes-troublesome back, Joel carries both bags. I take solace in the fact that the elephant he chose as his souvenir is larger than any of the hippos; it makes me feel the weight problem is as much his fault as mine—well, almost.

Carrying our newly purchased treasures, we rejoin Peter and drive to the Franschhoek Cellar for a wine tasting. Peter, once again, leaves Joel and me to ourselves. The bar, tables, display cases, and beams crossing the high ceilings are all dark wood. Huge windows, opening to views of vineyards, pour light into the dimly lit room. Large paintings of lush fields, hung on interior walls, compliment the natural views.

We are the only ones in the wine cellar—it's very different from in-season when the room bustles with tourists as lines wait outside. We easily slip into the quiet mood. The host comes by to help us select our wines. One will be red, one white, and one rosé. Soon six wine glasses and, for each of us, a small tray with bite-size, wrapped chocolates are set down before us. We are instructed on which chocolate to pair with each wine. I'm still in a foggy after-lunch state and hope the server will remind me which goes with which. I must admit, I am more interested in the chocolate than the wine.

Our first wine is presented. Before it is poured, we listen to a description of the grapes from which the wine is made, the process, the resulting fruitiness or spiciness, its balance, complexity, the effect on the palate, the finish, and more. The wine might have evaporated before the description ended had the server poured the wine before providing its history.

We sip the wine and nibble on the chocolate. I savor each. For Joel, savoring the small piece of chocolate must be a difficult task. When it comes to food, he goes all in, filling his mouth with a portion large enough to taste rather than locating a morsel and pinning it to his palate long enough to savor.

I sip, savor, look out the window, admire paintings. Patient Joel drums up as much conversation as he can while he waits for me to move along with the tastings. The server waits what must be an appropriate amount of time between servings, brings out the red wine and then the rosé. I don't feel rushed; I just feel good, and then better, and then even better.

Franschhoek Cellar; Joel is seated at the rear right.

Peter stops by as we finish the rosé. He, too, sinks into the relaxed atmosphere, partaking in conversation. It's almost evening when we arrive back at the hotel. We say our goodbyes to Peter. We'll be heading home tomorrow. With neither of us being hungry, Joel and I settle into the task of repacking before we relocate to the living room with the fireplace and the Port wine.

I'm ready to go home and eager to begin planning our next trip to Africa. Perhaps we could fly into Windhoek and go to the art museum we missed. We could fly to Etosha National Park to watch a parade of multiple animal species cluster together around waterholes in the dry, open plains. We could travel to the Serengeti, go in search of silverback gorillas, take a walking safari, and definitely go back to Botswana where being among the elephants felt so natural. Then we could wrap up at Sabi Sands, the first place we stayed, where we can be treated like royalty in the middle of a kingdom where lions rule, leopards and rhinos thrive, and elephants go about their business.

It's getting late. I'm tired, but happy. This has been an unforgettable three weeks.

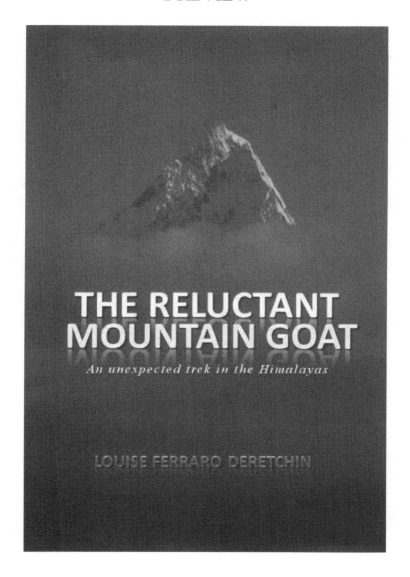

THE RELUCTANT
MOUNTAIN GOAT

An unexpected trek in the Himalayas

LOUISE FERRARO DERETCHIN

by Louise Deretchin

Chapter One
TRIPPED

I'm done with the ritual of coating my face with color. I blot my lipstick, smooth the front of my basic-black evening gown and check my rhinestone earrings in the mirror. I've taken my time, dragged my feet, but I can't delay any longer.

"C'mon. Forget the damn bracelet. We're already late," my pacing husband calls to me as I head down the stairs and remember the matching bracelet I had planned to wear. With his peppered gray hair cut short, and slim athletic body he looks absolutely scrumptious even though his lined face reveals a no-nonsense seriousness.

I dread going to large social events where smiles are the most important accessory and conversation is kept light enough to float across the room without landing on anyone's pet peeve. I'm strictly a small-group person; my husband, on the other hand, could live in a glass house with "Welcome" plastered all over it.

When the invitation to the gala arrived last month, he had asked if we could put it on our calendar. Of course I said yes. How could I say no when he was sweet enough to ask? Besides, after being coaxed out of the house the evening of a big bash, I usually surprise myself by having a good time.

The cocktail hour is half over by the time we arrive. Clusters of partyers in glittering gowns and sleek tuxedoes crowd the lobby and saturate the air with laughter-filled conversation.

Side-by-side silent auction items clutter cloth-covered tables. A train of guests divides its time between chatting and writing down bids as it inches along the tables. I fortify myself against the temptation of joining the line. Joel and I are still reeling from the expense of moving into a new home we bought at auction three months ago. It was my hand that flew up into the air to win the bid and then shook violently as I placed my signature next to Joel's on the contract that committed us to a new home.

As I struggle with myself, repeating the pledge Joel and I made not to bid on anything, a nameless face approaches with his hand extended toward my husband.

"Joel! So glad you could be here. Louise! I haven't seen you in a long time."

"Joel keeps me hidden." That's not true. I just happen to like doing solitary things—writing and painting or taking unscheduled walks.

Most people don't know who I am unless I appear by Joel's side. He steps away and I stand uninterrupted, entertaining my own thoughts until he returns. From my vantage point of stillness, I can spot the volunteers who have worked hard to plan this event. Their broad smiles and searching eyes radiate pride and purpose as they slip between guests to make sure everything runs smoothly. One of the volunteers in a shimmering silver gown approaches me after Joel joins the queue at the bar. She looks familiar; but I can't place who she is.

"Hey, Louise! You look great. I just saw Joel. He said you don't have a bid package. I'll get one for you."

"Oh, no. Don't bother. We'll take care of it."

"Don't be silly. It's no trouble at all. I'll be right back."

I don't want a bid package. But five minutes later, there I stand with temptation in my hand.

A chime signals it's time to enter the banquet room. Crystal chandeliers, soft lighting, floral centerpieces, tables set with china, silver, and wine glasses make the whole room sparkle. Proud of our self-control at bypassing the silent auction, my husband and I high-five each other and enter.

"Did you bid on anything?" friends ask before we can make it to our table.

"We tried not to," is our noncommittal reply.

We work our way past numbered tables and finally arrive at ours. It's right up front, much too close to where the action will take place. We won't be able to duck out unnoticed before the live auction begins.

We shake hands with the people at our table and take our seats. The din of conversation wanes as the master of ceremonies approaches the podium. We peruse the brochure of live auction items while short speeches are made and we wait for dinner to be served.

A forty-four-carat oval-cut citrine, a wine collection, a gourmet barbecue dinner at someone's house—no problem, these are things I know we can pass up. It'll be easy to sit on our hands. I read on. Then I see it. It's on the last page:

Package Six: *Eat, Pray, Love in Gokarna Forest Resort*
in Exotic Kathmandu, Nepal
Includes airfare for two with the two-week stay

Anxiety trickles through my body. I can't count the number of times Joel has said he wants to trek in the Himalayas and has tried to convince me it would be fun. Each time I greet his testing-the-waters with a noncommittal smile while *you-can-go-just-leave-me-out-of-it* pulsates behind my eyes. Walking on rocks for hours and falling into a crevice never to resurface hold no appeal for me.

I slip a quick sideways glance toward Joel and see he has reached the last page of the auction items list. I turn away and fix my eyes on a waiter, a chandelier, a door—anything but the brochure or Joel.

He turns to me; his expressionless face barely masks the hope that lies behind it. In a soft, even voice he says, "Did you see Package Six?"

Of course I've seen it! The words *forest* and *exotic* in the description of the package have been playing Ping-Pong in my brain for the last five minutes. They keep bouncing off my retina flashing images of a tree house with a vine used to descend to a communal commode. But when I look at his pleading puppy eyes, I can't bring myself to give a flat-out "No".

"I saw it." Big pause . . . "Would you like to bid on it?" Foolish even to ask.

"Yes."

Trapped!

"What are you willing to bid?" he asks. Most trips at charitable galas we have attended sold for $15,000 to $20,000 and sometimes more.

"Eight thousand," I offer—high enough to give Joel hope, low enough to let me feel safe we would not win the bid.

Dinner is done. Lights go up. The auction begins. After what seems like no more than a few minutes, the bidding opens for Package Six. The wine served at dinner must have put bidders in a generous mood. The final bids on Packages One through Five were high. I relax.

Joel's calm concentration does little to hide the eagerness behind it. Two bidders are bidding against each other for the Nepal trip.

"One thousand."

"Fifteen hundred."

"Seventeen hundred."

Their hands jut up one right after the other.

"Two thousand."

I start to sweat—the increments are too small.

"Twenty-five hundred."

"I have twenty-five hundred. Now let me have $3,000."

Silence.

Oh no! This is crazy. Don't they know airfare alone is about $4,000?

"Three thousand, three thousand, let me have $3,000. What about $2,700?" The auctioneer tries to tease a higher bid out of the second bidder. No dice. The auctioneer scans the room, "Twenty-seven hundred. Anyone?" No takers.

With gavel raised, in rapid succession he declares, "Going once. Going twice . . ."

I hold my breath waiting to hear "Sold" before Joel has time to react; but Joel's right arm, holding the paddle with our bid number, springs up faster than the gavel comes down. We enter the bidding war at $2,700.

"I have $2,700, now give me $3,000."

The remaining bidder ups the price; but in the rapid-fire bidding battle that ensues, he must sense the determination that has taken control of Joel's bidding arm. At $4,000 the other bidder quits. This time the gavel drops and the "Sold" means Package Six is ours. My heart sinks.

Early Sunday morning, I sit at my desk at home checking email, a band of sunlight slices across the room. I can't bring myself to look up Gokarna Forest Resort on the internet. I'm in denial and want to stay there. Joel, on the other hand, wants to see what last night's prize looks like.

Seated at his desk set against the wall, his back is turned toward me and his eyes are aimed at his computer screen. "Louise, you have to see this," he says with a voice that betrays his restrained excitement.

"I'm not interested. I want to be surprised."

"Gokarna Forest Resort is a FIVE-STAR resort!"

What? No planks in a treetop? I peek over his shoulder and see that the list of amenities includes a swimming pool and a spa. Okay, I can handle this—luxury and pampering for two weeks. Better yet, the resort is located far away from the Himalayas.

As it turns out, not quite far enough.

The Reluctant Mountain Goat is available on Amazon

ALSO BY LOUISE DERETCHIN

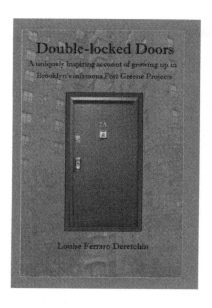

I grew up in Brooklyn's notorious low-income projects, an Italian American child cocooned in an old-world culture imbued with passion and protective love that created a minefield as punishing to negotiate as the traps spawned by the housing complex. Known today as the Whitman/Ingersoll Houses, the Fort Greene Projects housed 3,500 families of varying degrees of poverty. The concrete hallways, stairwells, and playgrounds provided excellent venues for thefts, assaults, and killings.

I made it past the hurdles and locked doors. Perhaps this memoir will help children growing up in public housing today find their own way through.

Double-locked Doors is available on Amazon

To SEE COLOR PHOTOS from *An Elephant at My Door* in color, follow me on Facebook and Instagram at @travelphotos4you.

If you enjoyed reading *An Elephant at My Door*, please take a minute to comment on it on its Amazon.com page.

Acknowledgements

Twenty-four days, seven camps and cities, twelve interior flights, guides for three cities, and not one glitch in our travels through four countries in Africa. For this I must thank UK-based Africa Travel Resources whose experts worked with us planning our adventure, arranging our stays, and taking care of us from the moment we stepped on the plane until we headed home. Not having to worry about where to be or when left me with the essential time I needed to record the experiences we had in southern Africa.

Many thanks go to my Houston, Texas writing buddies, Betty Jo Hall, Mary Harper, and Aline Myers, all fabulous writers, who wouldn't let any unanswered question, or questionable phrasing in my manuscript, slip by unchallenged.

A big thanks to Phaedra Greenwood, my Taos, New Mexico colleague, mentor, and friend for taking time from her own writing and documentary filmmaking to critique chapters after my Houston buddies and I worked through the kinks. Her input was invaluable even though, at times, it meant I would have to summon the energy to do yet another pass at the writing.

A special thanks goes to Ashley Henson for taking time away from writing and editing magazine articles to give *An Elephant at My Doorstep* a beginning-to-end checkup to test its readiness for publication. Her keen eyes picked things that slipped by everyone else.

I can't overstate the value of my family. My daughters, Jessica and Robin, and my husband, Joel, are my cheerleaders. Whenever I find myself bogged down in a chapter or just wanting to know if it worked, they are there as my readers with fresh eyes, gentle comments, and definite opinions. A special thanks to my husband, my most critical reader, whose careful readings are much appreciated and valuable.

Thanks to you all!

Louise

About the Author

Louise Ferraro Deretchin, Ph.D., a writer, painter, and former educator, grew up in Brooklyn and found her way to Texas. She is the author of *The Reluctant Mountain Goat*, a memoir about an unexpected trek in the Himalayas. Her essays have been published in literary journals. A memoir of her growing up in low-income projects was shortlisted in the Southwest Writers Contest. Her favorite place to be is hiking in the mountains of New Mexico. More information about the author and her artwork is available at LouiseDeretchin.com.

Sisters I
Oil on canvas

Printed in Great Britain
by Amazon

26470961R00181